Create Your Own Multimedia System

John McCormick

Windcrest® / McGraw-Hill
New York   San Francisco   Washington, D.C.   Auckland   Bogotá
Caracas   Lisbon   London   Madrid   Mexico City   Milan
Montreal   New Delhi   San Juan   Singapore
Sydney   Tokyo   Toronto

This book is dedicated to Beth and Jane, both of whom
contributed greatly to its creation.

pbk   1 2 3 4 5 6 7 8 9 DOH/DOH 9 9 8 7 6 5

Library of Congress Cataloging-in-Publication Data

McCormick, John A. (John Ash), 1947–
     Create your own multimedia system / by John A. McCormick.
         p.   cm.
     Includes index.
     ISBN 0-07-046034-5 (p)
     1. Multimedia systems. I. Title.
     QA76.575.M33   1994
     006.6—dc20   94-12268
                                                               CIP

Acquisitions editor: Jennifer Holt DiGiovanna
Editorial team: Joanne Slike, Executive Editor
               David McCandless, Supervising Editor
               Theresa Burke, Book Editor
Production team: Katherine G. Brown, Director
               Ollie A. Harmon, Coding
               Rose McFarland, Desktop Operator
               Cindi Bell, Proofreading
               Joann Woy, Indexer
Design team: Jaclyn J. Boone, Designer   WK2
             Brian Allison, Associate Designer   0460345

Contents

Preface

A brief word about how this book is arranged—in particular, why I discuss software before hardware.

I was originally taught to evaluate and specify systems by reviewing the software before the hardware nearly 25 years ago and it is just as appropriate today as ever. The idea behind this sequence is that the most important aspect of computers is what they can do for you, not what hardware they contain. For example, you want to create some type of multimedia system, but your selection of just what software you need is determined by what you intend to produce.

Once you determine what you want to do, you can then select the application software that can do the job economically and quickly, yet also allow expansion as your needs change.

If you choose your hardware first, you are limiting your choices of software to only those programs that can run on that hardware using that specific operating system. You can probably still accomplish your multimedia goals, but you might not be able to use the best tools for your needs, having restricted your applications software universe by preselected hardware.

Of course, many of you already own computer hardware and might want to continue with your selected platform, but if using your current computer system is not an absolute requirement, you certainly don't want to restrict your software choices from the start.

On the other hand, some hardware combination does exist that can run ANY software you locate; there has to be, or the software could never have been created! Before making a final decision on a platform, you need to ensure that your selected hardware is a practical choice from both a cost and support standpoint.

Nevertheless, you stand a far better chance of assembling the system you will be most happy with if you look first to your goal, decide which software capabilities you need to meet that goal, and only then choose the hardware needed to run that software.

Although I touch briefly on the basic multimedia systems that can be assembled by simply adding a multimedia upgrade kit to MS-DOS computers, this book concentrates on those who want to go beyond those meager production tools. While basic multimedia PCs provide an adequate playback platform for multimedia programs, they can be used for only the most basic of multimedia creations. Even if you are creating multimedia just for your own enjoyment, you will want a more advanced system.

This book can help you locate the most appropriate hardware and software to create the system most suited to your budget and needs. You learn how to create a sophisticated (but not necessarily expensive) multimedia production system using the descriptions of which software options are available as well as the sections on how to select or expand your computer hardware.

Starting from scratch, you can create a good basic production system for about $2,000—and considerably less if you already have a suitable computer. At the high end, professional multimedia systems can easily cost as much as $100,000, and we look at the components that compose these systems also. Most of you will probably choose a set of tools that emphasize only one aspect of multimedia, thus enabling you to assemble a powerful multimedia production system for less than $10,000 and probably less than $5,000. Not bad for capabilities that would have required a $500,000 TV studio and control room just five years ago!

Home users will probably want to add just one or two more powerful multimedia capabilities to their existing system, which can cost as little as $1,000, including the sophisticated hardware and software.

Perhaps most importantly, this book is targeted both at experienced computer users who need to learn about multimedia as well as the video producers, artists, and musicians who understand their fields but don't know anything about the role computers can play. Because this book addresses the needs of two very different groups, some from both sides might find certain (but different) sections too elementary.

Introduction

This book can help you evaluate your options when creating a multimedia production system and show you how all the pieces fit together. By "creating," I mean buying and connecting the components and installing the software, which is actually more like assembly than creation. Don't worry; you won't have to perform any complex assembly tasks that involve soldering irons or such. In creating a multimedia studio, selecting the appropriate software and hardware is the complex part of the job, while assembling those components into a system is usually trivial in comparison.

In this book, we briefly look at the low-end multimedia-capable computers that can be either purchased ready-to-run or created by adding an inexpensive multimedia upgrade kit to your basic computer. We also examine basic systems useful for individual hobbyists as well as sophisticated, team-development production facilities suitable for large-scale multimedia production. The main purpose of this book, however, is to show you how to assemble a computer capable of producing and playing multimedia. Creating a multimedia system is very different from merely adding low-end sound and a CD-ROM system to a standard computer. Whether you want to produce commercial CD-ROM multimedia titles, create business presentations, or simply intend to play with multimedia concepts for your own enjoyment, this book shows you just what you need.

What this book does not do is try to teach you how to produce multimedia shows. Hundreds of books are available that teach how to use specific multimedia production software and hardware. In addition, the products described in this book come with extensive operational documentation. Most software also provides tutorials on multimedia production.

In describing production software, a sample of which is shown in Fig. I-1, we look at the tools and techniques of multimedia creation. The creation of advanced multimedia projects, however, requires all the skills of a computer programmer, graphics designer, sound mixer, video editor, and television director. Any large-scale multimedia production effort will probably fail unless it is created by a staff equipped with these skills. On the other hand, even one person can produce spectacular multimedia presentations given a creative temperament and the right computer tools. The trick is in not trying to do too much too quickly.

As technology develops further, computers become more powerful, and users become familiar with multimedia, new multimedia applications will be developed, and the use of multimedia in existing

Figure I-1

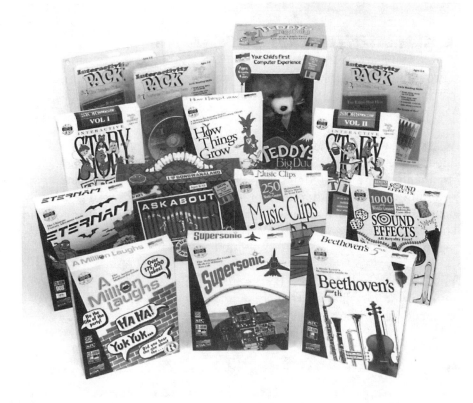

Some of the hundreds of multimedia entertainment and educational programs available on CD-ROM. Interactive Publishing Corporation

applications will become more widespread. High-end word processor programs such as WordPerfect are now including the ability to add sound and images to their documents, when just a few years ago word processors were battling to be the first to produce WYSIWYG (what you see is what you get) word processor/laser printer combinations.

Remember that multimedia is not just for business or academic professionals. Although the first personal video cameras were sold only to rich hobbyists, today every electronics store carries many comparatively inexpensive models. Many people see multimedia as the next step for home video fans and computer hobbyists, both of which must learn the skills and tools of the other to work with multimedia.

⇨ Explanation of terms

Throughout this book, the term *PC* refers to the IBM PC-compatible computer, that is, one that runs on an Intel-compatible microprocessor.

Windows indicates Microsoft's Windows in this book, unless specifically stated otherwise. Other windowing systems are also in use, such as the X-Windows standard for Unix computers for example. Except in Chapter 2 on operating systems (where other windows systems are discussed), however, I use the term Windows to specifically indicate Microsoft Windows 3.1 or later with multimedia extensions.

Finally, the Apple Macintosh computer, which comprises about one-tenth of the installed base of small computers, is referred to simply as a Macintosh or Mac.

Multimedia basics

T O fully understand a book on multimedia, some important questions need to be asked. What exactly comprises multimedia? What parts of a computer are important in multimedia? And what is multimedia even good for?

⇨ What is multimedia?

Multimedia generally includes a combination of three elements:

➢ sound

➢ images

➢ text

Of the three, only text has been the traditional province of computers. A basic multimedia-capable computer (or player) includes a method to reproduce sound and color images. The basic multimedia system typically has a CD-ROM player—especially if it is to meet Multimedia PC (MPC) requirements—but multimedia does not require much for basic power if the computer or player just plays back the presentations and does not create them.

How much text, image, and sound are in a multimedia production varies from application to application—and some presentations do not even use all three elements. Any combination of two or three of these elements is considered multimedia, however, because the same tools and skills are used. No real definition of multimedia other than this exists; most of us simply know it when we see it.

⇨ Hypertext

Hypertext is the basis for many multimedia productions as well as virtually all interactive multimedia applications. Thus, it is often included in any discussion of multimedia, despite the fact that many hypertext applications use only text.

The basic concept of hypertext is a bit difficult to grasp unless you have experienced it, but actual production can be quite simple. To understand *hypertext*, just assume that the italicized word is actually part of a hypertext application. If it were, all you need to do to see the definition of the term is to place the screen's cursor on that word and activate the hypertext feature (by pressing a key on the keyboard). This action would bring its definition up on the screen.

That example is the basis of hypertext—the ability to quickly and automatically access information related to highlighted terms without the annoyance of every term being explained in the main presentation. The simplest way to understand hypertext is to think of it as an automated book in which footnotes and endnotes are identified by highlighted words rather than reference numbers.

The tremendous advantage of hypertext is that you do not need to look at the bottom of the page, the end of the chapter, in the glossary, or in the back of the book for an explanatory note. You just move the cursor to the highlighted word and an explanation springs up on the screen. Hypertext links hidden sounds, pictures, animation, and charts to displayed words, phrases, or larger text groupings. To create hypertext, you need special software to create the links between words and the hidden explanations, animation, or sounds activated by highlighting selected words or images.

Data

Data form the basis of many multimedia productions. Whether you include actual text and numbers in the final production or just a simple narrated animation, if the purpose of the presentation is more than entertainment, it will almost certainly contain text and numbers. Even if your presentation is business charts, data were used to create those charts. Many productions make extensive use of data, either created specifically for the presentation or gathered from existing text archives, calculated in spreadsheets, or generated from database programs.

If you already use a word processor, you might think you know everything about text creation. In multimedia, however, there is both far more and far less to producing text than producing business letters and presentations using today's massively complex word

processors. Far more because you might not even want to use a separate word processor to create the text for your production. Far less because even if you create text for multimedia using a word processor program, you cannot use many of the special features provided by the word processor.

⇨ Images

Images used in multimedia applications fall into several categories. Each requires different production and manipulation software and hardware, and each has different storage requirements. Using images in multimedia is such a big topic and such a major part of multimedia that two chapters are devoted to image software—one for stills and the other for video.

Images used in multimedia productions range from simple clip art, such as that seen in sophisticated word processed documents, to digitized photographs, full-motion video clips, and even user-created animation. Clip art can be either still or video and can come from a variety of sources, including CD-ROMs, videotapes, and videodiscs.

Stock video, whether still- or full-motion, is professionally produced and sold either with an unlimited reproduction license or on a per-use fee basis. If stock video exists that complements your production, it is the easiest way to include professional-quality images in your presentation. Whether background shots of exotic places or action shots including professional models, a good selection of stock video can be a powerful tool for anyone producing multimedia and can greatly enhance a project at minimal cost. If you need to produce images in-house, you can use video or electronic still cameras. You can also scan existing art into the computer.

Alternatively, you can create your own images entirely within the computer using various graphics programs that generate everything from charts and graphs to freehand-drawn images and even attention-getting fractals. There are even animation programs and morph software that can produce the special effects seen in recent movies such as *Terminator 2*. Morphing is an important special-effects tool just now becoming available to personal computer users because it is so computation-intensive. In a morph sequence, one object metamorphasizes into another in a smooth series of intermediate steps. Thus, a fish can become a car to show how streamlining affects design, or, as in *Terminator 2*, a robot can change its shape from one object to another.

 Sounds

While most computer users are familiar with basic graphics software, outside the multimedia field only musicians and a few adventurous computer hobbyists are aware that computers can manipulate and generate music. It might be surprising to many readers that virtually all music today, other than symphonic and other classical music, is composed, created, and recorded digitally using either special-purpose computers or a simple desktop computer with an accessory board and editing software.

Sounds you can add to multimedia productions include voice, music, or special effects. Just as with images, you can purchase stock sounds collections or you can create your own. You can record speech and sounds using a traditional microphone or using Musical Instrument Digital Interface, or MIDI, files and programs.

MIDI is the ultimate in computer-generated sounds. Although you can edit and even compose sounds using nothing but a computer, the quality of the sound is entirely dependent on the system used to play back the music. Sampled sounds always suffer from compromises in dynamic range and frequency response made to balance quality with the massive storage requirements of full-fidelity stereo sound. MIDI, however, is a simple computer code recognized by synthesizers and converted into high-quality sounds.

You can picture MIDI files as the equivalent of a paper roll used to program a player piano. The sound quality depends on the synthesizer (instrument) used to play the program, not on how it was programmed originally. The sound could have been created by you manipulating MIDI files in an editor, a musician playing a MIDI instrument, or even a programmer writing MIDI code directly.

⇨ Editing

You might suspect that, in addition to editing text, graphics, and sounds separately, a multimedia producer must also have specialized software to blend, or cut, all three together. This software ranges from simple cut-and-paste programs that just insert different elements in the appropriate place to sophisticated control software that actually operates external devices, including slide projectors, VCRs, or videodisc players, to produce a *final cut*.

Using the same techniques and some of the same software, you can edit a multimedia project for the following:

> ➢ playback on the same computer/audio-visual system
>
> ➢ distribution on floppy disk
>
> ➢ posting on an electronic bulletin board
>
> ➢ mass distribution on videotape, CD-ROM, and videodisc

Low-end multimedia software often includes limited editing capabilities for images, sounds, and perhaps even text, but quality multimedia requires special video- and audio-editing tools, along with a separate program to mix all the elements together into a smooth whole, or at least a very expensive all-in-one production and editing tool.

⇨ Multimedia terms

Because multimedia is a synthesis of computer, video, and audio technology that has some new elements for almost every user, it is important to understand a few basic concepts along with the terminology.

⇨ SCSI

The small computer systems interface (SCSI) standard provides an easy, common connection for CD-ROM players, scanners, and external hard and magneto-optical drives, as well as other devices needed by multimedia authors. SCSI was once a very nonstandard standard, meaning that although different devices all claimed to be SCSI-compatible, they often did not work together. The latest boards and software drivers, however, allow users to connect SCSI devices together in a *daisy-chain arrangement*, in which you can connect up to seven devices to a single SCSI port (Fig. 1-1).

Figure 1-1

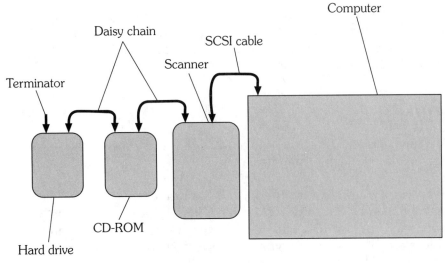

Example of daisy-chain arrangement.

Any serious multimedia production computer needs one or two SCSI ports. Macintosh systems come with one built in, as do a few PCs, but SCSI ports can also be added to other PCs very inexpensively. As a minimum you need at least one SCSI-2 port.

⇨ Scanners

There are handheld, sheet-feed, flatbed, and slide scanners, available for both color and black-and-white images. All scanners convert images into digital signals for storage and processing by computers.

Sheet-feed scanners are suitable for text scanning but not images because the mechanical feed mechanism often skews the page slightly.

Most scanned text is processed by optical character recognition software, which is capable of dealing with skewed text. Even a slightly out-of-line feed, however, is devastating for image-scanning because you must then straighten all those skewed lines manually. Another major disadvantage of sheet-feed scanners is that they cannot scan bound pages or portions of oversized images. Slide scanners convert 35-mm color slides into high-resolution computer images.

Because of their flexibility, flatbed and handheld scanners are the ones most commonly used for multimedia production image input. Fortunately, these scanners are also less expensive than the less versatile sheet-feed scanners.

⇨ Audio

We have already looked briefly at MIDI, but two other audio formats are also available for multimedia users.

Waveform audio is a digitized audio file format that can be manipulated by PC software. Unlike MIDI, it does not describe commands passed to a MIDI synthesizer. Instead, waveform audio drives an FM audio generator. Windows waveform audio format is designated by the .WAV extension.

The quality of waveform audio reproduction depends on the sampling rate used—the more samples per second, the higher quality (and the larger the storage requirements for a 1-second file). Waveform is also called pulse code modulation (PCM) audio. Audio boards take analog input from microphones or other sources, convert it to waveform audio files, and then convert it back to analog audio to be played back through speakers or headphones.

The other audio standard used in multimedia is the familiar CD audio, which is also digital but not in a form computers can directly edit.

⇨ Video

Video (the technology, not the images) for multimedia falls into two basic types—computer and broadcast-quality.

Video graphics array (VGA) and Super VGA (SVGA) are the current standards for displaying video on most desktop PCs. Multimedia designed for playback on computers should include VGA graphics board and monitor, unless the productions are being specifically targeted at lower-priced machines or monochrome displays, such as projection screens or notebook computers.

Broadcast-quality video in the United States means the National Television Standards Committee (NTSC) standard, but other standards exist in Europe and Japan. Phase alternate line (PAL) is the standard for most video sources, including video camera or VCR.

It is not easy to convert between computer graphics and television standards—the process requires a special video converter device that could be either an internal expansion board or an external unit. Going the opposite way, however, frame grabbers not only convert NTSC or PAL video to computer graphics standards, but they also capture single complete frames or images.

Inexpensive frame grabber boards can only capture one piece of a full television image, or only a single image, at a time. Professional-grade frame grabbers can capture full-motion video in real-time, converting it to another format and compressing the files before writing them to storage, but this process is difficult and requires expensive high-speed hardware.

Windows

Many people think multimedia requires Microsoft Windows and, for an MPC-compliant production, it does. While Windows is a fine multimedia platform, however, it is not the only method of using multimedia, even on a PC. Macintosh computers, for example, have long provided multimedia capabilities.

Microsoft Windows includes a set of multimedia extensions consisting of a set of dynamic link libraries (DLLs), which are tools that allow applications to communicate with any hardware supported by Windows. With DLLs, applications developers no longer need to

spend a vast amount of time writing custom drivers to interface their software with the hundreds of different hardware components.

Windows as the intermediary makes programming much easier, but it also means that developers must sacrifice any control over their program's operating environment and can then only work with hardware supported by Microsoft.

⇨ MPC

In a nutshell, MPC, which stands for Multimedia PC, is a trademark designation of the Multimedia PC Marketing Council. The initial minimum MPC standard (now referred to as MPC-1) called for the following:

> ➤ a 10-megahertz (MHz) 286-based computer with 2Mb of RAM
> ➤ a 4-bit (16-color) VGA graphics adapter with VGA monitor
> ➤ the usual array of serial, parallel, and joystick ports
> ➤ a 30Mb hard disk drive
> ➤ a CD-ROM drive with better than minimal performance
> ➤ digital audio
> ➤ Windows 3.0 with the Microsoft multimedia extensions (MME), a set of DLLs that provide links between Windows' applications and multimedia hardware

The minimum digital audio requirements for MPC include the following:

> ➤ an 8-bit digital-to-analog converter with direct memory access
> ➤ an 8-bit or 16-bit linear analog-to-digital converter
> ➤ a music synthesizer
> ➤ onboard analog (not digital) audio-mixing
> ➤ MIDI instrument controls

Don't be concerned if you don't understand all the complex terminology; virtually any audio accessory board now on the market meets those minimum MPC requirements.

Because all MPC systems require that the computer run Microsoft Windows 3.x, the original specification was obviously inadequate with regard to speed. Later MPC specifications addressed this need for a faster base computer to run multimedia, but just barely. (Note that in exchange for providing easy access to hardware components and a sophisticated working environment, Windows itself adds a massive resource-draining overhead to any MPC system.) MPC-2, this second standard, calls for a minimum of the following:

➤ an entry-level 386SX-based computer with 2Mb of memory

➤ a 30Mb hard drive

➤ a VGA graphics display

➤ a 4-bit digital sound subsystem (either for speakers or headphones)

➤ a CD-ROM drive with a minimum of 150 kilobits-per-second (kbps) data transfer capabilities and an average access time under 1000 ms.

Once again, this hardware is barely sufficient to run Windows itself without even considering the massive requirements of audio and video processing software. Multimedia producers require an even more powerful system. Thus, virtually every MPC-compatible computer and upgrade kit surpasses this extremely limited MPC-2 specification. If you are interested in producing multimedia, all you really need to know about MPC-2 is enough to know what capabilities most multimedia systems have. You can then target your users better when designing your programs.

Compression

Any multimedia discussion also involves compression techniques. Compression reduces the size of files created when storing analog sound or complex color images in digital computer format.

There are a number of different compression techniques, some of which matter to multimedia authors because users must have the same technology built into their players; others are only used internally in the production system. Most compression techniques reduce the quality of the information stored, resulting in lower-quality sounds or images. Some, however, do perform full-content compression, with less loss of quality. These more expensive technologies are what is needed for most production systems.

 # What aspects of a computer are important in multimedia?

A multimedia production computer requires three basic hardware elements: memory, storage, and computing power.

You might already be an experienced computer user who understands these terms; however, because multimedia production requires skills not typically associated with computers, there's a chance you might have only a limited computer background. Therefore, I define all the important specialized terms in simple but clear language. Definitions are given both to computer terms that might be confusing to media workers and to media-related terms that probably are not familiar to computer people. Therefore, we look briefly at the elements of memory, storage, and computing power—probably the most easily confused terms in the computer field.

 ## Memory

Not only are high-end multimedia production programs themselves complex and memory-hungry, but the images and sounds they process require a lot of space in memory so they can be manipulated by the software. As you will see, no computer ever has too much memory. Random access memory, or RAM, is another way of referring to memory. RAM is not really the same as memory; it actually describes a kind of microchip often used for computer memory, but it does have other applications. Nevertheless, you often see RAM used to refer to memory.

A basic IBM PC-compatible system that just plays back multimedia programs needs about 4Mb of memory; half of that is needed to run Microsoft Windows, which eats up about 2Mb of memory itself. The majority of multimedia produced for PCs is targeted at Windows-based systems, but some can run without Windows. Many business productions, such as training software, is designed to run on older PCs that do not have Windows.

A true multimedia production computer requires an absolute minimum of 8Mb of memory and really cannot perform well without 16Mb or more using most software. Even if running under the MS-DOS operating system, which occupies far less memory than Windows, professional-grade multimedia animation or 3-D software—such as the programs sold by computer-aided design (CAD) pioneer Autodesk—requires a minimum of 8Mb of RAM.

Storage

Storage is where programs and files are kept when they are not being used or when the computer is turned off. It might be useful to examine briefly the difference between memory and storage, which is a confusing topic for many people, and one made even more confusing by reporters and writers who often use the terms interchangeably on television and in noncomputer publications. The two are not equivalent at all, except in some very special cases not covered here.

Real memory is basically the amount of RAM or memory chips installed either on a computer's motherboard or as an add-in board used to extend system memory.

Video memory, a special category of high-speed memory, is not included in the usual discussions of memory requirements because it is installed on a video card and not available for general-purpose use by the computer.

There is also *cache memory*, which is part of a caching hard-drive controller or very high-speed (and very expensive) cache memory, which is used to increase throughput speed of the microprocessor.

Finally, *system memory* stores program segments, user commands, portions of the operating environment, and data (text, numbers, images, and sounds) during processing. This type of memory is that which is referred to in descriptions of minimum memory requirements for the MPC and such. System memory is used for temporary (often *very* temporary) storage and is also volatile, which means that anything in memory disappears when the computer is turned off or loses power.

True storage, then, is much more permanent and is where data are kept when the computer is turned off. It is also where the computer locates the programs and files to be loaded into system memory. Storage can be a special type of memory chip that can be kept activated by a small battery or a different type of chip that does not lose data when power is removed. Most storage consists of floppy, hard, or optical discs.

Computing power

A fast 80386-based PC (with a minimum speed of 25 MHz) or a basic color Macintosh system provides enough computer power to play most multimedia presentations and can also be used to add sound and simple images to a very basic multimedia production. Professional-grade, and even most amateur, multimedia productions, however, require a minimum of a 33-MHz 80486-based PC or an advanced Macintosh system using a 68040 microprocessor.

Serious multimedia production work involves editing and manipulating both full-color images and full-motion video. It is therefore difficult to produce on anything less than the fastest 80486-based PC or 68040 Macintosh system. An Intel Pentium-based computer, or even a workstation based on reduced instruction set code (RISC), such as the PowerPC or PowerMac, provides an even better production platform. When deciding how to spend your money, however, remember that it is more important to have large amounts of memory and storage than the fastest microprocessor ever created.

Good news on price

Fortunately, memory, storage, and processor power all have plunged in price over the past decade and, except for temporary aberrations in the price of memory chips, the price reductions show no signs of stopping. This affordability is what has led largely to the explosion of multimedia.

The tools and concepts of multimedia are nothing new—just turn on your television to see the ultimate in multimedia production values—but the drop in computer hardware costs have brought to the desktop all the studio production capabilities that a decade ago cost a television network more than a million dollars a decade ago.

 # What are the uses of multimedia?

Multimedia isn't an end in itself: it is a communications tool that can be used to communicate almost anything. As with every other computer advancement, one of the first applications was games. As soon as computers were used by individuals rather than accounting offices, they were used to play chess, checkers, and adventure games. For example, some of the very first computers ever built were switches, lights, and simple relays wired together to play tic-tac-toe.

 # Entertainment

No one should be surprised, then, that there has been an explosion of new computer games that link video and sound to the traditional formats, from adventure games to chess. Multimedia games often include full-motion video displayed in small windows; sometimes this video is just animated images, but more and more the video uses live actors, with a real or computer-generated background. These games featuring stereo sound and speech are often interactive, so that different choices made by the player result in different video sequences being played.

Of course, these programs need a lot of storage space, so the programs often come on a CD-ROM, or even several, but all play on standard computers that have a CD-ROM player and basic audio capabilities, purchased from an inexpensive multimedia upgrade kit. Other multimedia entertainment software includes children's stories, music videos, and even travelogues and museum tours. Many of these advanced multimedia applications play only on dedicated multimedia players, such as the Philips Imagination Machine CD-I player or Tandy's similar dedicated multimedia player.

 # Business uses

Multimedia can serve many different business needs. The primary uses are discussed in the following subsections:

➢ presentations

➢ point-of-sale

➢ video conferencing

➢ training (discussed under education)

✳ **Presentations**   Anyone who has sat through a boring business presentation—enlivened only by a few slides that are often in the wrong order or upside down—knows that most people ignore much of the information provided at any presentation, wasting the time of both the presenter and the audience. More importantly, when the presentation regards sales, this boredom can also mean a substantial financial loss.

By adding animation and sound to a business presentation, the message, regardless of content, has a far better chance of reaching its audience (Fig. 1-2). Not only can multimedia boost the attention of audiences in face-to-face presentations, but a well-designed multimedia presentation can also be sent to customers' offices or other sites for viewing at their leisure. This sort of presentation can be particularly effective when designed to be interactive, allowing the user to follow his or her own path through the supplied information.

Figure 1-2

Multimedia business presentation using color Polaroid Professional Presenter DP-2000 projection panel. Polaroid Corporation

An early example of this type of business-oriented multimedia presentation is the floppy-disk-based presentation produced by North Carolina in 1993. "The Better Business Climate" uses text and images to present demographic and economic information to company managers who are considering relocating to that southern state. Although this presentation lacks the sound and motion video that would be included in a full multimedia production, it is far more effective than if the exact same information were printed in a brochure. "The Better Business

Climate" demonstrates how even a limited combination of text and images can be a powerful marketing tool.

✳ **Point-of-sale**   Another area multimedia presentations can play an important business role is in retail stores, where they can provide important, attention-getting interactive information for potential customers. Whether used to supplement the efforts of the sales staff during busy times or to catch the attention of passersby, a relatively simple multimedia presentation can become a powerful part of point-of-sales marketing.

Consider the following advantages:

➤ Once the presentation is produced, there is no need to pay someone an hourly rate to run it.

➤ The presentation never forgets an important feature of the product, becomes exasperated with customer questions, or feels pressured to move on to a customer who seems more likely to make a quick purchase.

➤ Although some people never look at such a computer-based presentation, many customers will feel much more comfortable obtaining details in just such a way, especially if they are not planning to make an immediate purchase.

A multimedia presentation can also easily demonstrate special features of a product that even the best salesperson cannot duplicate in a store setting. This feature applies to products that must be assembled or are too expensive to carry in stock, as well as products that can't be operated in the store (such as a bicycle).

✳ **Video conferencing**   A final important multimedia application for business users is video conferencing. Although real-time video conferencing is not always a multimedia production, such conferences often use much of the same computer hardware. When they include video or audio clips, text, or charts and other images in addition to the voices and images of conferees, they become multimedia. Whether the conference is between different cities or continents or just between two or more individuals on a local area network, video conferencing can be a real time-saver.

 Education & training

Business, academic, and personal applications can benefit from multimedia training programs, simulations, or teaching aids. Whether simulating dangerous conditions that would be too hazardous to actually initiate in an industrial training environment, teaching children to count, or providing a simple way to instruct computer users how to run a new program, multimedia training can be a real boost in any educational environment.

Teaching disabled workers or children is a particularly powerful application for multimedia. Multimedia can provide the extra reinforcement some students need or visual or audible training, depending on the individual needs of the student. Another very important application for multimedia training is in industry, when workers need to learn how to operate expensive new equipment that has not yet been built or installed. Airlines, for example, use multimedia training simulators to train mechanics on new airplanes before a single airplane is built. Other exotic applications for multimedia training include simulations of hazardous waste spills and nuclear plant accidents.

On a more basic level, any business that uses customized database or spreadsheet programs needs to train its employees who use these programs. While many companies produce standardized training videos and software for off-the-shelf software, training for customized report generators or templates must typically be produced in-house to be cost-effective.

The software Instant Replay Professional from I.R. Corporation in Salt Lake City, Utah, is an example of a program that can capture still or animated screen images and quickly combine them with audio. The program can then be distributed throughout the organization for initial training or quick reference by users.

 # All-in-one solutions

If you already have a Windows-capable computer, you can add multimedia playback capabilities by buying a single multimedia upgrade package. This upgrade contains all the components you need to add CD-ROM, software, and audio capabilities to play any MPC-2 program. Along with playback tools, you also receive elementary multimedia production capabilities. Any serious production, however, requires extensive upgrades to the MPC upgrade, often making it more economical to just start from scratch in creating a multimedia system (Fig. 1-3).

Both the audio and CD-ROM capabilities of most MPC upgrades are inadequate for multimedia production. For example, the system shown in Fig. 1-3 is good to use as a target system for playback, but

Figure 1-3

Typical multimedia player complete with CD-ROM and audio capabilities.
Hertz Computer Corporation

is not for serious multimedia production. Although adequate for some multimedia playback, the CD-ROM drives supplied with basic upgrade packages seldom come with a SCSI port. Without this port, the system cannot be expanded to support scanners or other devices often used for multimedia production.

The audio boards provide fine sound reproduction for most multimedia programs but lack the sophisticated capabilities needed for high-grade recording and manipulation of sounds. In particular, you might waste money on a required (for MPC compatibility) MIDI interface if you do not intend to use MIDI in your productions. MIDI is a powerful tool for composers but is not used by every multimedia producer. If you are not going to use it, you need to spend that money on better digital sound capabilities. On the other hand, if you will be using MIDI, you probably need a better MIDI board than the one supplied with these kits.

If you want to orient yourself with multimedia using a kit, consider upgrade kits from any of the companies listed later in this section. All the upgrades cost in the vicinity of $450–$650 and are generally less expensive than the individual components. Detailed specifications aren't included for these kits because the individual components and precise requirements change regularly, making detailed descriptions outdated by the time you read this book.

Most kits also come with a variety of CD-ROM multimedia titles, and all include amplifiers and external speakers, making them a bargain for those who just want to play multimedia or produce the most elementary shows.

Sensory System 1 Multimedia Upgrade Kit
Cardinal Technologies
1827 Freedom Rd.
Lancaster, PA 17601

Cyberspeed
High Technology Distributing (Better Business Systems)
7949 Woodley Ave.
Van Nuys, CA 91406

Reveal Multimedia
Insight Direct, Inc.
1912 W. 4th St.
Tempe, AZ 85281

Double Thunder
Saturn Technology, Inc.
3945 Freedom Circle
Santa Clara, CA 95054

This list is just a sampling of the companies that offer multimedia
upgrade kits through the mail—ones you would be unlikely to find in
stores or advertised in magazines. Creative Labs, Aztech, Media
Vision, Orchid, and Sony are among the major companies who offer
kits in stores and dealer ads in direct sales magazines such as
Computer Shopper.

⇨ Looking ahead

The remainder of this book looks at the specific software tools you
need to produce professional-grade multimedia, as well as the
hardware necessary to support those tools. Our target is to build a
basic system that meets the minimum requirements for true
multimedia production, but we also look at far more powerful
professional-grade systems. The more powerful systems described in
this book are suitable for creation of virtual reality presentations—that
total immersion in a computer-created environment that represents
the ultimate in multimedia.

Operating environments

BEFORE you can choose your computer system to run your programs, you first must decide which software you want to use. Of course, if you've already set up your own computer system, you most likely want to stay with compatible equipment and software.

When possible, however, choose software first because software determines which hardware you need. Hardware exists to run any software, but software that does what you want to do might not exist for a particular hardware platform. If you've already decided on your target system (which is the hardware that is to be used to play back your multimedia production), then use a similar production platform. For example, if you want to create for Macintosh users, you want to develop your multimedia on a Mac.

In either case, you still need to select software, and the software you choose will influence the rest of the hardware you add to your system. For example, if you use Autocad animation software, you need a minimum of 8Mb of memory. If you are going to purchase video editing software, be sure to also purchase plenty of storage capacity. Remember that your video, audio, and other hardware must be compatible with the software you are using.

So you see, you do not know what hardware you need until you first decide which software packages you want to run. If you are starting from scratch, the actual sequence of events leading to selecting a complete multimedia production system is as follows:

❶ First, decide what you want to do.

❷ Next, find the software that allows you to do it.

❸ Lastly, select the optimum hardware configuration for the software you want to run.

There is nothing that I, or this book, can do about that first task; you must decide on your own what you want to do in multimedia. This book does, however, offer a lot of information and advice about the last two steps. Of course, your ideas about what you will do with the completed system are influenced by available software and hardware and which equipment is within your budget. You might find that you can afford to do some things that you never dreamed would be within

your budget, while you are almost certain to learn that some things you wanted to do are either impossible or too expensive.

The actual selection process involves going back and forth from what you want to do to what software you want to get, and what hardware you can afford. Each decision affects the others, but you must start someplace, and I have found that the sequence just outlined is the practical one.

Before you can select applications software, you need to decide which operating environment you are going to use. It is the basis of your entire system. That is why this chapter begins with a look at the major operating environments. Fortunately, the choices can be narrowed down rather quickly and easily to only a few practical candidates.

Of the many operating environments available, several choices are open to multimedia developers. Some are far more practical than others, however, either because they are multimedia-friendly or because ample multimedia software has been published that run under them. There is some multimedia software produced for every common operating environment. Those with a greater market presence and, very importantly, that provide an easy programming interface for multimedia software publishers offer the best selection of applications programs.

You have probably noticed that I refer to *operating environment* rather than *operating system*. This use of the term *environment* requires a brief explanation. An operating environment includes both the operating system and the add-on programs that overlay the operating system commands to create a more friendly work environment for both users and applications programs.

Operating systems such as MS-DOS (and the nearly identical PC-DOS and DR-DOS), OS/2 (Operating System/2), and Unix (with its many variations) provide the basic personality of the computers on which they run. Each offers a way for users and applications programs alike to communicate with the system hardware. These operating systems also provide an environment, or interface, with which users must

interact to perform basic operations, such as copying files and formatting diskettes.

In the case of MS-DOS, this is the dreaded C:\ prompt or some simple variation created by using the PROMPT command. Unix systems are even less friendly. The Macintosh operating system has for many years offered users a friendly graphical interface that contrasted with the complex Unix command structure and the less complex, but still rather stark, set of system commands proven so annoying to so many MS-DOS (and early OS/2) users. With the inclusion of the Program Manager in later versions of IBM's (and codeveloper Microsoft's) OS/2, the operating system gained a powerful and reasonably friendly graphical user interface that changed the work environment without modifying how the underlying operating system worked.

Microsoft Windows 3.1 is an example of an environment that is not also an operating system (which will probably change with the introduction of Windows 4, currently code-named *Chicago*). Windows computers are MS-DOS computers and must have MS-DOS installed before Windows can operate.

Whether built into the operating system, as with the Macintosh, or added on separately, as with Windows 3.1, the graphical user interface (referred to as GUI and pronounced "gooey") imposes a considerable overhead on the system, requiring more memory, greater storage space, and increased processor performance. In exchange, the GUI adds a user-friendly environment and a standard set of tools that let applications programmers create powerful software more easily. Other windows (with a small *w*) operating environments are available, the best-known being the X-Windows software for Unix systems.

Quarterdeck Office Systems' DESQview is an extremely powerful non-GUI operating environment for MS-DOS systems. Unlike Microsoft Windows and OS/2's Presentation Manager, however, DESQview is not particularly suitable for multimedia development because it offers poor support for graphics.

Although this book is not a history of the personal computer industry, in choosing your operating system, it is useful to have some knowledge of how the present systems developed and thus their strengths and weaknesses. If you have already decided on a base system, you can skip this section.

⇨ MS-DOS

MS-DOS (MicroSoft-disk operating system) is what fired the expansion of the personal computer industry and caused the boom in Redmond, Washington, that has made Microsoft Chairman and Harvard dropout Bill Gates a multibillionaire. Back when IBM was creating the original disk-based PC office machine, the company went to Bill Gates, who already had ported the BASIC language to several early computers, and reached an agreement whereby Microsoft would design and supply PC-DOS for IBM PCs.

This primitive operating system combined features of Unix and other operating systems, such as CP/M (control program/microcomputers). Although PC-DOS and the nearly identical MS-DOS were barely able to keep out of their own way, they did provide enough tools to allow users and applications programs to access all the primitive PC's features.

This operating system was floppy-only, and had an inherent memory use limit of 640 kilobytes (K). Because hard drives were very rare back then and early PCs often had no more than 64K (not 640K) of memory, these limitations were not important. As the PC grew, so did MS-DOS (and the term is now used to include both MS-DOS and the IBM-specific PC-DOS). MS-DOS gained many new features, including a way to access hard disks. With version 2.11, MS-DOS had become a mature operating system, but to remain compatible with programs written for earlier versions, it was prevented from unrestricted growth.

MS-DOS can be used as a basis for a multimedia production system all by itself. Any advanced applications software running in an MS-DOS environment, however, must necessarily provide special tools that duplicate the features built into some other operating environments. Some of the most powerful multimedia tools (the most common being from Autodesk) do operate under basic MS-DOS and provide all the special extensions they require. They thus retain more control over their environment than they could achieve using Microsoft Windows, which provides ready-made tools but also imposes its own restrictions on any software running under it.

Novell DOS 7

Digital Research (DR) created the CP/M operating system and also lost out to Bill Gates' Microsoft when it failed to develop a version for IBM's original PC. It then struggled for years to gain a piece of the MS-DOS operating system market by offering more features and better performance than Microsoft's MS-DOS. Unfortunately, DR-DOS never made much headway, mostly because MS-DOS was shipped already installed on most PCs. Thus, users had to be convinced that DR-DOS offered enough advantages to cause them to discard the already purchased and installed MS-DOS to buy and install DR-DOS. Only a relatively few people and businesses chose to do so.

DR was eventually bought by network giant Novell, providing that company with a complete spectrum of operating system and network products and leading to the introduction of Novell DOS 7 in 1993. DOS 7 runs MS-DOS programs, including Windows, but has a few command differences and can be difficult to install. Nevertheless, it does offer the powerful ability to multitask (run several programs simultaneously) without Windows and also includes a complete network (except for hardware cables and adapter cards) that can be used to link several office computers together almost painlessly. Sophisticated users might want to consider using Novell DOS 7 as the basis for their multimedia system, even if they run Windows on top of DOS.

Microsoft Windows

By the mid-1980s, PCs were pushing the limits of MS-DOS, and Microsoft had begun serious development of Windows. Windows operates on top of MS-DOS and addresses many of the limitations of MS-DOS.

One major problem with MS-DOS is that it is a single-tasking operating system; that is, you can only load and run one application program at a time. For many years, terminate-and-stay-resident (TSR), or memory-resident, programs were the only answer to this problem. Thousands were created to add useful features, such as pop-up calendars, to standard programs. TSRs, however, are notoriously unstable, especially when several are competing against each other and MS-DOS for the same segments of computer memory.

Quarterdeck Office Systems' DESQview and other programs were developed to run under MS-DOS and provide a way to load and run multiple applications programs simultaneously. Windows, however, had the marketing muscle of Microsoft behind it and slowly but surely gained market share. Everything changed with version 3.0 of Windows, which was a full-blown operating environment that addressed many of the shortcomings of earlier versions. The initial release suffered badly from bugs that caused unexplained system crashes, but Microsoft's deep pockets carried the day. The next release (Windows 3.1) finally produced a powerful, viable, and popular operating environment alternative to the stark MS-DOS prompt.

By the end of 1993, the research firm International Data Corporation from Framingham, Massachusetts, had estimated that Microsoft had sold 45 million copies of all versions of Windows from when Windows was first introduced in 1985. The newspaper also reported that Microsoft was predicting that Windows 4.0 would ship 40 million copies by 1995. Quite a feat, considering that Windows 4.0 wasn't even shipping as of April 1994. Windows was given such emphasis because of the breakdown of Microsoft's partnership with IBM on the new OS/2. Reportedly, IBM demanded that OS/2 be crippled to ensure that it would run on the then-popular PC AT computer.

Because Windows is a graphical and multitasking operating environment, it is well-suited to run multimedia programs and also to

support the multimedia creation tools needed by authors. In fact, Windows even includes the basic tools needed to create and integrate color graphics with sounds and text and thus produce simple multimedia.

Obviously, Windows is an important operating environment to consider when deciding how to begin assembling a multimedia production system. Windows, or the closely related NT (Newer Technology) operating system, will surely continue to add multimedia tools.

Windows 4.0 is not yet on the market as this book is being completed, but it is expected to be an integrated operating system and GUI environment with full support for 32-bit microprocessors. Readers need not be overly concerned with 4.0, whether or not it is available by the time this book is published, because Microsoft will keep it backwardly compatible with virtually all existing Windows applications. In other words, unless something drastic changes between now and the date of shipping, Windows 4.0 will look just like a new version of Windows to those who are already using Windows software. Windows 4.0 will almost certainly spawn the introduction of new multimedia tools and the addition of more advanced features to existing programs, but your older software should run just fine. Hence the nature of an upgrade, rather than the introduction of a new, incompatible operating environment.

Macintosh

The Apple Macintosh computers and their integrated operating system were developed to address the stark text-oriented interface of PCs that used the MS-DOS operating system. From the beginning, the Mac used graphical elements and quickly added sound and publishing (HyperCard) tools. Later, the QuickTime multimedia publishing environment was developed.

Although the Mac has long had a multimedia-friendly environment, it has suffered from very high prices and a tightly closed system that was difficult to modify or expand. Macs' weaknesses began to change when Windows' presence in the marketplace was felt. By

the end of 1993, Apple had cut the price about a dozen times and simultaneously made it easier to add accessories.

One important expansion device long included in the Macintoshes but missing from most PCs is the SCSI port. This port allows users to easily add a number of standard devices, such as external hard drives, scanners, and CD-ROM drives, simply by connecting a new cable. The real problem with early Macintoshes was that they offered no expansion slots and were restricted to the use of tiny black and white screens. Now, however, a variety of specialized cards are available that address the needs of multimedia producers. Actually, Apple made most of these changes before multimedia really caught on and has helped lead the charge into the new technology, just as it led the move to desktop publishing.

The other drawback of Macintosh systems was that their powerful Motorola microprocessors still left many Mac systems underpowered because of the massive processor overhead imposed by the same graphical operating environment that gave the Mac such a distinct personality. This penalty is becoming widely known to many PC users now that they are adopting the Windows GUI.

 Amiga

Commodore Amiga computers were the other early multimedia leaders and are still big in Europe, but the company has virtually ignored the U.S. market for years. Because of this lack of support, Amigas can't be considered for serious multimedia development, despite their many advanced features.

Third-party companies have worked with Amiga computers to produce powerful multimedia systems. If you are interested in this platform, I suggest you contact a third-party Amiga multimedia integrator such as

Computer Basics, Inc.
1490 N. Hermitage Rd.
Hermitage, PA 16148
412-962-0533

Computer Basics offers complete Amiga-based multimedia production systems starting at about $5,000.

 # Preferred systems

By the end of 1993, most low- and mid-range multimedia production systems were operating on Macintosh, Windows, or MS-DOS systems. These are the big three, and the two Microsoft operating environments easily share programs and files.

MS-DOS is already loaded on any Windows system, so MS-DOS software can either be run without booting Windows or, in many cases, run directly from within Windows. MS-DOS programs are also compatible with IBM's powerful OS/2 and Microsoft's competing NT. The Macintosh operating system, in many cases, can share files with almost any other operating environment. The applications software, however, is not compatible with MS-DOS/Windows, OS/2, NT systems, or vice versa.

Just to keep things complicated (or to make them simpler, depending on your viewpoint), Apple introduced a new computer platform early in 1994. This PowerMac is so powerful it can run emulations of Macintosh, MS-DOS, and Windows operating environments, and applications software for those environments, sometimes faster than those programs run on the hardware platform for which they were designed. The PowerMac is discussed in Chapter 9, but is included here in the software section because it bridges the barrier between Unix, OS/2, Windows, MS-DOS, and Macintosh operating environments—it can run all of them on a single piece of hardware. When and if enough native (PowerMac-specific) multimedia programs are available, PowerMac might well prove to be the new multimedia platform of choice.

 # OS/2

OS/2 is a powerful 32-bit operating system (MS-DOS is 8-bit) designed to be compatible with both MS-DOS and Windows and to

eliminate the memory and single-tasking restrictions imposed by MS-DOS. Intended for powerful business programs, OS/2 runs multiple programs simultaneously without the danger of one program crashing the others. It runs multiple programs so efficiently that, many times, programs designed just for OS/2 run faster than their MS-DOS equivalent on MS-DOS systems, even when OS/2 is running two programs and MS-DOS is only running one.

Some multimedia applications run under OS/2, which can run MS-DOS and Windows 3.1 software, offering a powerful 32-bit alternative that can really take full advantage of a computer's power. For the most part, however, OS/2 has been left behind in the operating system wars. A major problem with OS/2, in addition to the fact that you need about 16Mb of memory for a good basic platform, is that new versions of OS/2 probably won't run Windows 4.0 software because cross-licensing agreements have expired.

⇨ Windows NT

Windows NT is essentially a network operating system. When first introduced, it was not suitable for multimedia development, precisely because its power was devoted to making it a friendly multiuser environment rather than using the hardware's power for applications programs.

NT will improve and computer hardware will continue to become faster, but applications software will also continue to become more complex and power-hungry right along with the hardware. No network or multiuser operating environment will ever be as powerful an environment for multimedia production as single-user systems are, because multimedia development is the most processor-intensive application that runs on personal computers. During some stages of large-project multimedia production, it is advantageous to have workers linked on a network, but for processor intensive tasks such as editing video or audio, a one-user workstation is best.

⇨ Unix

Although OS/2 and Windows come on more than a dozen diskettes each, Unix, the granddaddy of all microcomputer operating systems, has now grown so large that a full implementation consumes several hundred megabytes of hard disk space. The Unix operating system itself costs at least $1,000, and many versions are more expensive. While MS-DOS and Windows both lagged behind hardware for most of their existence, Unix was developed for mainframe and minicomputers. Therefore, Unix was almost always ahead of the needs of the PC world, providing tools and hardware support for personal computers of which few, if any, users could make full use. Unix, and its Xenix clones, are referred to in the computer programming world as *robust operating environments*.

Compared to the very limited tools and commands provided by MS-DOS, Unix is so packed with tools and features that a full set of its documentation looks, to the uninitiated, like the multivolume Oxford English Dictionary. Considerable doubt exists as to whether any one person actually understands everything that Unix can accomplish.

One reason for this complexity is that, in addition to being a multitasking operating system, Unix is also designed from the ground up to be a multiuser operating system. Thus, many Unix-based computers can be linked together in the same way that MS-DOS and Windows' systems can but without adding a complex network operating system, such as Novell NetWare, which is needed for the PC.

Unix was primarily designed by the same programmers who invented the C programming language. Although Unix was not developed by the U.S. Government, it was produced by what was probably the world's second largest and oldest bureaucracy, AT&T, and it shows that heritage. In general, Unix is not a good operating environment for building multimedia unless you are running it on a powerful RISC-based workstation. The reason is simply because a personal computer just is not powerful enough to run Unix well and still have processor power left for actual multimedia production.

Text-editing software

ALTHOUGH the spotlight is on images and sound when people discuss multimedia, data (plain text and numbers) are still the basis of many productions. To focus on producing live business presentations or relatively small multimedia productions, the necessary text is such a small part of the finished product that nearly any word processor is suitable. You might even be able to use just graphics-generation software to create a few headlines or sentences on charts.

Any large-scale multimedia project, however, especially those intended to be used on a standalone basis, probably involves a large amount of text, as well as charts filled with numbers. For these applications, you need a good word processor, but not one overloaded with tools you won't use. You can also use a dedicated text editor, if you are working with existing text files.

For business presentations that must be regularly adjusted to fit changes in data, such as quarterly reports or product descriptions as presented in multimedia catalogs, data are often generated from spreadsheets or even databases.

⇨ Word processors

Today's powerful word processors such as Microsoft Word, WordPerfect (WP), or even the strongly Windows-oriented Lotus Ami are massive. They each have hundreds of features, of which any particular user only uses a relative few. These business-oriented word processors have, over the past few years, become document word publishers that can easily substitute for a full-featured page layout and desktop publishing program, as long as the documents being produced are relatively simple and short.

Before you load one of these massive word publishing programs onto your computer, sacrificing a dozen or more megabytes of precious hard disk space for tools you won't be using, stop and analyze just what type of text manipulation you need to perform. Word processors include spellcheckers and thesauri, both of which are useful for most text creation and editing functions. They also provide a selection of

fonts, special characters, outliners, formatting tools, chart and column generators, mail merge, math features, graphics tools, footnotes, table of contents generators, and so forth. If you already use one of these programs, it will almost certainly be more efficient to continue to rely on it (no retraining is involved). If you are selecting a new text editor, however, consider just how many of those features you really need and how some might actually interfere with your work before you invest the time and money to install and learn it.

For instance, if you need plain ASCII text files as input for a hypertext or other multimedia publishing program, you must ensure that your chosen word processor produces pure ASCII. Some word processors insert unwanted carriage returns at the end of each line when exporting a file designated as DOS or ASCII.

A major problem facing newspaper, magazine, and book publishers when they accept documents on diskette is the different file formats created by various word processors. Creating text in a text editor rather than a word processor eliminates that problem. Because the software is designed to produce ASCII code, but not perform formatting, text editors are usually simpler to learn and use.

Nevertheless, most companies rely on one of a handful of basic word processors to produce their text. Whether you work on in-house productions or are an independent developer who receives files by clients, you need to convert the text files you receive into a format that your authoring software accepts.

⇨ WordPerfect

I begin with this word processor because it is the most popular one, and I regularly use it to create plain text. The latter reason is mostly because I am familiar with the software. WordPerfect does, however, typify the features packed into most modern word processors. I use a very old version of WordPerfect (WP), both because my many macros would need to be translated to move up to a later version and because, although there have been two major upgrades, neither contains any features I would use.

This creeping feature-itis, common to most business programs, must be considered when you will not use the word processor for any tasks that really use those costly and complex tools. If you are only going to produce simple multimedia documents, the complexity of WP 6 for Windows is actually a big advantage because it includes all the tools needed to integrate images and sounds within a text document. This feature makes it a sensible choice for some users, but none of these multimedia tools is an acceptable substitute for the powerful standalone programs used to produce true multimedia.

Microsoft Word

Microsoft Word is WP's biggest competitor and offers just about equivalent capabilities. Realistically, there is little to choose between these two word processors. If you have one already available, stick with it.

Each word processor will continue to be regularly updated with exciting new features and bugs, which is why I stick with an old version for most of my work. It also has bugs, but I am familiar with all of them by now, and some have even proven highly useful.

Ami

I am including this graphical interface word processor because it is bundled with many computers that come preloaded with Windows and a Windows version of Lotus 1-2-3. Ami is a terrific word processor with neat desktop publishing features. As with the big two, however, it is overkill for the sort of text editing and creation that multimedia producers encounter.

XyWrite

XyWrite is the premier word processor/editor chosen as a standard by most publishing companies, from giant hardback book publishers

to small newspapers and magazines. There are three reasons for XyWrite's massive popularity among editors:

- ➢ speed
- ➢ flexibility
- ➢ lack of upgrades

XyWrite is probably the fastest word processor ever designed for MS-DOS systems. As such, it was a vital tool when a powerful computer was powered by a 4.77-MHz 8088 Intel chip. It has retained its popularity because as computers became faster, the tasks have also become more demanding, and editors still need a very fast editor. XyWrite's other powerful feature is the ability to customize its operation to suit particular documents or publishers' needs.

Its last advantage, lack of upgrades, is considered a disadvantage by some users who want every product they install on their computer to do everything. Being the fastest editor and word processor isn't enough for them; they want good outlining tools, better printer support, even graphics and faxing capabilities. Serious users, however, have applauded XyWrite III for remaining aloof from this urge to expand. The basic program remained the same for enough years so that it became a major standard in the publishing industry.

XyWrite had only one drawback: it was very difficult to learn. The recently introduced version, however, has pull-down menus that make it easier to learn and use. But many editors see this as the first step on that slippery slope toward the feature-itis that made many other programs so bloated they lost their original appeal as being best at a particular task.

Do not confuse other XyWrites with the XyWrite III that is such a powerful editing tool. There is also the IBM-sponsored version of XyWrite, called Signature, that was designed for Windows operation, for example, as well as the XyWrite IV program with its WYSIWYG (what you see is what you get) formatting and other desktop publishing tools.

Conversion programs

The best situation exists when you are using a second program that can import the original's file format directly. But importing only works occasionally. Even if you limit your choice of editing and authoring software to those compatible with the file formats you already have, the next assignment could come with a couple of megabytes of text files in a completely different format. The best solution is to be prepared with a powerful file conversion program that can convert between as many of the several hundred proprietary formats as possible.

A conversion program is one piece of software that must be kept current through upgrades, because even popular word processors, such as WP, have a tendency to change file formats regularly. Thus, not only do you need to convert files created in WP 4.1 (the version being used to write this book), but you also must convert version 5.1 and even version 6.0 (WPSIX0) format files just to keep current with one word processor.

I am intimately familiar with such problems because, as a reporter and author, I must convert daily between my base word processor format and any of a dozen or more used by various editors, including the plain ASCII file format required by my editors at Windcrest/McGraw-Hill. Conversion is not as easy as you might think, even with the text-export option provided by nearly all word processor programs that convert their own files into plain ASCII.

⇨ General conversion

Personally, I have always leaned toward using Word-for-Word (WFW), from

Mastersoft
6991 E. Camelback Rd.
Scottsdale, AZ 85251

to handle most of my file conversion tasks. Although WFW Professional can handle about 90 text-file formats, it is strictly a PC-based utility. The inexpensive Doc-to-Doc from

MCS Group
2465 W. Chicago
Rapid City, SD 57702

is also worth looking into if it converts the formats you encounter. It is an easy-to-use program with lots of powerful conversion features, one that every wordsmith should have available.

The problem with many conversion programs is exactly the same one you encounter with the "text" conversions included with word processors—the file output format that converts files into "standard" ASCII. The trouble is that these conversion systems almost always leave a hard return at the end of each line, which you must then remove manually before most other programs can format the text properly. You can strip these hard returns out of small files by using search-and-replace (S&R) tricks, either from within WP or (for corrupted files that cause my system to crash) from WP's Program Editor.

In WP, you can usually just S&R for double occurrences, replace them with a tab or other unusual character, S&R the remaining "s" with either nothing or a blank space, depending on the file, and then replace those tabs with tabs again to get decently formatted text. Of course, if you export ASCII from WP, when you finish editing, all those "s" characters go right back in. It's a roundabout solution, but a simple one that is quick, painless, and easy to semiautomate. You can also produce text in "clean" ASCII by setting very wide margins before exporting the file from WP and then removing the few remaining hard returns, but this is not a universal solution. These tricks, however, are no solution for a production shop that needs to clean up hundreds of files produced in a number of different formats or for a multimedia producer who might be importing an entire book for inclusion in a project.

Surprisingly, no easy-to-locate commercial programs tackle this simple-seeming but annoying problem of hard returns. I could locate none among the nearly 50,000 programs described in my various databases. I even tried CompuServe (CS), the large commercial electronic bulletin board system that carries software and hardware support for many products.

Because CS has an active desktop publishing forum, it seemed a likely place to find TEXTCON, a shareware program I knew of that promised to intelligently strip out those extra hard returns. I did need to search for it because its name had been changed, but I finally did locate the file. It almost seemed anticlimactic that this little shareware utility did exactly what it claimed. TEXTCON analyzes files and intelligently removes the extra hard returns. If you have similar ASCII file problems, check out TEXTCON, written by CrossCourt Systems' Chris Wolf back in 1986.

I talked to Chris, whose company is based in East Lansing, Michigan, and he said the program is sold directly for $25 for the command-line version I tested, or for $35 for a menu-driven version that also includes support for DCA/RFT formatted output in addition to straight ASCII. Both programs work only with ASCII files, but CrossCourt does have a program that converts WP 5.0 and 5.1 to ASCII that Chris says is superior to the WP DOS utility.

If you encounter problems with hard carriage returns during file conversions, I urge you to try TEXTCON. The best way to find it is to become familiar with the shareware files found on major bulletin board services (BBS)—something you need to do anyway to keep up with developments in the computer field. Magazines, newspapers, and books just aren't current enough to solve all your problems. A version of TEXTCON is included on the disk provided with this book.

Wang

If you are working with a branch of the U.S. Government or one of many old, established companies, you are likely to run across Wang Laboratory word processor-compatible files, which pose a special problem. Because Wang was well into office automation before the invention of the standardized PC, it developed its own standards. Unfortunately for users and the company alike, Wang did not adapt to the changes that occurred in the industry in the 1980s.

A legacy of strangely formatted text remains that certainly runs into the billions of words, all of which must be converted to a newer format if it is to remain useful. Format conversion is always a challenge, even between programs running under the same operating system. The problem is even worse when files must be exchanged between incompatible platforms, such as Wang and PC.

Although users are rapidly migrating away from the company's proprietary formats, government agencies will continue to use Wang-created documents for years, either in their native VS format or on PCs. But whether agencies make the changeover now or delay the inevitable, sooner or later a multitude of documents will need to be converted from VS to some PC format.

MCS Group offers a solution with its Pride document conversion software, which provides two-way conversion between VS formats and popular PC-based government word processor formats such as Enable, .WK1, Word, Multimate, WP, Wang PC, DCA/RFT, and ASCII, as well as some less-used formats. The conversion process between platforms retains text formatting such as italics, margins, and tabs as well as more exotic features such as superscripts and subscripts. Pride lets you view and convert a single document or batchprocess up to 2,500 files at one time and supports most LANs. Don't be surprised if conversion takes some time across platforms.

WordDoctor Plus is a much less expensive conversion program from MCS Group with the same basic features, but it converts only between PC-based word processor formats, including Wang PCWP, SITA and APS Archive, and not between VS and PC platforms.

Yet another conversion program, Doc-to-Doc, is similar to the more expensive MCS programs, but the only Wang format supported by it is Wang PCWP. Other PC word processor file conversions supported include all those major PC programs listed above. At less than $45,

Doc-to-Doc is probably the least expensive professional document conversion software on the market.

Other data sources

Business presentations in particular often need to draw upon text and numbers generated by spreadsheets or other nontext programs. A basic non-GUI spreadsheet such as Lotus 1-2-3 can be a powerful editing and chart creation tool for formatting text and numbers. Many publishers, and therefore writers, use 1-2-3 as nothing more than a sophisticated way of generating tables and text charts that would be difficult or impossible to create in any word processor, regardless of its table-generation capabilities. The ability to move around entire columns or rows of text and export them in plain ASCII files makes 1-2-3 a useful text formatting and editing tool.

You might also find that you need to export existing spreadsheet data to a form that can be used in a presentation. These data can be reformatted right in the spreadsheet, or archived data files can be converted to ASCII using Word-for-Word or other conversion programs.

Databases

If you are in the business of publishing a catalog, your major source of data will be the files contained in the inventory database program that the company uses to track products. Your database must therefore have a powerful report-generating capability and you must have a way to convert the almost universally adopted dBASE file format into a usable layout format.

Still-image creation software

I N this chapter, we define illustration software as those programs used to create illustrations for inclusion in documents, on overhead transparencies used in presentations, or for screen and slide shows. All of these can be multimedia productions.

Some people restrict the category of illustration software to only a few programs that emulate an artist's drawing board. They rely mostly on electronic simulations of paint brushes, pencils, rulers, and French curves. This artificial restriction would never limit a non-electronic artist, so why should it be applied to computerized illustration programs?

Most illustrations include freehand drawings (bit-map graphics) and enhancements to CAD-like lines and curves (vector graphics). Effective presentations often also contain computer-generated images such as graphs and charts. Even such exotic items as fractal images are used in both business presentations and multimedia shows. (Fractals are those creations of chaos mathematics that simulate natural images such as plants and landscapes.)

Illustration software can be used to create what many people consider art, either abstract or photo-realistic. This sort of art is important and included in many business-style illustrations, but its major use is in creating alternative realities for entertainment presentations. For example, an architect often uses a photo-realistic view of an as-yet-unbuilt structure to liven up a presentation. Home users also enjoy working with this type of software.

Corporate users, along with their counterparts in government, tend to create illustrations meant to convey a concrete rather than aesthetic message. So, in addition to what some would call pure art, these illustrations almost always contain text. Not just plain type, but enlarged, elongated, shadowed, and otherwise embellished letters and numbers.

Because charts and graphs are also regularly included in presentations, illustration software must be able to either create such graphics elements directly from imported raw data (presentation software) or import and enhance graphs and charts when created using other software.

The broadly defined category of illustration software includes both paint and draw programs, as well as more advanced presentation software. The difference between the high-end paint software and presentation (including chart-generation) software is becoming as blurred as the difference between high-end word processors and desktop publishing systems. This book does not attempt any artificial separation of the two groups of programs. In general, paint and draw programs are simpler than presentation software, with fewer or no special effects and a more limited selection of tools.

The technical difference between draw and paint software is that paint programs generate raster images—that is, paint software uses bit-mapped graphics. Every part of each individual element is specified in the file, and therefore each data bit in an image can be individually changed.

Draw graphics software

Draw programs are less expensive and less than related computer-aided design (CAD) software. Their lack of complexity is mostly connected with such engineering-related items as precise size and position of lines and elements. Thus, these programs are unsuitable for drafting, but actually more useful for those wanting to produce illustrations rather than technical drawings. Draw programs are normally more versatile and easier both to learn and use than full-featured CAD software.

Draw programs (and CAD software) create vector or line-segment images where each line element can be rearranged independently of adjacent objects or even independently of those of which it is a part. Vector graphics images use beginning and end points, or beginning points, direction, and length, to define each line element.

Paint software

Paint programs could be considered limited versions of presentation software. While paint programs can be used to create the

sophisticated, highly stylized charts and graphs commonly associated with business-style presentations, they do not normally include a way to create charts and graphs automatically from an imported data set, an important feature of many presentation programs.

Paint programs have tools that emulate traditional artists' tools, such as paintbrushes, and are therefore more versatile than basic graph and chart presentation software. In a paint program, you can "lasso" and move any piece of the image, whereas in a draw program you can only manipulate individual lines or sets of lines. Paint software is bit-map based.

Presentation graphics software

The varied presentation graphics software on the market falls into several specialized areas, with some concentrating on creating graphs and charts from data sets and others being sophisticated versions of paint programs. Still more combine the two and even add animation. The most powerful aspect of presentation graphics programs is usually the ability to import vast data files directly to automatically create a variety of graphs or charts.

As many as 30 or 40 types of graphs are available in the software. These powerful business tools are particularly important for those individuals who must create new presentations on a regular basis using new data sets each time. These programs can be used for presentations to different, or potential, clients as well as productions to internal personnel that use regularly updated data.

Freehand presentation software, in contrast to the data manipulation programs, typically includes sophisticated ways to create and manipulate text but is primarily concerned with producing images rather than data-related graphics. Some presentation software combines both data import charting and freehand enhancement tools, but even these usually stress one or the other set of features. Animation and slide shows are two somewhat-related features also found in presentation software. A discussion of animation is included in Chapter 5.

Slide show graphics software

Slide shows are normally created by the same high-end presentation software used to create the initial images. A slide show is just a sequential display of existing images, shown directly on a computer screen or displayed to a larger audience using a projection television or an overhead projector equipped with a computer-controlled flat-panel projection screen.

There are also standalone slide show programs that can integrate images from different paint or presentation graphics programs. Most users, however, will want to select a full-featured program that includes its own slide show utility. Although a desktop computer is typically used to create the graphics initially, it is common to use a portable, or even notebook, computer to transport the presentation, either to a conference room or directly to a client's desk.

Scientific graphics

A more specialized category is the scientific or engineering graphics programs. They are used to generate hard copy or display data on a workstation monitor. Their main function is to help make complex data more intelligible via scientific charts and graphs. Scientific and engineering-oriented graphics programs are related to business-oriented programs in the same way that draw programs are related to CAD. They bring more precision and more special features to the user because the data are often more complex.

Fractals

A relatively new graphics type called *fractals* is unlike either raster (bit-mapped) or vector graphics. Fractals will be used more and more in high-performance graphics programs when any natural object is to be represented.

Bit-mapped graphics cannot be enlarged because only the original number of data bits that were specified when the image is initially created actually exist, and thus all available information is included in the original drawing. Any magnification creates a blocky image, such as what you see when a newspaper image is magnified.

Vector graphics images can always be enlarged because they specify line segments that can be magnified. No additional details are presented, however, once the image scale is increased beyond that originally created. Thus, these illustrations appear empty when enlarged because, while the distances between elements increase, no additional detail is added.

Fractal images are entirely different because they are based on a set of data, along with an algorithm that formulates those data into an image. The more you enlarge the scale of a fractal, the more detail becomes available, making these images more suited to real-world images. That definition is a rather false representation, however, because the details are more in the nature of "fill" than actual information. Still, the resulting enlarged illustrations appear just as complex as before. If you need to present complex scientific data by simulating natural elements such as landscapes or water or just want to really add some pizzazz to otherwise dull presentations, nothing can match fractal technology.

Fractal illustrations are unlike the usual, rather simple overhead projection charts, graphs, and headlines in most illustration software applications. These simple charts have for decades been created by art departments using no computers at all. Fractal illustration software, however, creates images so complex that they can only be generated by a computer. For graphics applications, the computer only speeds up production that could be done by hand. Graphics created with fractal technology, however, must use the powerful calculating ability of the computer.

Unfortunately, although fractal programs do run on MS-DOS, Windows, or Macintosh systems, few workstation programs specifically list fractal technology as part of their rendering repertoire. The Fractals Artist Toolkit, for both MS-DOS and Sun platforms, from Small Systems Communications Products in Kensington,

California, is one of those. The program generates fractal images and includes some already-generated fractal images. For Macintosh users, Koyn Fractal Studio (Koyn Software, 1754 Sprucedale, St. Louis, MO 63146; 314-878-9125) is an excellent choice for generating intricate fractal designs.

⇨ File conversion

Rather than create every image that is to be used in a presentation, many authors choose to import and modify existing graphics. This concept is especially important when creating a final image based on an existing image, such as a company logo or an actual physical object.

Just as there are a wide range of programs designed to convert between different word processing formats, so too are there a number of graphics formats. Thus, you must either select editing software that can import and export images in a variety of formats or purchase a specialty conversion utility program.

North Coast Software from Barrington, New Hampshire, offers a dual-purpose solution to Windows graphics users called Conversion Artist. This utility lets Windows 3.x users both convert and view 32 bit-map graphics file formats. Many of the supported file formats can be either imported or exported, with the notable exception of EPS (encapsulated PostScript), which is available as an export format only. EPS images can, however, be viewed from Conversion Artist. All in all, you can export an image to any of 17 file formats and import any of 31 formats. Fifteen 24-bit True Color formats are supported.

Conversion is quite fast, at least on my Zeos 33-MHz 486 PC. Despite the fact that some pages were missing from the documentation, I had little trouble installing and using the software on the second try. I say second try because I ran into a lot of trouble with what was apparently a bad file or two on the first attempt. But because Conversion Artist comes with both sizes of disks, all I had to do was switch disks and everything worked well.

Besides converting between file formats, Conversion Artist also can reduce the number of colors in an image, going all the way from 32-bit images to 16-color and gray-scale. I won't list all of the compatible file formats, but I didn't notice any missing; even the Video Toaster format from Amiga is included, as are other non-MS-DOS formats from Silicon Graphics, Macintosh, SUN, and OS/2. Batch conversions are available, but no overwrite warning exists for duplicate file names, so use caution. Of special interest to government users is that Conversion Artist supports import and export of the WordPerfect raster format (WPG).

A highly versatile screen capture utility is included, as are a choice of eight dithering methods. RLE, LZW, G3, G4, and Packbits file compression options can be applied to some files. Separate add-on optional programs include a Dycam digital camera interface module, advanced image editing, and a JPEG compression module.

Although conversion, screen capture, and color reduction are powerful features of Conversion Artist, if you want to edit images, this is not the program to buy. You won't find a better graphics conversion program for less than $150, but don't confuse Conversion Artist with a program such as Pizzazz Plus from Application Techniques in Pepperell, Massachusetts, which also has a screen capture utility but is mainly a print enhancement program. Pizzazz Plus has extensive graphics enhancement editing capabilities but very limited conversion capabilities.

Both programs are very useful. Pizzazz is more sophisticated, but the two are not interchangeable. If your work involves enough graphics manipulation that you need one, you might still need the other.

Using graphics in business presentations

Both the general business community and government agencies are very interested in presentation and drawing software. The reason for including graphics in most presentations or publications is relatively simple—text and talk alone can be pretty boring. That simple truth,

along with the obvious fact that graphs can summarize and present complex data in new and useful ways, accounts for most office uses of graphics programs.

Putting the same information contained in an oral presentation into overhead projection transparencies or slide shows offers advantages. You not only give the audience something to look at to break up the monotony of a straight lecture, but you also reinforce the message by presenting it to the audience in two different media simultaneously.

In addition to putting accounting-type numbers into graphs or charts to make the data more understandable, there are also scientific applications for graphics programs. These programs can take complex or incomplete data and present them in an entirely new format that can bring new relationships to the forefront. Graphics representations are also important tools when summarizing vast quantities of data. Color provides even more information. It is often considered essential, both to make graphics interesting and to display subtle differences in complex data presentations.

The usefulness of supplying data both in tabular and graphical form has been underlined lately by the move toward adding sound to further enhance the understanding of highly complex, especially scientific, data. I am not talking about adding cartoon sounds to presentations in a multimedia extravaganza, either. If carried too far, that can actually distract attention from the information being presented. Serious scientific efforts using supercomputers are making complex information more accessible. Can it be very long before the graphics-with-sound concept is applied to the complex statistical information involved in many nonscientific disciplines?

⇨ Platforms

While personal computer graphics programs (particularly Macintosh software) have come a long way in the past few years, the growing importance of graphics, along with the growing complexity of the software, are good reasons why large businesses might need to use workstations or even minicomputers for their graphics work. Of

course, if data are being charted or graphically analyzed and those data were originally generated on a larger-scale system than a PC, it is probably easiest to use a graphics program running on the same platform. There are other reasons, however, for moving beyond personal computers for graphics work.

First, obviously, is speed. Even the fastest graphics boards and 486-based systems are not a match yet for a dedicated graphics workstation. With the 586 looming on the horizon and ever faster graphics coprocessors, however, the speed question might become moot. Second (at least for the PC), the range of colors is quite limited. The Macintosh platform is usually best for top-quality graphics in a smaller desktop system.

But, speed and color aside, other limitations exist with PC graphics programs. For example, few or no PC graphics programs have the range of graph types available on some of the more advanced packages that run on larger platforms. Polar charts in particular, because of their complexity, are slighted by many low-end programs. Many higher-end programs also allow multiple graphs on the same screen. They can present both graphs and the data used to create them onscreen at the same time, rather than linking them from hidden files.

Also missing from virtually all low-end programs is the ability to both import and enter data easily from the keyboard. Some PC software concentrates on data import; other programs optimize keyboard data entry.

Workstation or minicomputer graphics packages are better at handling very large data sets, whose large numbers of points provide sophisticated curve-fitting tools with more information to analyze. Multimedia producers working with this type of data can generally get preprocessed files from the appropriate department.

Users have always known the importance of transferring image files between different applications programs and operating environments. The use of graphics programs increases daily, however, and ever more complex tasks are being tackled by graphics designer professionals and casual users alike. It is therefore becoming very

important for departments to consider if using graphics programs that run on a variety of hardware platforms can save training time while increasing versatility. It is also sometimes cost-effective to do some preliminary or final work on one platform and carry out the bulk of the design activity on one or more other systems.

Some presentation graphics programs, such as Computer Associates' CA-DISSPLA, run on everything from PCs to Cray supercomputers. The HP 9000, Apollo, MS-DOS, Sun, Unisys, Convex, Concentrix, DEC, AIX, Cray, AViiON, Prime, and IRIS are just some of the platforms for which Computer Associates produces special versions of their presentation graphics programs.

Will graphics work (and multimedia) become more important for a particular department as time passes? If so, will it eventually be important to move users to much more sophisticated software running on more powerful platforms? If this evolution is a real possibility, it will become even more important to choose software that comes in Unix and other workstation versions.

 # Buying tips

Most presentation software is used to create graphs from numeric data. Despite the fact that the programs might have many other features, graph production is often a major consideration.

In choosing among graph and charting programs, the user should consider more than just whether the software can handle the data format already in use. Ease of learning and use, especially when a program will be used infrequently or by several people rather than a designated operator, will prove very important. Because some sort of menu control system usually makes a program much easier to use, the design of menus and their usefulness is also important.

The amount of computing power, memory, and storage space are additional important considerations. A terrific program won't be of much use if it turns out to need more memory than available when tackling big data sets or if it runs too slowly.

Computer Associates' CA-DISSPLA, for instance, runs in less than one megabyte of RAM but needs a minimum of 30Mb of disk storage, and CA-TELLAGRAF takes up 60Mb of space on a VAX. Information International's Leonardo needs 8Mb of RAM and nearly 20Mb of disk space on a Sun system. The hardware requirement champion is probably the InterCAP Illustrator II that runs in 8Mb of RAM but needs a whopping 200Mb of hard disk space. Although these RAM requirements are not too unusual, Illustrator II takes a significant chunk out of nearly any workstation's storage space. Nothing is wrong with Illustrator II's storage requirement; some illustration software simply has large hardware requirements because it has a large feature list.

A prime consideration for those who frequently need to generate many charts and graphs should be how many different types of charts and graphs a program can provide. Graphics software should provide templates, macros, style sheets, and other guides that help ensure a consistent presentation. Otherwise, it won't be very useful for creating graphics, either for presentations or for publication, unless it is only used to create a few illustrations in a given project. Consistency of appearance is very important when creating a number of illustrations for a project.

Slide show features, which can be important on PCs used to operate projectors at presentations, are not usually important for the larger workstations. If you are creating images on a workstation, however, and want to produce slide shows to be run on a PC, this feature, as well as file compatibility, is of prime importance.

If you are operating in a mixed computer environment and will not be working with graphics created with only one program, it is vital that your software be able to import, export, or (preferably) do both with files in a format compatible with your other programs.

Data also need to be moved between systems when being graphed or charted, so make certain that, if your data are coming from dBASE or Lotus 1-2-3, the graphics program can import that data format. Delimited ASCII files can be exported and imported by most programs, although this might not prove satisfactory and is seldom a good substitute for a program that can import data in the original format.

Lastly, flow charts, decision tree charts, or organization charts might be important in a particular office. If so, the easiest and most cost-effective solution might be to purchase a separate program, such as allCLEAR, from CLEAR Software. This program uses simple English commands and an artificial intelligence engine to produce simple or complex charts quickly and easily. allCLEAR runs only under MS-DOS but is so powerful and easy to use it is a good investment for many offices. It is especially useful because many of the listed illustration programs do not include any easy method of creating this type of box-and-text chart.

Graphics creation tips

As with desktop publishing, the most important rule for creating effective and pleasing illustrations is to keep things simple. An M.C. Escher etching may be eye-catching, but it has little place as the background for a representation of complex statistical data.

In general, a very simple message can sometimes be effectively dressed up using a Peter Max/Yellow Submarine-style illustration. The more complex the information becomes, however, the less the background should be permitted to detract from it. Background is not the only consideration, either.

Just as good design dictates that desktop publishing users strictly limit the number of fonts used on a single page and throughout an entire document, so too does good graphics design require a limited number of chart or graph types. With a wide range of graphs available, it is tempting to make use of all that variety to spice up a document or presentation. By making viewers constantly play catch-up with your style, however, you defeat what should be the prime purpose of including illustrations—making the message clearer!

Designers, especially technically oriented individuals who do not normally design graphics, should remember that not all graph types are equally understandable by all viewers. Polar representations, for instance, are essential for displaying some data, but the chart type itself might be mystifying to viewers.

Similarly, while multiple charts can explain some item in detail, it is not a good idea to place unrelated charts, even those of the same type and style, on the same page or projection image. You can use multiple charts without causing confusion if the charts are very simple, but what is the point of placing them in close conjunction if they contain unrelated information?

When presenting complex or related information, it is possible to combine graphs or place a large number of variables on a single chart. Unless this is done carefully, however, it will confuse more than it will clarify, depending somewhat on the kind of graph being used.

Some pie charts, for instance, can contain a large number of factors and still be meaningful. Line or bar charts, however, can quickly become unintelligible if too many elements are included. It is far better to use identically formatted graphs placed in close proximity, with each displaying only one or two of the related factors.

A good way to present complex information is to begin simple and use advancing illustrations, where more information is added to the same chart or a graph is built up during the presentation. In print, this concept can be accomplished by placing a sequence of illustrations in the same location on succeeding pages, with each illustration becoming more complex by the addition of more data. This technique also prevents the audience from skipping ahead.

Consistency is important and can be accomplished without constantly using the same types of charts or graphs, which is not always practical. The use of a simple and consistent background for all related charts and graphs can make the presentation as a whole more understandable, especially when you are covering several unrelated topics. In the latter case, you might want to use several different backgrounds, each keyed to the current subject.

Finally, a note on design that should be obvious but needs mentioning. Color can be a very powerful tool when used correctly in an illustration. Some thought should be given, however, to just how much information you want color to convey and whether critical data should be illustrated in more than one way. Remember, a significant part of nearly any audience could be color-blind! In some cases, it

might be best to view completed illustrations in black-and-white before committing to using specific colorful designs. If the information isn't clear in gray, it won't be clear in full color to a measurable portion of your audience. Print illustrations might also be copied on a black-and-white copier.

⇨ **Conclusions**

Some type of advanced still image-creation or editing software will be needed by all but those who are authoring the most basic of multimedia presentations.

It is important to remember the difference between paint and draw (or CAD) programs. Paint is a freehand graphics creation system where individual image elements are created or edited. A paint or bit-map image can be reduced in size with good results, but it cannot be enlarged much because the original doesn't contain any more details than are possible to create using a very limited number of image points. Bit-map files contain a description of the color and intensity of every image element at the bit level.

Vector, or draw, and CAD programs represent images by formulas, rather than by defining each picture element. They can therefore be enlarged to any extent, although it might not prove useful to do so because there might not be any underlying detail to display. Fractals provide image fill that keeps images relatively busy and interesting, no matter how large they are made.

File conversion and compatibility between the image creation software and image editors, animation programs, or multimedia authoring systems are very important for almost every multimedia creator. Whether cross-platform compatibility is important depends entirely on the particular work environment. If your business uses both Macintosh and MS-DOS systems, it might be important to have software versions that run on both. Normally, it is only important to convert raw data or finished images from one platform to another. It isn't typically important that both systems run similar editing software.

5

Video & animation software

CHAPTER 5

VIDEO images will form the heart of your multimedia production, whether still or full-motion, full-screen or window, computer-generated or live action. Collecting, creating, editing, and integrating video images will be the biggest challenge to you, the multimedia producer, and to your hardware and software.

⇨ Clip video

The easiest way to get high-quality images for your multimedia production is to purchase ready-to-use stock art on floppy diskette or CD-ROM. You can also obtain stock stills and video footage on video tape, but you need a video capture board to use it in your production. A video capture board is required by most multimedia development platforms anyway, but it is not essential for simple productions.

One of the best collections of video clip art is from the MediaClips series published by

Aries Multimedia Entertainment
310 Washington Blvd.
Suite 100
Marina del Rey, CA 90292

The CD-ROM collections are royalty-free; once you pay for a disc, you can use any of the images in any of your creations without paying per-use royalties as you would with some video and sound clips. A typical disc contains approximately 100 high-quality still images, 50 or more audio clips, and 25 or more full-motion video clips (which can only be used with Microsoft-sponsored MPC and Macintosh systems).

Titles of directories that contain MPC (Windows)-, Macintosh-, and PC-compatible files include the following:

➤ Wild Places, which features still images and sounds of unusual locations

➤ Deep Voyage, with colorful underwater images along with motion video and sounds

➤ World View, featuring images of the world from space along with other space-related clips

> Tropical Rainforest, with video, still, and audio clips of colorful plants and animals

> MPC Wizard, a suite of test and tune-up tools systems that measure CD-ROM drive performance; CD-Audio, WAVE, MIDI, and other sound systems on MPC machines; VGA graphics configuration (many 265-color VGA drivers are included on the disc); and hints for optimizing Windows and multimedia performance

This disc also includes a number of the best royalty-free sound and image files from the MediaClips series. Other MediaClip titles available in early 1994 are Business Backgrounds; Full Bloom; Island Designs; Jets & Props; Majestic Places; and Money, Money, Money.

Macintosh MediaClip images are 8-, 24- and 32-bit (QuickDraw) color. PC and MPC images are intended for 512K RAM video boards with Super VGA (SVGA), or 256-color capability. Available Aries images include QuickTime animations and PICT files. For quality video clips, these images are very inexpensive.

Although these clips are royalty-free, restrictions do exist. First, you can only use 20 percent of the files on a single disc without obtaining special permission from the publisher. Second, you must include a credit line for the artist and Aries Multimedia Entertainment.

One company that provides 8- and 24-bit PICT color and 24-bit TIFF files for Macintosh users is

East*West Communications
1631 Woods Dr.
Los Angeles, CA 90069

Another company,

The Audio Visual Group
398 Columbus Ave.
Suite 355
Boston, MA 02116

markets PICT photo files and QuickTime movies.

⇨ Animation

Animation has a basic advantage over other video. It uses images that do not exist in the physical world! Desktop animation brings entirely new capabilities to business.

Animation offers the following benefits to users of multimedia:

> ➤ An advertising firm can use animation to show a client how a new product will look in an upcoming campaign.

> ➤ An engineer can perform a what-if study on several design variations while the actual product is still on the drawing board.

> ➤ A rock group can produce a music video without building sets.

> ➤ An educator can make a preschool program interesting to the Sesame Street crowd as well as show graduate students what researchers think is happening inside a black hole.

> ➤ Companies can offer training before the actual product exists, as Boeing Aircraft did in early 1994 when it trained aircraft mechanics to repair an airplane for which the first prototype is still being built.

> ➤ Business people can add spice to a business presentation by not just showing charts of last year's sales and next year's projections but, rather, an eye-catching animated progression from one to the other.

In traditional animation, which nearly all of us have seen demonstrated, you can create an animation in one of two ways. You can either paint an entire new image for each display frame or use a constant background and just repaint the images that move.

Mr. Disney himself hosted a television program where he demonstrated how animators in his studios used a long scroll of background images that included sky, ground, buildings, and plants. The animators moved this scroll as necessary behind the glass frame that positioned the sequential cell paintings of the animated characters in the foreground.

The same character- or cast-based (also referred to as *sprite*) animation applies to computers, as does the frame-based animation, where the entire image, including the static background, is recreated for each image.

The advantages of using a fixed background and only animating the characters or moving objects minimizes the work required to create the animation and maximize the reusability of characters. In older cartoons, the animators did much more actual drawing, yet some sequences were still repeated. The background might change (or it might not, if the producer didn't want to spend the money) but the characters performed the exact same movements as in previous sequences.

The problem with character-based animation is that the amount of processing required for the computer to create such animations is enormous. Each character must be blended carefully into what, to the computer, is a new background each frame. Even though the background might actually be a duplicate of the last one, because the new positions of the animated portions of the image cover and uncover new pieces of the background, the computer must process each new frame completely.

Animation on a computer looks just like the animation Walt Disney made so popular. It is based on the same persistence of vision that causes the human mind to ignore the brief flickers that occur as one image is replaced with another in a film. In fact, The Walt Disney Software Company actually sells a low-end animation program called The Animation Studio, but it is not targeted to business users. Both the background and moving images of the animation created on computers are essentially built up from the familiar tiny rectangular bit-map images we see when paint software magnifies a portion of an image for fine editing.

⇨ Advanced topics

Windows programmers can actually create their own animation by using Windows 3.1's BitBlt(), which controls bit maps using raster

operations including AND, XOR, OR, and COPY. Windows icons are created by blending AND and OR masks with the background. Programmers can create animations using the timing functions SetTimer() and WM_TIMER or GetTickCount().

This type of programming is for two groups of users: very advanced programmers who want to use low-level Windows functions to create otherwise difficult-to-build animation while learning more about Windows, or hackers who have more time than money needed to purchase higher-level animation tools such as the Microsoft Multimedia Development Kit (MDK). The MDK provides some, but not all, of the tools advanced programmers need to manage the development of simple animation. Included in the MDK are a bit-map editor, file converter, device drivers, and sound manipulation tools, along with the media control interface that offers a simple way to integrate audio and video sequences.

For details, see *Windows-DOS Developer's Journal*, vol. 4 no. 2, "Animation Under Windows 3.1," by Thomas W. Olsen.

⇨ Dirty rectangles

Slow VGA graphics response times plague developers who work on fast systems and then see their smooth animations turned into jerky images with VGA graphics systems, which are the likely target of many PC multimedia productions. The dirty-rectangle method, explained in *Dr. Dobb's Journal*'s "Graphics Programming" column by Michael Abrash (vol. 18 no. 1), creates images and stores them in nondisplay memory, instead of drawing them directly onscreen, where they will be delayed by video graphics board limitations and any necessary processing.

⇨ Video performance

The speed of the latest 486 and Pentium computers is amazing. You might be seduced into thinking that the Super VGA graphics board you bought, with or without local-bus video, is responsible for some

of the speed you are seeing. The chances are, though, that it is not. ISA and many local-bus video bus boards have a maximum bus transfer rate limited by a 300-nanosecond access time. Thus, it doesn't matter how fast the board is because the system processor can't supply the board with graphics information any quicker.

If the graphics on your new system seem a lot faster and you don't have a graphics accelerator board (such as the ATI Ultra, Diamond Stealth, or similar technological heavy-hitter), then all that improvement actually comes from your processor. The faster processor can now provide video information to the VGA interface card just as fast as, or much faster than, the card can take it. The slow performance of older systems where the VGA controller was not the system performance bottleneck was often due to the fact that the microprocessor could not keep up with the maximum bus transfer rate.

If you are using a word processor or a database, the speed of your video is not important. If you are developing multimedia, however, video display adapter speed can be critical, and you need the fastest you can afford. Remember though that the applications you create might not have that same high-speed video. Many multimedia productions that look great on the development system really bog down when they go out into the real world and are run on basic 386SX MPC-2 systems.

Software

Some of the programs discussed in this section are appropriate for home users—all of them are if you can afford them—but even the least expensive also contain features for professional multimedia developers. Some of the programs run on DOS, some under Windows, and others under Macintosh or even both Macintosh and Windows. The programs that can run under both are actually different versions but have similar interface and features.

Previous versions before Windows 3.1 both lacked the power and features needed for animation and were simply too crash-prone. Hence, the two mainstays of business animation, Brightbill-Roberts'

Show Partner F/X and IBM's Storyboard Live!, ran under MS-DOS. Both are getting rather outdated as this book is written, but they could be updated to provide a more friendly work environment.

⇨ Autodesk Animator Pro

Animator Pro is probably suitable for many home hobbyists. (It even has a smaller sibling, the $200 MultiMedia Explorer/Animator.) A combination of high-end engineering application and artistic tool, it contains tools for easy production of business applications. For example, the sophisticated text tools allow you to scroll text and even recall and reuse text stored in a buffer.

The less expensive version of Autodesk's animation software might even be a fine choice for some advanced producers because it includes many of the sophisticated tools found in Animator Pro. It does not support high-resolution, full-screen animation, however. But because your target playback machine might not have this capability anyway, the simpler-to-use Animator could be the better choice. If you really need the best 2-D animation software that DOS offers and are willing to work with the highly complex and difficult interface, Animator Pro is your best choice.

Installation is straightforward. The program can run in a system having only 4Mb of memory and can be installed in 5Mb of hard-disk space. Eleven megabytes is required for all files included in a full installation. These memory requirements should not pose a problem, however, because no multimedia workstation can function properly without much more free hard disk space and memory.

The excellent documentation explains much about the hardware requirements and includes a large chart showing exact minimum memory requirements for all display options. For example, minimum playback and paint at 320 × 200 pixel resolution requires less than 2Mb of memory. A full-featured (Autodesk calls this "all stops out") 2550 × 3300 animation needs 55Mb of memory. Because fast animation work must be run directly from memory, the more memory available, the larger the animation can be before you must start swapping to hard disk and thus slow processing.

Animator Pro comes ready to run with a Microsoft-compatible mouse and Summagraphics SummaSketch digitizer tablet (which is a good choice) but can be configured for any other device with the appropriate .idr driver file.

An optional C language-based graphics programming language, called POCO, is supplied with Animator Pro that gives programmers access to many sophisticated tools. The program itself comes on high-density floppy diskettes, but there is also a CD-ROM with additional files packed with the program. Animation Player, an included program, lets you play back Animator Pro sequences in Windows and offers a simple way to add sound to your creations.

 WARNING Some versions of Animator Pro come with a hardware lock. If these devices tend to give you trouble, you might have a problem. The lock is included with programs sold outside the United States and Canada and attaches to the parallel port. Problems sometimes arise when you have other programs that also use a hardware lock, but Autodesk claims that its software will work while other hardware locks are installed as long as Animator Pro's is also installed.

You can contact Autodesk at the following address:

Autodesk
2320 Marinship Way
Sausalito, CA 94965

⇨ PC Animate Plus

PC Animate Plus, for $200, offers very limited paint capabilities for creating images, but it does offer powerful animation tools if you import images. In addition to a variety of tools, another professional-grade element in this inexpensive software is the ability to work with relatively high-resolution images. This software cannot compare to Autodesk's Animator Pro, of course, but it is well above the limits that might be expected from such an inexpensive program.

PC Animate Plus is a DOS program and requires very little memory. It can run on a system that cannot even load Windows. If most of

your images will originate as clips, scanned images, or screen captures, Animate Plus might be the animation tool you need to bring your images to life. Learning to use PC Animate Plus is relatively simple because the interface is easy to understand.

You can get more information from

Presidio Software
2215 Chestnut St.
San Francisco, CA 94123

 # Deluxe Paint Animation

This Electronic Arts program is well-named; it is a deluxe paint program. Both the image creation and animation features, however, are seriously restricted by the software's very low resolution capabilities. Although later versions might change this shortcoming, early editions of this $135 program would only work with CGA-quality images, not even reaching the base VGA level of graphics resolution. Animation in this program can be as simple as dragging an image across the background while holding down a key that tells the software to record a sequence of images.

 # Keyframe animation programs

Very high-end animation software, such as the multi-thousand-dollar Topas Animator from AT&T or Autodesk's 3D Studio, use a sophisticated animation tool known as *keyframing*. AT&T also has a very high-end 2-D animation program, called Rio, which uses keyframing for sophisticated flat-animation sequences.

In a way, keyframing is how art directors worked in the old Disney. In keyframing, you select a few key animation scenes and leave the intermediate frames to the creation of underlings (in this case, the computer). Keyframing requires a great deal of processor power and very sophisticated software, but the results are actually fairly easy to create. Final images are extremely realistic.

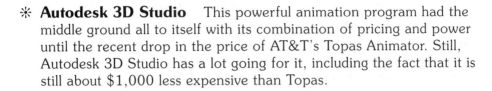

✳ **Autodesk 3D Studio** This powerful animation program had the middle ground all to itself with its combination of pricing and power until the recent drop in the price of AT&T's Topas Animator. Still, Autodesk 3D Studio has a lot going for it, including the fact that it is still about $1,000 less expensive than Topas.

If you really want an attention-getting presentation, you might want to link up files from 3D Studio and Autodesk's AutoCAD drafting program to create a cyberspace virtual environment. All you need is the company's $2,495 Cyberspace Software Development Kit, which is based on the C++ programming language. The kit includes C++ class libraries, diagnostic utilities, and sample demo programs complete with source code.

What's so different between an animated 3D Studio presentation and Cyberspace? Simple! Animation programs use objects, move them around in fixed paths, and change the way they appear through simulating reflections from different light sources. Cyberspace adds physical properties, such as mass, density, and elasticity, to those objects. Drop a bowling ball in Cyberspace, and you can almost feel your toe break!

WARNING All versions of 3D Studio come with the parallel port hardware lock mentioned earlier, and the very fastest computers seem to have a problem with it. According to Autodesk, all you need to do is turn on your printer and leave it on while running the program to eliminate the trouble that can intermittently occur on 66-MHz or faster systems.

✳ **Topas Animator** This expensive software ($7,500 for Macintosh and $4,995 for PC), was marketed for years by AT&T's Graphics Software Labs, but was actually created, and is now sold, by CrystalGraphics.

The latest upgraded Macintosh version costs only $3,000, despite faster performance and other enhancements to the earlier $7,500 AT&T-labeled version. Previously, there were two PC versions, the $2,000 low-end desktop version and the $4,995 professional

version. CrystalGraphics, however, has dropped the price of the top PC program to $3,995. Both Macintosh and PC versions are extremely powerful and relatively easy to learn. (Crystal Topas is a $1,000 PC version of the CrystalGraphics program that features 3-D animation with texture mapping and fractals.)

Powerful features in Topas 4.0 for the PC include a way to create objects so they appear engraved. Documentation for the newest versions is also reportedly much better than that shipped with older versions. Both Macintosh and PC versions of Topas Animator support direct VCR control through Videomedia and Diaquest hardware, making it easy to record your creations to video tape. Like Autocad's 3D Studio, Topas uses a parallel port hardware lock, something quite common for these very high-priced programs.

For more information, contact

CrystalGraphics
3110 Patrick Henry Dr.
Santa Clara, CA 95054

Action!

Action!, a Windows-based animation program, is a $500 business-oriented presentation program that uses the slide show as its operating metaphor. Action! uses thumbnail slide images common to Aldus Persuasion and other presentation programs. The icons in Action!, however, can be rearranged to change the order of the show and are not limited to still images. Rather, they can have duration or even include animated elements, allowing business users an easy transition to video technology.

This software comes from the well-known Macintosh software developer that publishes MacroMind Director (renamed MacroMedia Director). Producers with limited knowledge of (or interest in) sophisticated video techniques can just pick and choose the transition and animation effects they want to include in their presentations.

Action! is a business presentation-oriented animation program, however, which is both its strength and its weakness. Business presentation users include a lot of text in their images. Action! supports scalable TrueType and Adobe Type Manager fonts, which means clean text images, with no rough edges or the sloppy appearance of text that is evident in many low- to mid-range animation software packages.

Because this program can import Windows Metafiles, it can easily base animation sequences on charts generated by most graphics packages. Sound files can also be attached to Action! sequences. Animation speed and flexibility, however, are compromised by the same object-oriented manipulation process that makes Action! a good business-oriented presentation tool.

This program could perform a lot better on very fast computers recommended in this book for serious multimedia production. But Action! is a business package and is a better choice for those who simply want to add a bit of animation and sound to more traditional business slide shows.

For information, contact

MacroMedia
600 Townsend
San Francisco, CA 94103

Animation Works Interactive

This Windows animation program earned an Editor's Choice rating in the August 1992 issue of *PC Magazine* for its power and relatively low $495 price. Animation Works was a good mid-range animation program in its early incarnations, but lacked the ability to export compiled animations, which limited its playback performance considerably.

A later version supposedly corrects many playback performance problems in Windows. The early version could run on a 286-based system, but that base is totally unacceptable for multimedia

development. Newer versions will probably be restricted to 32-bit systems, but even the earlier versions ran better when installed on faster systems.

For more information, contact

Gold Disk
5155 Spectrum Way
Mississauga, ON, Canada L4W 5A1

MacroMind (or MacroMedia) Director

This Macintosh program provides multimedia authoring and animation in the same package, so it belongs here and in Chapter 8 on authoring software. It is relatively expensive at about $1,200. Its main strength is the ability to edit and transfer QuickTime movies. The version I saw, however, lacked the ability to import TIFF image files, and the user interface was quite complex.

The Electric Image Animation System

This software is a powerful high-end animation program for the Macintosh. At $7,500, it produces almost photo-realistic backgrounds and smoothly animated objects with reflections. Despite its power, this software is actually relatively easy to use with an integrated project control window. It requires a very powerful Macintosh to perform well, though.

The recommended hardware includes a CD-ROM drive (sample Electric images are included on a supplied CD-ROM), a 32-bit color monitor, and at least 8Mb of memory.

For more information, contact

Electric Image
117 East Colorado Blvd.
Suite 300
Pasadena, CA 91105

 # Morph

A look at animation wouldn't be complete without mention of Morph. Morph is an inexpensive QuickTime or PICT animation creation tool that introduced many computer users to the possibilities offered by desktop animation. WinImages: Morph is a $200 animation program for the PC platform. It includes texture mapping, but not ray-tracing or fractal features. Ray-tracing makes images more realistic.

You can order Morph from

Gryphon Software
7220 Trade St.
Suite 120
San Diego, CA 92121

You can order WinImages: Morph from

Black Belt Systems
398 Johnson Rd.
Glasgow, MT 59203

 # Others

Other inexpensive animation programs for the PC and Macintosh are available from

Caligari
1955 Landings Dr.
Mountain View, CA 94043

and

Strata
2 W. St. George Blvd.
St. George, UT 84770

⇨ Video editing

After creating an animation sequence in a computer, you can insert it as part of a larger project. Once you have a video sequence recorded on tape, however, your job has only just begun. The next step, after buying stock footage or sending someone out with a VHS or 8-mm video camera, is to edit all the pieces together. Editing can be done either on the original (online editing) or using a copy (offline editing). In either case, you need to control the videotape player and recorders you will be using to make the final cut. Video editing is a mixed subject as far as this book is concerned; editing involves both hardware and software at the same time, but the hardware (in this case, cables) comes with the software.

Probably the premier midrange video editing program for the Macintosh is Video Toolkit from Abbate Video. This $300 program provides the cable required to connect to the Macintosh serial port and various camcorder and VCR control connectors. With Video Toolkit, you can assemble and edit videotapes even in the field from a PowerBook. A wide range of common video hardware is supported, along with Crtl-L, VISCA, Panasonic 5-pin, and serial port (RS-232/422) protocols.

Contact Abbate Video at

Abbate Video
14 Ross Ave.
Floor 3
Millis, MA 02054
508-376-3712

Videomedia, with its $2,000 OZ software, supports all video editing protocols and is a good choice for high-end video editing. Contact them at

Videomedia
175 Lewis Rd.
San Jose, CA 95111

Other Macintosh and PC video editing software and combination software/hardware packages include the following:

Edit Master ($2,500+; Mac & PC
CV Technologies)
184 Veterans Dr.
Northvale, NJ 07647

V-Station Editor/2 ($1,195; PC)
V-Station Editor/3 ($1,495; PC)
FutureVideo
28 Argonaut
Aliso Viejo, CA 92656

VideoDirector ($200; Mac, PC)
Gold Disk
3350 Scott Blvd.
Santa Clara, CA 95054

ErV2 ($250; IBM)
Homerich Communications
175 N. Old Wassau Rd.
Stevens Point, WI 54481

The Executive Producer ($600; PC)
Imagine Products
581 S. Rangeline Rd., Suite B
Carmel, IN 46032

Media Editor ($450; PC)
Interactive MicroSystems
9 Red Roof Lane
Salem, NH 03079

EDDi Pro ($2,500; PC)
Paltex International
2752 Walnut Ave.
Tustin, CA 92608

AutoCut ($1,000; Mac)
Pipeline Digital
45-508 Lolii St.
Kaneohe, HI 46744

Video Edge ($700; Mac)
Silicon Valley Bus Company
475 Brown Rd.
San Juan Bautista, CA 95045

EdiQit A/B Roll ($5,500; PC)
Strassner Editing Systems
10419 McCormick St.
North Hollywood, CA 91601

StudioNet ($4,000; Mac, PC)
Technical Aesthetics Operations
P.O. Box 1254
Rolla, MO 65401

PC 300 ($2,300; PC)
United Media
4771 E. Hunter
Anaheim, CA 92807

Production management tools

I N any multimedia project, whether a one-person job or having a staff of hundreds, proper management of all individual elements and all phases of production is necessary. Someone must track two components of each part of the project at all times: the location of each sound, text, and image element and the precise stage of each element's production.

Whether you are working on a project for internal use or producing a presentation under contract for a client, you will also be required to produce periodic reports on the progress of the project. Therefore, you need to track progress, both internally within your multimedia production software using authoring software and externally, using a traditional project management tool such as an outliner, calendar, or full-scale project management program.

Storyboarding software

Storyboarding is where a director and the writers produce a visual outline of the final product. A storyboard normally includes one representative screen shot from each movie or animation sequence. At the very early stages, there might only be a rough sketch or text description of the sequence.

Typical entries would be the following:

➤ opening title sequence

➤ introduction

➤ first

The storyboard is a common tool found in multimedia authoring software. It is often linked to the full movie sequence, complete with sounds. The gross editing process might just be reorganizing the storyboard elements.

Although storyboarding is a powerful production tool, it does not produce task progress reports, file tracking, or other report elements that go into true management of a complex project. For example, a storyboard can show that a particular show element still lacks most or all of its components, but it cannot help you locate files on other systems or show just who is at fault for slowing the project. Because storyboards are part of most authoring tools, they are covered in Chapter 8.

 Outliners

The outline format is familiar to everyone who took a high school English course. That does not mean that it is not a powerful management tool. You can use paper and pencil, key the outline into a text file, use a word processor's primitive outline feature, or use a sophisticated outliner program with collapsible elements to create your outline. But beginning such a complex task as a multimedia production without some formal outline that covers project stages and elements is unthinkable.

Beginners might confuse the function of the outline with that of the storyboard, but while the storyboard might form a portion of the outline, it is far from being a project outline in itself. For example, the following items are found in outlines but are not part of any storyboard:

➢ perform market analysis or review client's request

➢ develop budget

➢ get project approval

➢ determine skills required

➢ select and hire staff

➢ produce or refine storyboard

➢ collect images

➢ convert images to proper format

Not all of these elements are part of every project; each project has its own unique pieces. You should be able to see, however, that even the most sophisticated storyboard tools cannot replace a project outline.

I strongly recommend using an outline program that allows you to collapse and expand lower-rank elements in the outline. This way, you can maintain the simple, easy-to-visualize nature of the basic outline, yet also track the performance and even the location of various parts of the project as they move from computer to computer or worker to worker.

The classic standalone outliner was ThinkTank, published by Living Videotext. It was powerful, but inconvenient. You had to import the outlines it generated into a word processor and then strip off unwanted header codes before you could really use the outline in a text-creation environment.

This inconvenience would not be a drawback for creating an outline used just as a management tool. Unfortunately, ThinkTank is no longer available, nor is there any comparable, easy-to-learn, standalone outliner. To find a good outliner today, look within a word processor or project management program.

Project management

Other books on multimedia do not even mention project management. Those books are intended for those who want to enjoy commercial multimedia programs or want to experiment with basic multimedia production projects. You might be reading this book, on the other hand, because you are concerned with producing large-scale or highly professional multimedia applications. You might need to manage a large and complex project, one involving input and work by many people. Such complex activities require that someone, usually the producer, manage and track the progress of others' work, some of which depends on the progress achieved by still more people.

Project management software can help with three areas: planning, scheduling, and control. Of course, these three together determine the really important aspect of any job—cost! Cost by itself, however, is not directly addressed in project management programs; instead, cost savings are the result of proper planning, scheduling, and control.

Bottlenecks in large projects can be difficult to anticipate without a great deal of experience. For example, a complex morphing sequence might take days to complete properly. But it can't be started until the drawings or photographs are produced that provide the beginning and end points for the morph sequence. Meanwhile, a composer might be finished with an earlier project and waiting to receive the results of the morphing process to create or edit sounds for that part of the total project.

Coordination between the creation of documentation, advertising, and the ongoing multimedia production is essential in any commercial project. It can, however, be difficult to manage in such a way that everything is completed at the same time and no one left waiting with nothing to do during the production process.

Fortunately, computer software has been designed just for this type of management. Although project management has absolutely nothing to do with multimedia, any manager working on a project of any scale can benefit from the use of such software.

Project management software is not as well-known as other software such as word processors, spreadsheets, and databases. They are, however, excellent examples of applications that have changed how business management problems are approached. Just as word processors and spreadsheets process words and numbers, project management software manipulates schedules, pinpointing critical elements in a plan and allowing easy performance of what-if analyses. Nearly 100 project management and project scheduling programs are on the market, but only a few have found widespread acceptance.

Any operation that has a definite beginning and end can be planned using project management programs. Projects that can be planned need to have clearly definable tasks that are interrelated or independent, and at least some of the tasks must be completed in a certain time relationship to others.

A popular example cited by most project management publishers is building a house. You must obtain a building permit before starting any construction and build the foundation before raising the walls, but

you can plaster and paint one floor while still installing the plumbing on another.

Other good applications include starting a new business or new venture in an existing company, publishing a magazine, broadcasting a television show, or planning a convention. In our case, it is producing a multimedia project, which is very much like simultaneously producing a television show while publishing a magazine.

You might also find that the graphics created by project management software can be used in your multimedia projects, especially if they are training programs.

 # Schedulers vs. managers

Project management programs deal with time, costs, and resources involved in project planning. They provide critical path analysis and usually generate two types of graphics to assist planners. Project schedulers deal mainly with time and are much less sophisticated. If you need more software help to manage a multimedia project than that available with calendar programs and an outliner, what you really need is a manager rather than a scheduler.

There are two major types of project managers. One is designed for construction and engineering-type projects, and the other is intended more for office-style business applications. The nonengineering (nonconstruction) programs are often easier to learn and use, but they might not provide the management tools you need for something as complex as multimedia production.

 # PERT and Gantt charts

The major management tools provided by project management software include two special types of charts: *PERT* and *Gantt*.

The PERT (program evaluation and review technique) chart (Fig. 6-1) consists of a series of boxes, similar to a programmer's flow chart.

Figure 6-1

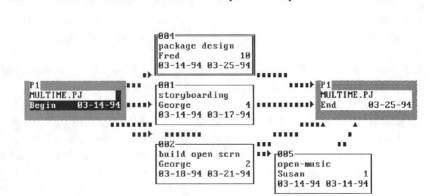

Unique name for this task.

Sample PERT chart for simple project named MULTIME.PJ. Computer Associates

The boxes are all linked together in various ways, with each box containing the description of one complete task and including the time needed to complete the task along with any resources required (Fig. 6-2). The PERT chart is also called a *network chart*.

Figure 6-2

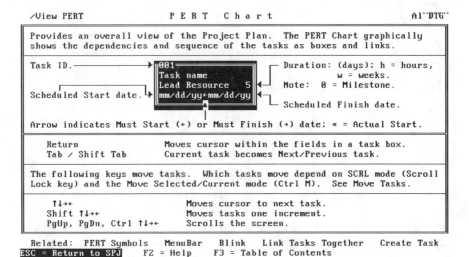

Help screen in SuperProject Expert showing how to interpret PERT chart.
Computer Associates

PERT charts are especially useful when it is difficult to specify the exact duration of tasks. Thus, it is a statistical analysis method well-suited to research and development situations or multimedia projects, where the artistic nature of many tasks make it difficult to pin down specific times.

A Gantt chart is similar to a horizontal bar chart (Fig. 6-3). It shows all the tasks side by side on a calendar, showing the start, finish, and duration of each task. The Gantt bars overlap where two tasks can be worked on at the same time and do not overlap when one task must be completed before another can be started. For example, you cannot start copying the software or printing the documentation until those segments of the project are completed. You can, however, compose and arrange music while collecting images, as well as simultaneously produce some of the text for the documentation and use in the project itself.

Figure 6-3

```
Task Gantt                    SuperProject Expert              MULTI``DTG``
     View        Edit     Select    File     Output     Help

  1 Day Per Symbol                              April 94
  ID     Heading/Task     Resource   14    21    28   04    11    18    25

  P1   MULTIME.PJ
  001    storyboarding
  001                     George
  002    build open scrn
  002                     George
  004    package design
  004                     Fred
  005    open-music
  005                     Susan
  006    get/scan photos
  006                     Paul
  008    write text
  008                     Sam
  008                     Beth
```

Name of heading/task or resource.

Sample Gantt chart for simple project named MULTIME.PJ.
Computer Associates

Each task in the Gantt chart is listed according to required start and finish dates. The required dates are earliest and latest start and finish dates needed to keep the project completion date on schedule. In addition, each bar is shown in a different format, as shown in Fig. 6-4, indicating which tasks are critical to the timely completion of the project (critical path) and which are not. For the other tasks, you can see the amount of leeway allowed in the completion date without affecting the overall schedule (float time).

Figure 6-4

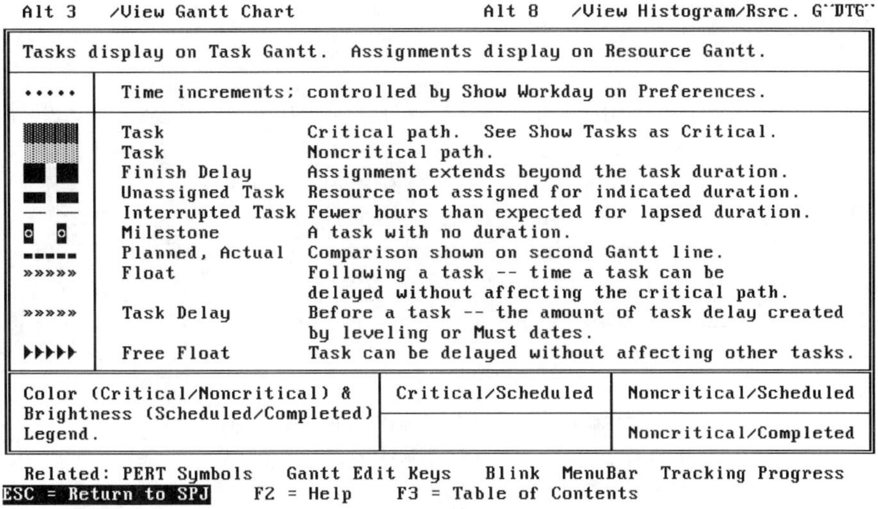

```
Alt 3   /View Gantt Chart                    Alt 8   /View Histogram/Rsrc. G`DTG``
┌─────────────────────────────────────────────────────────────────────────────┐
│  Tasks display on Task Gantt.  Assignments display on Resource Gantt.         │
│                                                                               │
│  •••••   │ Time increments; controlled by Show Workday on Preferences.        │
│                                                                               │
│  ▓▓▓▓▓  │ Task              Critical path.  See Show Tasks as Critical.       │
│         │ Task              Noncritical path.                                 │
│  ■■ ■■  │ Finish Delay      Assignment extends beyond the task duration.      │
│  ■■ ■■  │ Unassigned Task   Resource not assigned for indicated duration.     │
│  ──── ──│ Interrupted Task  Fewer hours than expected for lapsed duration.    │
│  ◊   ◊  │ Milestone         A task with no duration.                          │
│  ▄▄▄▄   │ Planned, Actual   Comparison shown on second Gantt line.            │
│  »»»»»   │ Float             Following a task -- time a task can be            │
│         │                   delayed without affecting the critical path.      │
│  »»»»»   │ Task Delay        Before a task -- the amount of task delay created │
│         │                   by leveling or Must dates.                        │
│  ▶▶▶▶▶  │ Free Float        Task can be delayed without affecting other tasks.│
├──────────────────────────────┬──────────────────────┬─────────────────────────┤
│ Color (Critical/Noncritical) &│ Critical/Scheduled   │ Noncritical/Scheduled   │
│ Brightness (Scheduled/Completed)│                    ├─────────────────────────┤
│ Legend.                       │                      │ Noncritical/Completed   │
└──────────────────────────────┴──────────────────────┴─────────────────────────┘
   Related: PERT Symbols   Gantt Edit Keys   Blink   MenuBar   Tracking Progress
   ESC = Return to SPJ      F2 = Help    F3 = Table of Contents
```

Help screen in SuperProject Expert showing how to interpret Gantt chart.
Computer Associates

⇨ Critical path

A main function of project management planning is to determine the so-called *critical path*—the series of tasks that regulate how long the entire project requires. By determining the interrelation of all tasks, along with which ones cannot be started until others (predecessors) are completed, a planner can determine which steps are critical and which ones have leeway or slack time and won't delay the entire project if postponed. Determining the critical path allows the planner to allocate resources where they are most needed to ensure timely completion of the project.

Finding the critical path can also help when analyzing the exact amount of time required to finish certain tasks. For example, if you know a certain job takes from 10 to 15 hours to complete but that two others take a total of 35 hours, and the first can be completed any time before the other two, you might not need to refine your estimate further. Although the extra hours might affect the budget, it certainly won't matter to the final completion date whether the noncritical task took 10 or 15 hours.

 # Resource leveling

Resource leveling is often the most important part of planning. When you plan a project, you allocate resources to each task in a way that seems reasonable to you. Sometimes, however, you find you have scheduled the same carpenter, artist, printing press, etc., for two different tasks simultaneously. Project management involves resolving these conflicts. Some programs do this for you automatically by rearranging all task timing to avoid resource conflicts. This process is called *resource leveling*.

In general, it is most economical to have the same number of resources (computers, workers, etc.) working every day. Resource leveling is intended to help the project manager avoid renting extra equipment on certain days or hiring temporary help while on other days equipment and personnel are idle. Resource leveling is especially important for projects using contract workers for some of the tasks.

All project management programs make resource leveling easier by indicating where problems lie, but some programs are more sophisticated and can offer suggestions for leveling automatically. You can always level resources by taking resources away from those tasks with float times. If a task is critical, however, you can't take away any resources without lengthening the total project's duration unless you can "crash" some other critical task by adding more resources to it thereby reducing its completion time.

 # Activity codes

Activity codes is the last major feature you need to look at when choosing a project manager. The number of activity codes that can be assigned to each task is an important indication of the flexibility of the program. Because many separate activities might be involved in the completion of each small task, the ability to indicate which activities are involved on each task and how much of a certain activity is needed over the duration of the project is very important. Using activity codes allows you to create reports that show activity totals, such as how much management is involved in the entire project.

Choosing a program management package for your multimedia project depends on many factors:

➤ size of the project

➤ number of workers

➤ complexity of project

➤ type of organization

➤ style of management

 # Software

A few of the most popular project management programs are described in this section. Depending on your specific needs, one will be best for you.

Primavera Project Planner

At $4,000, Primavera's software is entirely out of the class of the other programs described here. It costs five times more than some of the others and is far more complex. The software is not, however, difficult to use.

One of the major differences between this and the other programs is in tracking progress and generating reports that pinpoint variations from the budget. While other programs are entirely suitable for planning even fairly large projects, Primavera's software is intended to track the daily progress of each step in the project, relying more on report-generation than fancy onscreen graphics. A special AutoCost feature enables easy cost-to-completion analyses. The documentation for this software starts with 190 pages of tutorials, carrying the user through all stages of project analysis for building a multifamily housing project. Learning to use this powerful program really is not difficult, especially with all the available help screens.

You can specify up to 10,000 tasks per project but only 96 resources per project. Primavera is compatible with ASCII, Lotus, and dBASE

III files and is both menu- and command-driven. It does not support a mouse. Primavision, an enhanced graphics program for $1,500, is an available option that allows you to produce charts on various plotters.

Although Primavera can be used for small- and medium-sized projects, it is used almost exclusively by the largest engineering firms for major projects. With new, easy-to-use features, it can also be highly useful for multimedia producers managing multiple projects.

SureTrak Project Scheduler is a low- to mid-range $500 project management program from Primavera for smaller projects. It is suitable for full management of projects with up to 4,000 activities. Primavera Project Planner and Primavision come from

Primavera Systems
Two Bala Plaza
Bala Cynwyd, PA 19004

SureTrak is from

Primavera Systems (SureTrak Division)
1574 W. 1700 S.
Salt Lake City, UT 84104

Advanced PRO-PATH 6

Advanced PRO-PATH 6 is low-end software that comes in two versions. One version is $199 and supports 250 tasks per project. The other is a 150-task version costing $149. Both versions have a maximum of 30 resources per project. You can link relatively short projects together, but this software really is not suitable for handling large projects.

This software package was cumbersome to use and did not have the features the other programs have. Even the quality of the print in the documentation is poor. The software does have its good points, however, high among them being its price, which is by far the lowest of those tested.

Along with being less-sophisticated (including its inability to produce PERT charts), PRO-PATH 6 takes up less memory, with the 150-task version operating in only 128 kilobytes (K) and the larger version only requiring 160K. This substantial savings in price and system requirements certainly makes this a worthy candidate for small projects, such as building a single house, but it is really not suitable for larger projects, even with its linking features. If most of your projects are small, however, you could handle an occasional larger job with this program rather than buying a much more sophisticated program that you would seldom use to capacity.

PRO-PATH 6 has a user interface that reminded me of the fairly crude screens I always associate with inexpensive software on home computers. The program also returns you to the main menu often, which can become something of a bore.

What may be a fault to me, however, might well be a virtue to less-sophisticated users. The plain screen and simple commands make it almost childishly simple to use, while providing some very useful management capabilities. This program will not impress the board of directors, but it just might be the easiest one to use for someone with little computer or project management experience.

Although the manual's print quality is bad enough to strain the eyes, the actual information is presented well, and the documentation is thorough and understandable. The software also comes with an interactive tutorial. If you have mostly small projects and you won't be using the software daily (where its clumsiness would soon drive you batty), then Advanced PRO-PATH 6 is certainly a usable product, possibly even a bargain. Advanced PRO-PATH 6 supports LOTUS and dBASE II, as well as ASCII text files.

For more information, contact

SoftCorp
2340 State Rd. 580
Suite 244
Clearwater, FL 34623

Project Scheduler 5

For $700, Project Scheduler 5 emphasizes the integration of work groups. It is thus very useful for managing multiple projects.

For more information on Project Scheduler 5, contact

Scitor
393 Vintage Park Dr.
Suite 140
Foster City, CA 94404

SuperProject for Windows

This program is well-integrated with Windows, using Dynamic Data Exchange to provide data-sharing between programs. The Project Manager's Assistant module of SuperProject offers users a complete guide to developing projects. For complexity, capabilities, and ease-of-use, this $900 program falls in between Advanced PRO PATH 6 and Project Scheduler 5.

For more information, contact

Computer Associates International
1 Computer Associates Plaza
Islandia, NY 11788

Symantec Time Line

This company's $700 Time Line, especially when combined with Guide Line, which is a collection of prebuilt scripts that speed project development, is the mainstay of low-end, general-purpose project management programs. Time Line should be given serious consideration by any multimedia producer who faces tasks just a little too complex to track mentally but who doesn't need a major mid- or high-end package that might require more effort than the entire project. The $200 On Target program offers easy management for nontechnical users.

For more information, contact

Symantec
10201 Tone Ave.
Cupertino, CA 95014

 # Microsoft Project

Microsoft Project is available on many platforms and is a versatile and sound mid-range project management program. It costs about $700.

For more information, contact

Microsoft
One Microsoft Way
Redmond, WA 98052

 # MacProject II

This powerful, $500 mid-range Macintosh project management software uses critical path techniques. MacProject Pro costs $600 and offers even more management tools.

For more information, contact

Claris (Apple Computer)
5201 Patrick Henry Dr.
Santa Clara, CA 95052

InstaPlan and Micro Planner for Windows

These are two $595 project management programs. For more information, contact

Micro Planning International
3801 E. Florida
Suite 601
Denver, CO 80210

 # Harvard Project Manager

Harvard Project Manager is a well-respected $700 mid-range project management program with many useful features. For more information, contact

Software Publishing
3165 Kifer Rd.
Santa Clara, CA 95056

 # Mini-glossary for project management

This glossary of related project management terms can be used as a guide when reading publishers' descriptions of their programs.

ASAP Acronym for as soon as possible (critical tasks).

ALAP Acronym for as late as possible (noncritical tasks).

critical path The sequence of tasks that affects when the project will finish. Finding this path (which the software should do for you) helps eliminate time wasted on nonessential tasks.

float How long a noncritical task can be delayed before affecting the completion of another task. For example, if long task A and short task B must both be finished before task C can begin, there is no advantage in completing B before A, but if A finishes first, B will delay C.

Gantt chart A chart that shows when a task starts and finishes by displaying a horizontal bar proportional to the task duration. Each task in the project has its own bar.

histogram A bar chart showing how many resources are used by each task throughout the project. Histograms are useful for resource leveling, or ensuring everyone is busy but not overworked.

milestone(s) Milestones mark the completion of major tasks and are a good measure of progress. They are very important elements of project management, and clients are very interested in them.

PERT chart A project evaluation and resource tracking chart, also known as a network diagram. PERT charts are flow charts that show how all tasks are connected. They are essentially work-flow charts.

resource Machine, program, worker, or team involved in completing a task.

resource-driven Tasks whose completion time is dependent on the availability of resources, not time.

resource leveling A project management tool that involves arranging all tasks to avoid resource allocation conflicts.

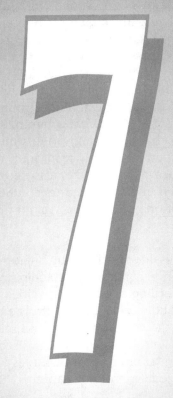

Audio production
software

AUDIO production, video production, and authoring are all interrelated. Thus, this chapter, Chapter 5 on video software, and the next chapter on authoring software contain product information that has necessarily been arranged somewhat arbitrarily. Many multimedia production programs include both audio- and video-editing tools, along with some authoring capabilities, so specific software is listed in the chapter where its strongest capabilities lie. Again, this arrangement is somewhat arbitrary and leads to the consequence that the chapter on authoring software is the shortest, even though choosing an authoring program is a critical choice for any multimedia producer. Chapter 8 is also short because many of the programs discussed in other chapters contain enough authoring tools that if you select one of them you might not need a separate authoring tool.

Not much fancy processing is offered by analog and digital audio-editing and production programs. Most audio production software starts and stops a recording sequence, specifies the quality (higher quality means larger audio files), and controls an external audio source device, such as a videodisc, audiotape, or videotape. There are, of course, exceptions; a few programs directly edit these files. Musical instrument digital interface (MIDI) files are very different entirely, as you will see later in this chapter.

Audio file types

Three types of audio files are used in computer productions. Two involve actual sounds, analog or digital. The third, MIDI, contains absolutely no vestige of sound in any form but is nevertheless by far the most sophisticated audio format for multimedia producers. Each of the three formats is discussed in the following subsections.

Analog audio

Analog music, still encountered in some multimedia productions, is suitable only for well-reproducible speech, using a very limited range

of frequencies and quite low fidelity. Beyond filtering, mixing, and amplification, no special processing is involved in creating the physical or electronic analog representation of analog sounds. Old vinyl records, audio tapes, television, radio, and the telephone are the most familiar analog sound formats.

The recording industry has relied on analog storage of music since the day Thomas Alva Edison invented recording. Edison pressed a vibrating needle against a revolving wax-coated cylinder, creating a physical copy of the sound vibrations passing through the air. Analog vinyl records, which have so recently been replaced by compact disks (CDs), use the same technology developed by Edison. The only changes to date are advances in amplification electronics and more precise physical duplication techniques.

⇨ Digital sound

Digital sound recording, on the other hand, was not possible until computer processing became fast enough and inexpensive enough to be put into common use. Essentially, the difference between analog and digital is the difference between something continuous and something discrete (divided into specifically sized pieces).

As seen in Fig. 7-1, sound waves are often represented graphically as a smoothly oscillating curve. Within the limits of resolution imposed by the printing process, or the particular hardware used to capture and present a similar image using a microphone, amplifier, and oscilloscope, this continuous curve is an exact representation of the actual sound, capturing every nuance of frequency and volume change.

To create a digital representation of a sound, the intensity of the sound is measured at selected periods of time—the shorter the period, the more data you collect. This measurement frequency is known as the *sampling rate* (Figs. 7-1, 7-2). The more samples you take, the more accurately the digital record can represent the original analog signal.

Figure 7-1

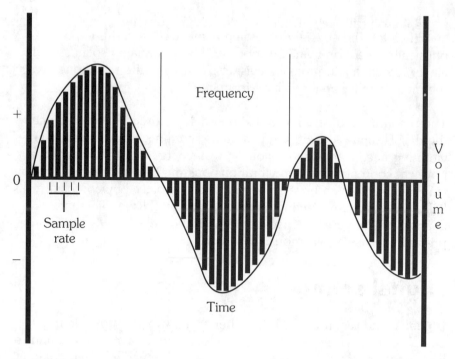

High sampling rate for sound wave.

If you made the time interval between samples infinitely small, you could get an infinite amount of information, precisely capturing all the features of the original. At the same time, however, it would be impossible to store and process the data simply because of the amount of data generated. Fortunately, the human ear is nowhere near as sensitive as electronic equipment, and the sample intervals need be only small enough that the human ear cannot tell the difference between the original sound and the digitized reproduced sound.

CD audio and digital audio tapes (DAT) sample and reproduce sounds so well that human hearing finds the reproduction perfect. This technology requires a large amount of data storage, however, and multimedia producers can choose several lower levels of quality using slower sampling rates. Thus, you can store as much as 16 hours of speech-quality sound on the same CD that only carries about 70 minutes of CD-quality music.

Figure 7-2

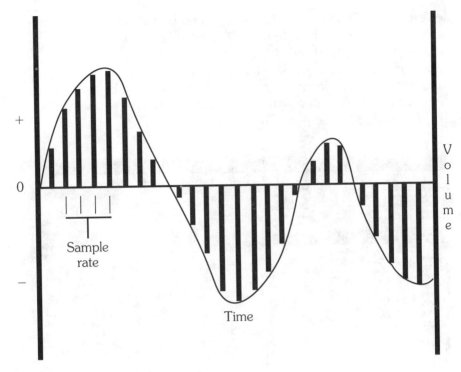

Lower sampling rate for sound wave.

As you can see, converting an analog sound into digital format and back again means your digital file is actually just another way of representing a real sound. When you convert it back to audio, it will (more or less) faithfully represent the original in volume changes, tempo, and frequency.

MIDI

The third type of audio that multimedia producers work with is so totally different that most people who first encounter it have difficulty understanding just how different it is, even from digitally recorded sounds.

MIDI is both a physical standard for connecting computers to musical instruments and control devices and a programming language. MIDI

files are simply numbers, as are analog and digital sound files. Unlike the others, however, they do not represent actual sounds in a different form. Instead, MIDI files are a series of instructions to musical instruments (actually, electronic representations of instruments). These instructions control the speed with which notes are played, their duration, volume, and the type of instrument they are supposed to sound like (Fig. 7-3).

Figure 7-3

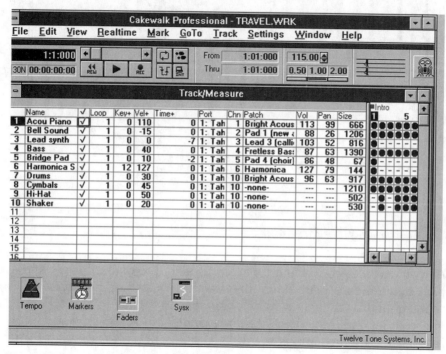

MIDI software editor interfaces. Twelve Tone Systems, Inc.

MIDI files are not created using an analog-to-digital board that converts sounds into computer files. Rather, a MIDI recording session consists of you pressing keys on a MIDI keyboard (or even a MIDI saxophone) while the hardware records what key you pressed, how long you held it down, and, with a velocity-sensitive keyboard, how quickly you pressed the key (Fig. 7-4). No actual sound, in any form whatsoever, is recorded when working with MIDI.

Figure 7-4

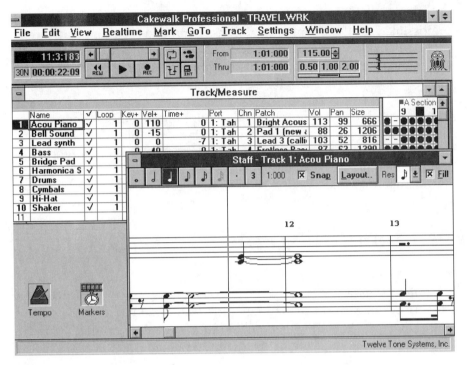

MIDI software editor interfaces. Twelve Tone Systems, Inc.

The main advantages to using MIDI files instead of the analog and digital alternatives are ease of editing and small file size (on the order of 1,000 times smaller). To give you an idea of the power you gain in working with MIDI instead of real sounds, imagine you want to repeat a single musical phrase in a recorded passage—specifically, a single instrument's sound. If you used analog or digital files, this process could be a major undertaking and probably would not work very well no matter how great an effort. Depending on the recording, it might be flatly impossible. But not with MIDI. You just copy the phrase and specify the new instrument. At the same time, you can also have it played in a different key, on a different instrument, or at a different tempo, just by changing one or two simple MIDI commands.

Other tasks that are easy to accomplish in MIDI are completely impossible for audio-editing programs. Even audio-editing software that does a good job of cutting and pasting audio files cannot change the sound of a piano into that of a banjo, or take a complex musical passage and remove several instruments.

In fact, with MIDI you can even edit entire music clips, speeding or slowing them without affecting frequencies, or duplicating them and designating that they be played simultaneously, but on different instruments. If you want a MIDI sequence played faster or slower, you just change the time signature.

Multimedia sound

Many of your productions will target Microsoft-sponsored Multimedia PC (MPC) standard systems as playback devices. We first discuss what MPC provides as a set of standards for recording and working with both MIDI signals and digitized audio that has been captured with a user-supplied microphone or from another source.

The waveform or sampled audio is recorded, using pulse code modulation (PCM) processing, which is the same standard used to record and play back data on CD-audio discs.

PCM breaks down microphone (analog) input signals into digitized sound, using a common analog-to-digital converter microchip and a sampling rate that balances the need for small file sizes with the required fidelity. Playback is accomplished by reversing the process. The numbers are fed through a digital-to-analog converter using the same sampling rate, and then the resulting music, speech, or other sounds are amplified.

Frequency response is only the first of three important features that determine how well sound is reproduced. The second feature is a sound's *dynamic range*, or the difference between the quietest and loudest sound reproduced. The third reason for using digital sound reproduction is that it eliminates any noise.

The dynamic range provided by a digital recording using a 16-bit sample size is 96 decibels (dB). This range, much higher than that provided by even the best old vinyl records, is what is provided by CD audio recordings. Greater dynamic range shows why CD audio so quickly replaced the old LP as well as why much of the older audio amplifier equipment could not perform well with CD audio.

The minimum standard required under the MPC-1 standard is 8-bit recording. You are familiar with the 48-dB dynamic range provided by systems that meet the minimum standard because 48 dB is almost the exact same dynamic range provided by standard AM radio.

Sound requirements for even minimum MPC storage demonstrate why Microsoft included a CD-ROM drive as a requirement for MPC systems. Even the poorest quality sound recordings for MPC require 8 bits of data to be stored for every sample, and each sample occurs a minimum of 11,025 times each second. Thus, one second of low-quality digitized sound requires 11 kilobytes (K) of storage, or more than a half-megabyte of storage for every minute of sound.

Stereo is crucial to realistic sound reproduction, but the MPC-1 does not require stereo reproduction capability. Fortunately, nearly every system compatible with MPC-1 is shipped with stereo capabilities, so they can be used for those applications that do provide stereo. At the very least, they can play CD audio discs in stereo.

Basic MPC sound does not meet the same high standards as CD-audio records because the MPC sampling rate is far below the 44.1-kHz rate (44,100 times each second) to record music for top-quality CD sound. The rate at which samples are taken and recorded determines the high-frequency response of the entire digital recording system.

Human hearing operates over a range of about 20 cycles per second (hertz) to almost 20 kHz for people with perfect hearing (under ideal conditions). The sampling rate required to reproduce a sound properly is more than twice the top frequency, which means that the minimum MPC standard (requiring a sampling rate of 11.025 kHz) is acceptable for recording decent monophonic sound such as speech. A second 22.05-kHz sampling rate is available for use under the

MPC-1 standard. Even this lower standard was far above that used by the telephone company, until recently, when competition and more sophisticated equipment led to better-quality voice and data connections.

To achieve top-quality sounds to integrate into MPC productions, use only the MIDI input port or the millions of megabytes of prerecorded MIDI sequences already available.

⇨ IBM Ultimedia

While the other multimedia giants (the members of MPC) believe that, one size fits all in the multimedia, IBM took the opposite approach. IBM decided that a single giant multimedia market did not exist, but rather, a plethora of potential applications, each with a different target audience requiring a special emphasis on its own set of multimedia features.

Among these diverse end users were those who viewed business presentations, students, business trainees, and even department store customers treated to multimedia point-of-sale sales pitches for other products while they are waiting to pay for their current purchase.

As might be expected, IBM's Ultimedia has different minimum hardware requirements for what the company considers true multimedia, based on IBM's proprietary Micro Channel. Micro Channel was an alternative computer architecture designed with special audio features that has barely been used as of yet. The base system proposed by IBM to counter the MPC standard was the following:

> ➢ the PS/2 Ultimedia M57 SLC

> ➢ an enhanced 386-based, 20 MHz computer with XGA (IBM eXtended Graphics Array)

> ➢ a CD-ROM drive with CD-ROM XA (eXtended Audio)

> ➢ a 16-bit (versus 4-bit) MIDI audio card

Equipped with a 160Mb hard drive, this system is obviously much more powerful than either the original MPC 286-based specification

or the now-promoted 386SX. With an introductory base cost of $6,000, however, it was also about $4,000 more expensive than a basic 386SX system that was MPC-2 compatible. Essentially, IBM's position with this high entry-level specification is that, while Ultimedia systems are very capable business computers, they are intended to be sold primarily as multimedia presentation systems that can also be used secondarily as business computers.

The MPC specification, on the other hand, was obviously set low enough that the vast majority of businesses, and even many home computers, already have the computer portion of the multimedia-compatible system and only need to add a sound board and perhaps CD-ROM player.

In addition to being a powerful multimedia presentation system, IBM's base system is also a good basic multimedia creation package. Included with the Ultimedia system's CD-ROM was Storyboard Live, IBM's MS-DOS multimedia authoring system, and Audio Visual Connection, a sample development system for the included OS/2 operating system. Windows was also included with Ultimedia, along with MacroMind's Action!, a windows MPC development package.

Despite early confusion in the marketplace, Ultimedia is not a standard in the sense that MPC as a standard guarantees compatibility. Ultimedia is IBM's brand name for a series of well-equipped audio- and video-capable computer systems that make excellent multimedia platforms. Moreover, they set a base system for which business multimedia developers can target their productions. Unfortunately for IBM, this effort has largely failed. Most developers should target MPC-standard systems because far more of them are available.

⇨ Audio standards

A developer must be concerned with multimedia standards, along with which ones are most widely accepted, because while you can create a fantastic presentation that works just fine on your expensive development system, it won't do anyone much good if it won't play

back on the target system. We look at this problem here rather than in the chapter on graphics because, while most business systems have VGA compatibility as a base, no real standard for sound production systems exists.

If your production is intended for in-house use, you can easily target your production to a known base. For you, then, standards are not especially important, just as the MPC standard does not concern you if you are creating a standalone videotape or videodisc presentation.

If, however, you are creating a commercial product, or a business presentation intended to be run on a potential client's system (rather than your own presentation system), you cannot add fantastic MIDI sounds to the presentation if the target machine lacks MIDI capabilities. In fact, MIDI is an excellent example of the pitfalls of adopting too sophisticated a standard.

If you record audio on a videodisc, videotape, or to a CD-ROM, you know what the person playing the program will hear. This might not be true for MIDI files, however, as we shall see in the section devoted to MIDI. The quality of digitized or analog sounds varies with the playback system, but at least they are recognizable. With MIDI, you cannot even be sure of this, because even the type of instrument the MIDI files selects to play depends on the specific hardware attached to the playback system. Thus, you may have recorded a piano, but you might get back dog barks—far-fetched perhaps, but actually possible.

⇨ Creating audio files

Most computers are not supplied with a way to input sounds, but this is changing. Assuming yours did not come with audio input/output capabilities, you will need an audio board (discussed in Chapter 14) and editing software.

In any case, multimedia producers cannot work with the relatively primitive sound capabilities built into even those systems with audio capabilities—except to spoken words. For this undemanding

application, even the most primitive microphone and recording hardware is probably acceptable for any but the most sophisticated applications, where analog would not be an acceptable format anyway.

Both Microsoft Windows 3.1 and Macintosh computers are provided with simple audio playback and editing tools. SPEAKER.DRV is a special driver provided free of charge with windows. It even lets you play .WAV (Windows audio file) files through your system's existing speaker. Because this driver was designed solely to generate error beeps, however, it usually does not provide acceptable audio. In some cases it is beneficial to use this output device because your target systems might not have any better audio capabilities.

⇨ Audio-editing programs

Special sound-editing programs can do more than just start or stop recording sounds or control external playback devices, which are the common tools provided in multimedia authoring software. Standalone programs can also cut and paste sound sequences, record and edit multiple tracks, and add special effects.

You should also look for the ability to down-sample existing files from high-quality rates to lower-quality sound, such as reducing a 44-kHz sampled file to 22-kHz. The ability to reduce resolution from 16-bit to 8-bit, for example, will also prove very useful.

Much of the best audio-editing software, especially for the Macintosh, comes packed with high-end audio boards, simply because the system's available audio hardware is not capable of multimedia sound production. Of course, most PCs do not even have the basic sound recording capabilities of a Macintosh, so this shortcoming is even more evident in the PC world. Thus, to get the most out of your sound, make certain your third-party sound-editing software works with your specific sound board.

⇨ SoundEdit Pro

This $295 Macintosh sound program from Macromedia operates on a minimum of a 68020-based Macintosh with 2Mb of memory and a hard drive.

It works with either stereo or monaural sounds at 11-kHz, 22-kHz, and 44-kHz sampling and supports a range of file formats including the AIFF (audio interchange file format) standard shared by Windows and QuickTime. It uses the Apple Sound Chip, which offers only 8-bit stereo playback on most Macintoshes. With additional hardware, SoundEdit Pro will support more sophisticated recordings, but only using CD-ROM source files or an expensive sound board. Newer Macintoshes offer superior sound capabilities.

While the 2Mb memory requirement might make this program seem attractive, remember that it is achieved at the cost of using what is called *virtual memory*. Data that would normally be kept in working memory are instead sent to the hard disk. Thus, your file-editing capabilities are only limited by the amount of hard disk space you have available, but you will also have very poor performance because editing is done from your slower hard disk rather than in the much faster system memory.

Your basic editing tools consist of CUT, COPY, PASTE, UNDO, and CLEAR. More advanced tools allow you to fade sounds in or out, add echo, and alter pitch. The very important Crossfade tool, however, was missing from early versions. While SoundEdit Pro lets you record multiple tracks, it really isn't a multitrack editor. Instead, it blends the recorded tracks into a single new file.

Quite frankly, the early versions of this program just do not work very well, even adding noise to some playbacks, but it may be worth taking a look at the upgraded version.

For more information, contact

Macromedia
600 Townsend St.
San Francisco, CA 94103

Sound Designer II

This software, which comes packed with DigiDesign's $1,300 Macintosh sound digitizer board, is strictly an audio editor, with no MIDI capabilities other than the ability to recognize MTC (MIDI time control) codes and export its finished files to most MIDI sequencers. Because of the capabilities of the DigiDesign hardware, this editing software is capable of sampling and working with CD-audio quality sounds, making it suitable for serious multimedia production work.

The mixer lets you blend up to four mono or stereo channels into a single file, while a 10-band equalizer and parametric equalizer allows you to customize sounds.

Something that needs to be heard to be believed is the software's audio morphing capability, which does just what you might imagine— it smoothly transitions between one sound sequence and the next and not just using crossfading.

Audioshop

This $90 Macintosh program is not for serious multimedia producers, although later versions might improve.

Although Audioshop works better than the more expensive SoundEdit Pro (Audioshop does not skip and crackle during playback), it too is limited by the 8-bit mode. Audioshop is a fine program to add a bit of sound to QuickTime movies but is not suitable for professional work. Audioshop does, however, offer track sequencing from CD-ROM.

AudioTrax

This $300 Macintosh package includes the powerful ability to blend high-end MIDI files with good-quality 8-bit speech, easily creating a fine-sounding production.

MIDI editing capabilities in this software are very limited, but the same company also publishes a high-end MIDI sequencer. Other audio-editing features are weak, but the software does offer for CUT, COPY, and PASTE, as well as volume control and noise reduction.

⇨ Wave for Windows

This inexpensive, $150 audio program for Windows is probably all you need for working with most audio files in a Windows environment.

If nothing else makes it valuable to you, its ability to alter the length of a sequence of music or other sound without altering pitch or quality makes it essential for business presentations. A great deal of processing is required to accomplish something such as this, which is normally the province of MIDI sequencers that do the same thing in the blink of an eye. But remember, MIDI does not work with actual sounds, while Wave for Windows does.

You can use Wave to play music and narration simultaneously, and a four-band parametric equalizer adjusts sound quality. CUT, PASTE, and the other usual tools are all available, as are many sophisticated editing tools you might never need.

For more information, contact

Turtle Beach Systems
1600 Pennsylvania Ave.
York, PA 17404

⇨ MIDI

MIDI files are created in one of two basic ways: either you play a MIDI device, such as a keyboard, while the software records your actions and converts them into a MIDI file and into standard music notation or you just simply open a MIDI editing program and either place marks on a template showing duration and intensity or place

notes on a standard music staff. Recording and editing MIDI files occurs in MIDI sequencer software.

This software is also what you use to control a MIDI playback device (synthesizer) or edit existing MIDI files. Modifying existing MIDI files is probably what multimedia producers do the most.

Creating music either with an instrument or, as a sight-reader would, using music notation, is strictly a task for musicians, even though this task seems deceptively easy, even for nonmusicians, because of the sophisticated MIDI sequencer software. Of course, anyone who can play the piano can produce MIDI files directly from a compatible keyboard. You don't even have to be a very good musician because mistakes are easy to edit out. Even the tempo can be adjusted to make a duffer sound like Van Cliburn.

An important item to note is that compatibility problems could occur between Motorola-based (Macintosh and Commodore Amiga) and Intel-based (PC) computers because they record information in exactly the opposite format. The 68XXX series microprocessors place the most significant digit first in a byte of data, while the 80X86 Intel processors store the least significant digit first. I won't go into this in any further detail because if you do not know what a least significant digit is, you really are not prepared technically to worry about them beyond needing to know that a problem with MIDI file compatibility might occur.

Another basic problem is standardization. Although MIDI is a programming language and a standard control system, it is not quite standard enough. Part of the MIDI file consists of a signal that tells the synthesizer playing back the file exactly which sound it should be. This can be anything from MIDI ID 0, an acoustic grand piano, to ID 40, a violin, or even ID 127, a gunshot.

This flexibility is part of the power of MIDI, but a drawback is that those numbers refer to the "general MIDI instrument sounds standards." Not every synthesizer recognizes each ID code as the same sound, which can lead to real problems.

Windows' Multimedia Extensions support two different types of MIDI synthesizers. Thus, .MID files often have the same music recorded twice, once for extended synthesizers that use MIDI channels 0 through 10 and again for base-level synthesizers that use channels 12 through 15.

There are two types of MIDI files: a type 0 file, which supports only one track or instrument, and a type 1 MIDI file, which can play multiple voices simultaneously. A third MIDI file type, Type 2, does exist, but it is not Windows 3.1-compatible although it can contain several independent voices. MIDI sequencer software can do little or nothing to help with the incompatibility problems.

The MIDI sequencer software discussed in the following subsections all accept MIDI signals from external devices, turn them into editable files, and provide sophisticated tools that can be used to edit MIDI files just as easily as we normally edit word processor files.

Although the programs can take existing MIDI files and work with them, you also need a MIDI board and synthesizer, or a soundboard capable of playing back MIDI signals in audio form, if you want to hear what you have created. Some, mostly Macintosh-compatible programs, also allow you to integrate audio files such as speech into MIDI files.

A complete list of MIDI software is provided in Appendix E, and MIDI hardware is covered in Chapter 14.

CakeWalk Professional

One of the most sophisticated PC MIDI programs you are likely to need in multimedia production is TwelveTone Systems' $350 CakeWalk Professional.

This sequencer software is capable of supporting 256 tracks (separate simultaneous sound sequences) and supports all common SMPTE/MTC formats. Some reviewers have found the interface to be a bit intimidating and less than user-friendly, but I like CakeWalk, and it fits my needs.

A very important feature is the *score view* that presents notes in an editable score complete with notes. Any musician who can sight-read music will find this a very sophisticated and easy-to-use interface. The software can operate on any PC AT compatible system because MIDI doesn't require the sort of processor power that audio-editing requires.

The program can simultaneously support up to 16 MIDI devices with available multimedia extensions. Real-time recording controls include 16 assignable faders; if you adjust sound levels during recording, the software can play back the same sequence at the adjusted level.

For more information, write to

TwelveTone Systems
P.O. Box 760
Watertown, MA 02272

 # Studio Vision

This $1,000 program runs on top of Opcode MIDI system software, so the two together provide powerful MIDI and audio capabilities for the Macintosh.

Other programs allow you to integrate audio with MIDI sequences and could be all you need to accomplish that task, but if you want a single program that allows you to extensively edit both MIDI and audio files, this software is probably your top choice. Compatible input file formats include AIFF, Sound Designer II (SD2), and STDM (standard MIDI). The software only outputs SD2 and STDM files.

 # Master Tracks Pro 5

MTP5 is a powerful Macintosh sequencer that lacks any digital audio component. The many special filtering tools provided by this $500 program can be applied to specific MIDI events, making it easy to produce incredibly complex changes with little effort. To accommodate the common problem of MIDI crush (too many signals sent through the MIDI port in a given period of time), MTP5 allows you to easily adjust

the number of control event signals sent so you can compromise between quality of the final production and hardware limitations.

 # Master Tracks Pro 4

The Windows version of the above program is a powerful editor that lets you modify any part of a MIDI event easily.

Authoring software

THE main purpose of authoring software packages is to integrate existing clips into a final production. Most authoring software packages, however, do include extensive editing tools for video and even audio sequences. One thing to note is that although CD-ROM production requires a type of authoring software, it is entirely different from what is discussed in this chapter.

Several types of programs can be considered authoring software. They are categorized by the type of final product they produce.

➤ presentation-oriented software

➤ card-based authoring

➤ icon-based (also called event-driven) authoring

➤ time-based authoring

No one tool will be perfect for every task. If you are tackling a variety of presentations, from simple slide shows for speeches to interactive training sessions, you might need to learn several different types of authoring programs. In any of these types of programs, the term *event-driven* means that the final multimedia production is highly interactive.

Typical applications that you might be called upon to develop are the following:

➤ standalone point-of-sale (also known as kiosk) presentations

➤ simulations

➤ training programs

➤ business presentations

➤ product demonstrations

➤ games

Although the most sophisticated software can be used to create all of these presentations, it is usually not practical to use a powerful time-based presentation authoring program to create simple business presentations (slide shows), any more than it is practical to use dBASE to keep track of your children's birthdays. You can do it, but

it takes much less time and effort if you use a tool designed specifically for your task.

Also, depending on your level of sophistication, different types of authoring programs are available within each category, based on the actual programming approach. For example, if the word *programming* disturbs you when discussing creating a computer-based multimedia presentation, you certainly don't want an authoring program whose major features are accessible only to those with C++ or BASIC programming skills. Nor do you want features that are most easily controlled using a powerful and complex scripting language that is essentially a new programming language in itself, a language that even experienced programmers need to learn to get the most out of the software.

The easiest authoring systems to learn and use involve simple on-screen programming that consists of moving icons around and pasting them into various arrangements. Action!, IconAuthor, and Passport Producer are this type of authoring programs, making it very easy to produce slide shows or related presentations.

HyperCard and similar programs are an example of authoring systems that use a scripting language to develop a finished application. Fortunately, this simple language is so simple that it is easily accessible to even the most computer phobic. More complex programs that use a special control language are Tempra Media Author and Macromedia Director.

Although this book is not a tutorial on multimedia production, a brief example of authoring is appropriate. The following is a sample of how to program in Tempra Media Author.

The first step in creating a presentation in Tempra Media Author is to define the background for the image by defining BColor (Background Color) and setting the hue and type of background (such as solid). Next, determine how it is to be placed on the screen (such as a left to right wipe). You can then select "text" and load in any prewritten text to fill the screen, specifying when, where, and how large the text is to be displayed. Each step of the presentation is created in the same way. Fortunately, the software makes everything a lot simpler than it

appears here. Nevertheless, it is more complex than just grabbing an icon and moving it into its place in a sequence of other icons.

More sophisticated multimedia authoring software requires using a traditional programming language, most often either some form of BASIC or C, the language in which the Unix and much applications software is written. Pascal, a programming language written to teach programming rather than to be a working language, is also used as the basis for programming some authoring software. Windows-based presentations might require you to write custom drivers or call dynamic link libraries (DLLs).

Presentations that are mainly text, with sounds and images providing only a background for what is essentially a data presentation. They thus require using special document authoring tools that have powerful indexing features. In many, if not all, situations, this requirement means using the CD-ROM as the distribution media. CD-ROM authoring tools are discussed in Appendix A, which describes overall CD-ROM publishing.

Thus, you can see that several programming interfaces are used for authoring software, no matter what type of authoring process that program is based on. The main programming interfaces are the following:

> icons

> scripting language

> traditional languages, such as BASIC and C

> document-oriented tools

Presentation-oriented software

Presentation-oriented programs are not generally interactive and often lack true multimedia features such as sound or motion. They are exemplified by programs such as WordPerfect's DrawPerfect that create fancy, full-color business slide images and printable graphics for handouts. You can link a number of these images together and display them in a sequence, so they do perform the rudimentary tasks associated with multimedia authoring. Although they are easy to use and even better than multimedia authoring software for producing simple slide shows, they are not suitable for what this book considers multimedia production.

The major difference between simple presentations and most multimedia presentations is not sound, which can be added in several ways (including having a person narrate the presentation). No, the real difference is the lack of interaction between the viewer and the presentation. Virtually all multimedia presentations allow the viewer to interact with and modify how items are displayed. Basic business presentation programs are just slide shows, however, showing one item after another serially.

The top end of presentation-oriented graphics program overlap low-end multimedia production tools. Aldus Corporation's Persuasion, a presentation program available in both Macintosh and Windows versions, adds advanced transition effects between still images and the Macintosh version is QuickTime-compatible. Computer Associates' CA-Cricket Presents is another program that integrates charts, text, and tables to build simple slide-show presentations on either Macintosh or Windows-based computers.

Card-based authoring

Card-based authoring is both the simplest and most familiar of authoring tools. In fact, it is so common on Macintosh systems that many users fail to realize what it is. I am referring to HyperCard, the original and nearly ubiquitous authoring tool found on Macintosh computers.

Actual card images are used in HyperCard, but any similar presentation device that features individual hyperlinked pages as the main navigation and display device is also a card- or page-based system. In such a system, it is easy to progress from one page of information to the next, or jump around through the deck from an "index" card that usually presents a number of subsequences you can

121

move to directly. All cards are linked to the one before or the one after or both, but many also contain links to other cards or images, which allow easy branching.

 # Icon-based authoring

Icon-based authoring is similar to HyperCard but is more complex and used for more sophisticated presentations. Instead of just designing and linking cards one at a time, icon-based tools use flow diagrams, linking icons that represent either existing or still-to-be-created clips. This type of presentation is also sometimes known as event-driven because no real formal path exists that forms the core of the presentation. What the viewer sees is very much dependent on what choices he or she makes along the way. Multimedia games are an example, but icon-based authoring is also used in sophisticated tutorials and other productions.

 # Time-based authoring

Time-based authoring is a more formally structured presentation, usually with rigid time gaps between the initial display of one image and the next. It is similar to a straight-line HyperCard presentation with only one set of sequential pages and no branches. It adds to the process though, the element of machine control of events—the process goes from start to finish in a controlled, time-oriented manner, much like the simple slide shows created with a presentation program.

What qualifies this type of presentation as a sophisticated multimedia authoring tool is the fact that a more sophisticated time-based multimedia presentation also allows user intervention in the sequence of events and individual timing, thus allowing for a more individual presentation.

 # Authoring programs

Some authoring programs are briefly described in the following subsections, but a longer list is included in Appendix G. Remember that some of the programs discussed in Chapter 5, also have authoring capabilities but were placed in that chapter because of their special graphics capabilities.

Authoring software is probably the most critical single software selection you will make for your multimedia production system. I urge you to write many companies listed for detailed descriptions of their products, rather than relying on a brief description here or in other books. You might find all the authoring tools you need in a program that is actually more oriented to graphics creation and editing. If so, use it. On the other hand, you might need the sort of easy-to-use multimedia authoring tools found in HyperWriter!, especially for business training environments with a known playback system.

New features are always being added to these programs. Rather than give what might be outdated information about a program, I only provide very general descriptions of those programs.

A major problem to note with advanced multimedia productions that run on computers is the fact that, although the authoring software can do a fine job of creating the final cut, the production might only be playable on the system used to produce it, unlike videotape recordings. While MIDI and other tools are great for producing top-quality multimedia, they cannot be played back on any machine not equipped with similar, compatible equipment. This is NOT the fault of the production software!

If you spend a lot of your company's or your client's time and money producing an advanced production that cannot be distributed to the target audience, it is your fault! You must make certain that you do not produce quality beyond the ability of the target systems to reproduce, something that many of these programs can easily lead you to do if you are not careful to limit your ambition.

HyperWriter!

HyperWriter! is the hypertext program I use. Multimedia tools are limited, but it can easily link a presentation to audio/video devices and even play animation files. HyperWriter! is also very easy to learn and use. A major attraction is that you can use it to produce royalty-free, standalone documents that can be played back on even notebook computers from a floppy diskette. It is difficult to imagine a simpler hypertext authoring program than this Ntergaid software. Creating a link that triggers a video event, graphics display, animation sequence, or sound is extremely easy in HyperWriter!. Just make the appropriate selections from a pull-down menu.

HyperWriter! is a true authoring program, having no audio/video creation or editing tools, but it can easily integrate .FLI VGA animation files at 320 × 200-bit, 256-color resolution as well as other images or audio files created by other programs. Standard Pioneer and Sony videodisc players are controlled through the usual serial port interface. Digital audio cards compatible with a Creative Labs Sound Blaster can play back prerecorded sounds.

Computer-based training can use HyperWriter! to control a videodisc presentation. The quality of images is extremely high, and display of the images is through any television or right on the computer screen using a digital video board. A single 12" videodisc can contain movies complete with sound or can store up to 40,000 separate high-quality still images. Controlling the video disc player is extremely easy in HyperWriter!. Just create a link to a word in the text and specify the beginning and ending frame numbers for playback when that sequence is triggered.

⇨ Tempra Media Author

Tempra Media Author from Mathematica is an MS-DOS authoring tool that can, if necessary, run on a very limited system. Tempra Pro provides photo-realistic image editing tools, while Turbo Animator supports sophisticated protected-mode 32-bit processor power on 386 and higher systems to produce 8- and 16-bit animated videos.

Tempra Media Author supports MIDI, CD, and digital audio as well as multiple video devices such as videodisc players. Tempra allows you to integrate MIDI sounds, as well as CD and other audio. It has no MIDI-editing capabilities, however, but does work well with graphics programs from Mathematica.

As with HyperWriter!, Tempra Media Author can be used to create standalone, royalty-free multimedia presentations. In fact, you can select a special Demo Builder utility from a menu if you are creating a demo program. The software takes the multimedia production you have created and places all the files needed to play it back on a series of floppy diskettes.

This multimedia authoring system is intended to create complex presentations. This characteristic is either good or bad, depending on what you are creating. Tempra Media Author and HyperWriter! together make an excellent choice for mid-level production. Use HyperWriter! to produce hypertext presentations that might or might not use sound and graphics, and use Tempra Media Author to produce graphics- and sound-intensive presentations. Neither can really be used to produce what the other one does easily.

Control for Sony VISCA protocol devices such as Hi-8, 8-mm, or VHS videotape players and camcorders is built into Media Author. In fact, it can operate up to seven VISCA decks in a daisy-chain arrangement, similar to SCSI devices. Sony and Pioneer videodisc players are also compatible for audio, still frames, or full-video playback.

Hypercard

Hypercard, described earlier in this chapter, is the card-based authoring system shipped with all Macintosh computers. You can use this very basic program to integrate text cards with sound and animation.

Supercard

This Aldus program is a more sophisticated development system that can be used as a front-end for database programs. A major feature of

Supercard is the ability to create and scroll around gigantic 32K × 32K pixel cards.

Visual Basic

This Microsoft programming language is used to organize and present multimedia elements in a Windows environment. Creating event-driven multimedia presentations is done using language code similar to that used in GW-BASIC. Tools are provided for controlling various external media devices such as VCRs and laser disc players.

Authorware

This Macromedia icon-based program comes in both Macintosh and Windows versions. You don't need to learn any scripting language to build complex presentations using Authorware.

Basic computer platform

CHAPTER 9

THERE can be no single most important chapter in a book such as this but, if there were, this would probably be it. So, although this chapter focuses on the PC, even if you plan to buy a Macintosh, this chapter is crucial for you to read. This chapter covers a lot of topics. If you fail to select a suitable base system, not much else matters. You won't be happy with your system, nor as productive as you should be.

PCs and Macintoshes are mostly discussed completely separately, with Macintosh-specific information covered in Chapter 10. I emphasize PCs in this comprehensive chapter simply because there are about 100 million more of them. I own both. Macintoshes are perfectly suitable for multimedia production. Nevertheless, as most users will select PCs, this chapter focuses on them.

Having selected the software you want to work with based on the information provided in the previous chapters, you can now choose basic hardware needed to accommodate your selected software. Whether you are on a tight budget or not, you should not skimp on basic hardware. You do not have to bust the budget at this point, but you must at least plan ahead carefully to ensure that whatever computer you select will have room to expand.

Some quick rules might help you get in the right frame of mind to read and fully understand this chapter. I like to think of them as McCormick's Rule of Nine:

> ➢ No computer is ever fast enough.

> ➢ No computer ever has enough storage.

> ➢ No computer ever has enough memory.

> ➢ No computer ever has a large enough power supply.

> ➢ No computer ever has too much cooling capacity.

> ➢ No computer ever has too many expansion slots.

> ➢ No disk drive is ever fast enough.

> ➢ No video is ever too fast or too high-quality.

> ➢ No computer ever has enough total expansion capacity.

That is quite a list. You might think I have been far too dogmatic in some of my assertions but, believe me, in 14 years of working with personal computers, I have never seen any one of these rules violated. Cheer up! Things aren't hopelessly complicated. The really important rule is the final one listed—keep it firmly in mind at all times. If all you do is ensure that your computer has a lot of room for expansion, you can't go wrong. If you do, and you can expand your system, you can always change it. Figure 9-1 shows a good hardware configuration.

Figure 9-1

Fast Micro Express PC with 256K video RAM on local-bus video board. Micro Express

Now let's go through those rules one at a time and see how to apply them in the real world.

No computer is ever fast enough

"Fast" refers to the overall speed of the microprocessor that forms the heart of the computer. In a PC, the microprocessor is an Intel or

Intel-compatible chip of the 80X86 family. The 80C86 family
consists of the following:

> 8088/8086 used in the first IBM PC and the IBM PC XT

> 80286 used in the IBM PC AT

> 80386 SX

> 80386 DX

> 80486 SX

> 80486 DX and 80486 SLC

> Pentium

Table 9-1 provides a comparison of the different chips.

Table 9-1

Chip comparison

Date introduced	Chip	$new	$93	MIPS New	MIPS* Now	Transistors
June 78	8086	$360	NA	.33	.75	29K
Feb 82	286	$360	8	1.2	2.66	134K
Oct 85	386	$299	91	5.	11.4	275K
Aug 89	486	$950	317	20	54	1.2Mb
Mar 93	Pent	$900	850	112	..	3.1Mb

No computer can outperform its microprocessor. Other features, such
as speed and efficiency of caches, can also affect how fast the
computer is in performing real world tasks, but not as much as the
microprocessor. Any special design features only tend to maximize the
rest of the system so it can keep up with the MIPS rating of the
microprocessor. I did not list specific clock speed ranges for the chips
because new variants are being developed all the time, but minimum
acceptable speeds are discussed within each category.

The chips in the table are listed in approximate order of increasing
power, although the fastest in one category might offer speed
advantages over the slowest in the next one. An interesting sidenote is
that the Pentium chip, which was code-named P5 during development,
was expected to be named the 80586 because it is just a more

sophisticated version of that microprocessor. Intel changed the name, however, because while a number could not be copyrighted, a name could. Intel was concerned about potential competitors using similar-sounding names, as they did with the 386 and 486 microprocessors.

All chips below the 80486 are unsuitable for any realistic multimedia production system and are not discussed in this chapter. Systems based on the slower microprocessors are perfectly adequate for playing most multimedia, but they cannot be considered as serious development platforms; not even for home hobbyists.

Math coprocessor

Note that there are two 80486 chips listed in the table. The 486SX does not differ from the 486DX (usually just written as the 486) in the same way the 386SX does from the 386, so this requires a bit of explanation.

All 386 chips (DX and SX alike) lack what is known as a *floating-point math coprocessor*, or a set of circuits that perform advanced mathematical functions much faster than software emulations using standard microprocessors. For the 80386, the SX version refers to the ability to use less expensive 16-bit memory despite the 386SX chip being 32-bit software-compatible.

The 486SX, on the other hand, is a full 32-bit microprocessor that uses 32-bit memory. In this case, the SX refers to a crippled version of the standard 80486 chip with the built-in math coprocessor actually being turned off during manufacturing, leaving the chip without coprocessor capability. Thus, the 486SX is less expensive, but also unsuitable for most multimedia production because advanced audio and video manipulation software often require the math coprocessor. Most other software, even spreadsheets, make little use of math coprocessors, despite all the coprocessor battles of the late 1980s. Computer-aided design (CAD) and other image-related processing, however, often involve the math functions speeded by the coprocessor.

As you can see, despite the large number of Intel-compatible microprocessors, we have already narrowed the field to two: the

486DX and Pentium chips. Your choice of computer actually gets even easier, despite the seeming complexity: buy the fastest microprocessor you can afford. It should have a minimum clock speed of 50 MHz, and faster is better.

Hobbyists can get away with a 33-MHz 80486DX if selected software is not too sophisticated. Make certain, however, that other components can support a faster chip, because you will probably decide to upgrade that slow processor in the near future if you continue with multimedia work. It is not necessary to purchase a Pentium-based system until the prices drop substantially, which might have occurred by the time you read this book. It is a good idea to also ensure that any 486-based computer you buy can be upgraded to the Pentium.

Don't worry too much about special chip designations. A 486DX2-66, for instance, indicates a dual speed 33- and 66-MHz microprocessor. While this chip is not as fast as a straight 486 66-MHz processor, the difference should not be very noticeable for any but the most advanced PC users. Even those users might actually need to move beyond the PCs entirely and use a RISC-based workstation. (This category is so specialized that it is not covered in this book other than at the end of this chapter, which introduces a new kind of RISC computer that is both Macintosh-and PC-compatible.)

There is also an SL microprocessor category. For example, a notebook computer might be advertised as being powered by an 80486 SL. The SL is a variable speed chip that slows down intelligently to conserve battery power in portable systems. There is no performance advantage or disadvantage to using an SL microprocessor in a desktop or tower computer.

Cache

Besides microprocessor clock speed and efficiency (note that Pentium chips actually do more work during a single clock-tick than a 486 can, so a 50-MHz Pentium is actually faster than a 50-MHz 486), processor speed is affected by the speed and size of the hardware cache provided for the microprocessor. Both Pentium and 486 systems have built-in

caches directly on the chips that keep data and instructions in very high-speed memory ready and waiting for the processor to use. Many computer makers, however, also offer off-chip caches that further improve performance.

 NOTE A word about non-Intel chips. Intel has competitors in the fast microprocessor market, and more could emerge. These other chips are all high-quality semiconductors and should be considered equivalent to Intel-brand chips (unless you own Intel stock). There are no low-quality or second-quality 486 chips. Despite Intel advertisements, there is no real advantage to using Intel versus the competing Advanced Micro Devices, Cyrix, or any other licensed IBM variants.

No computer ever has enough storage

Storage, in a computer, is that hardware where data and programs are stored when the computer is turned off. Secondary storage, which is used to store data not often accessed, is discussed in Chapter 17. This section discusses only primary storage. Primary storage, since the introduction of the IBM XT, has meant hard or Winchester disk storage.

Two factors have brought us to where a gigabyte (Gb) of online storage is considered a reasonable amount to have in a desktop system. The first factor is that operating systems, environments, and applications software have grown tremendously in size. While a word processor program, complete with spellcheckers and thesaurus, could be installed and run on a PC with only a floppy diskette drive back in 1982 (and remember, that computer only put 360 kilobytes on a floppy diskette), in today's Windows environment the operating system and graphical user interface alone occupies about 30Mb of hard disk space. A sophisticated program, such as WordPerfect 6.0 for Windows, needs another 30Mb of space, *before you even add your text files*.

Unless you are running a plain MS-DOS system with only a spreadsheet and a simple word processor, this almost manic growth in

software size (due to new printer drivers and the desire to remain competitive by adding bells and whistles to applications) requires any other computer user to have a minimum of 200Mb of hard disk space just to operate a few basic programs and store files.

The second factor that must be considered is that multimedia uses the two most storage-intensive types of files: images and sounds. While a screen full of text only needs a 4K or smaller file if stored in ASCII text format, the same screen if stored as an image can fill a 100K or larger file. Complex images, especially color, need much more space. Many color images take up several megabytes of space per image.

Most of the sound and image files used by a multimedia producer are kept on some form of secondary storage such as CD-ROM. Still, many files need to be kept on the very high-speed hard drive(s) that your computer must access dozens or hundreds of times per second. As an absolute minimum, any multimedia production system should have 500Mb of fast hard disk storage. A gigabyte or more is therefore perfectly reasonable for a basic system.

Because of price wars between hard drive manufacturers during 1993, prices of hard disks fell by nearly half. By early 1994 there was no indication that this trend would not continue. Despite these low prices of gigabyte-size drives, however, I do not recommend putting all your files on one large drive. If the drive fails (as all of them eventually do), your entire system will be inoperable until it is replaced. Unless you have been diligent in making backups, you may even lose important files. If you can afford the $1,200 needed to install a single 1Gb drive in early 1994, spend about 10 percent more and install two 500Mb drives instead. Moving up, two 1Gb drives are better than a single 2Gb drive, and so on. File management is slightly more complex with two drives, but the added security of having two drives that can be store copies of crucial programs and files should make this worthwhile for most professional-level users.

Drive performance is also crucial, but covered later in this chapter. It is also discussed in Chapter 16, when we look at how to determine how large a hard drive you need.

 # No computer ever has enough memory

The arguments defending this statement are similar to those for hard drive storage. While MS-DOS has been streamlined to where more lower memory than ever is available to programs (mostly by slipping items into normally inaccessible high memory) few multimedia production programs run under MS-DOS. The ones that do generally require a lot of memory (Autodesk's multimedia programs need a minimum of 8Mb of memory just to load, for example).

Windows, which is a popular operating environment, requires a minimum of 4Mb of memory to really work properly. Eight megabytes are not too much if you want to run several programs at once. (And if you don't want to load multiple programs, why are you using Windows?)

IBM's powerful OS/2 and graphical user environment need a minimum of 16Mb of memory to function. Some applications programs require 10- to 20Mb above the operating system requirements. (Windows NT is even worse, but it is mainly a network operating system, so you do not need to worry about it.)

Operating systems, graphical user interfaces, and applications programs are not the only factors that increase minimum acceptable memory size. Programs that run in, say, 10Mb of memory might be called upon to work with files that themselves are several megabytes in size. While the software could process such files a segment at a time by constantly swapping pieces back and forth between memory and hard disk, even the fastest cached hard drive is not at all fast compared to solid-state memory. Thus, swapping data to the hard disk slows down production tremendously.

Another memory hog is the software cache. We have talked about the microprocessor's own hardware cache and look again at hardware disk caches, as well as video caches, in other chapters of this book. But software cache programs also can greatly enhance a computer's performance. Windows comes with its own cache, as do some versions

of operating systems. There are also third-party cache software suppliers, some of whose programs even speed CD-ROM access.

A software cache is just a reserved area of main memory used to buffer, or temporarily store, data being read from or written to the hard disk or other storage area. The larger the cache, the more performance improves, up to a certain limit. This limit could be several megabytes in size, so you need to add a couple more megabytes of memory to your base system requirements if you want to be able to add a very cost-effective software cache.

The final memory eater is even hungrier and can make an even bigger difference to multimedia producers—the RAM disk. Often seen in early days when hard drives had average access times of 30 to 40 milliseconds (ms), RAM disks lost favor as drives were improved, especially after caching hard drive controllers became common. RAM disks are now making a comeback, however, with the more sophisticated users.

Simply put, a RAM disk is a section of memory set aside to emulate hard disk storage. This may sound just like a software cache, but it isn't. The data stored in a cache are just there for a brief time until they can be processed or written to disk. RAM disks are used to store entire programs, utilities, or often-used files.

A good example of using a RAM disk would be if you were working with a large text file, such as a book. Searches and other text-processing tasks will be much faster if you first create a RAM disk designated by a letter, just like a hard disk partition. You can then copy the file into that "fake" drive, and load the file into the word processor by specifying the file name and designating the path as being to the RAM disk. You could also copy the word processor's spellcheck dictionaries into the RAM disk and direct the program to look for them there.

Using the RAM disk this way can greatly speed processing of large files. It also works with the gigantic video and sound files used in multimedia production. The only problem is that files and applications software might need 20 or more megabytes of space to run from a RAM disk. Thus, you must ensure that any multimedia production

computer you choose has the space to upgrade the RAM capacity to 32Mb or even 64Mb.

Many computers have space for 128Mb of memory right on the motherboard. This location is ideal because you do not have to fool with accessory boards or special drivers when adding more memory. This trend to accommodate more and more memory is sure to continue as faster processors are installed. For example, in late 1993, Zeos International was offering a $3,500 Pentium system with room for 192Mb of memory right on the motherboard.

Fortunately, it is very easy to upgrade memory. Just open a PC's case and carefully insert more single inline memory modules (SIMMs) that contain the correct-speed chips. Fortunate also is the fact that memory prices keep dropping. You can even purchase used memory, as long as it is tested and guaranteed. Used memory removed from scrapped computers can be just as reliable as new memory, but manufacturers cannot reuse microchips and still call their computers new. Thus, because the price of memory continues to drop, you should probably buy just a bit more memory than you are likely to need at first and upgrade it later as your needs change.

Certainly there are price fluctuations. The most notable ones occurred in the 1980s when Japanese chips were declared to have been dumped, and high tariffs were placed on them and the U.S. manufacturers could not meet the growing demand. The second came in mid-1993 when the only factory in the world that made a critical chemical was destroyed by fire. Such events cause temporary blips in microprocessor and memory prices, but the trend in both areas is toward decreasing costs.

 # No computer ever has a large enough power supply

People tend to give little or no thought to the power supplies that provide the highly regulated voltages needed to operate computers. Power supplies are important however, especially for those who load a computer with lots of hardware. A prime example of the importance

of power supplies occurred in late 1993 when the respected computer maker, Gateway 2000, began shipping Pentium-based computers with inadequate power supplies. The systems started to fail in the field. The company did stand behind its products, but the message is clear: small power supplies are no bargain if you expect to expand your system!

This sort of engineering error seldom occurs, but it is common for a business or individual to purchase a bargain computer with some of the cost savings from the 125-watt power supply. While 125 watts is adequate for a modern low-power hard drive, video board, 4Mb of memory, and even a 486 33-MHz processor, what happens when you add a CD-ROM drive, 12Mb more memory, video capture board, SCSI-2 port for a scanner, and more?

I can tell you. In the vast majority of cases, nothing seems to happen, at least at first. But, as you push a small power supply to its limits, your system will start to experience unexplained crashes, overheating, and even premature hardware failures. Asking a 125-watt power supply to provide 120 watts or more of power continuously seriously erodes its ability to handle normal power line fluctuations.

Thus, accept nothing less than a 200-watt power supply, and take that only if you intend to run a minimum multimedia workstation. A 300-watt power supply should be the minimum for any Pentium-based system, and this requirement certainly applies to any 486-based computer that you expect to upgrade to Pentium later.

No computer ever has too much cooling capacity

Heat destroys computer components. It's that simple. In the ancient days of the IBM mainframe dinosaurs (yes, I am that old), our major concern when operating something like an IBM 360-65 was keeping it cool enough. We used special subfloor pressurized cooling systems with air conditioners whose capacities (and weight) were measured in tons, and we even applied local cooling to critical components using a large window air conditioner on a rolling cart. Of course, this portable

air conditioner actually heated the entire environment, but it did cool that critical piece of hardware.

Today, we take cooling for granted, and with good reason. Early PCs had tiny power supplies that drew less power than a desk lamp. This scenario changed recently, but few people have noted it. Let's try a simple experiment to demonstrate the new levels of power: the incandescent lamp providing local light for your reading probably has a 60- to 100-watt bulb. Right now, reach out and grab that bulb with your bare hand...Ouch! I hope none of you actually did that because even a 60-watt bulb can get really hot!

Now look at your tightly closed computer and picture between three and five of those bulbs inside. This example should clearly show you why your computer needs at least two cooling fans, or one large one. Early Pentium chips ran hot enough to literally fry an egg. Every expansion board or megabyte of extra memory you pack into that system further increases the heat, thus increasing your chances for system crashes and shortened component life.

No computer ever has too many expansion slots

This section boils down to whether you want a desktop or power configuration. I ignore minitowers because they serve no purpose; they offer the same number of slots as a desktop but cannot support a monitor on top.

Early PC users quickly learned that a couple of open slots just were not enough. Lack of expansion is one of the major reasons why Apple's early Macintosh computers faced so much resistance from experienced computer users. A sealed system that could not be easily upgraded with new hardware was just not acceptable because needs change, and new products constantly hit the market.

A few years ago, I would not have hesitated to say that any serious multimedia production workstation had to be a full-height tower—you simply needed that much expansion space. By early 1994, however, I

can say that a full-sized desktop unit is acceptable for many users, and the difference is SCSI-2. SCSI, which is sometimes called SCSI-1 to distinguish between early and later versions, was developed to provide a simple way to expand a computer's hardware without adding a new control board for each device. SCSI-2 is simply a faster and more compatible version of SCSI.

The SCSI standard lets you daisy-chain everything from scanners to optical devices to hard disks on a single port and eliminated the need for most internal expansion. SCSI did exactly that for the Apple Macintosh computers. Yet it still did nothing for Macintosh video or memory upgrades, leaving customers with the sealed Macintosh systems complaining bitterly about the then sky-high proprietary Apple pricing.

Unfortunately for PC users, there was just one thing wrong with the SCSI-1 standard: it did not work. The standard just was not standard enough. When you bought a SCSI device, such as a flatbed scanner, it often did not work with the SCSI port you installed to run a CD-ROM drive. So you could not daisy-chain the two devices.

Years of user complaints along with the development of SCSI-2 resulted in an inexpensive SCSI adapter board, such as the one from Trantor Systems, that can easily install and configure itself for any SCSI device you choose to connect. SCSI-2 is not perfect, but it is workable. Because most SCSI devices can now be daisy-chained, you can connect enough external devices to a desktop system to make it a practical multimedia workstation.

Nevertheless, I still strongly suggest you use a tower system to get as many available expansion slots as you can. I recommend a minimum of five expansion slots and seven still is not too many (Fig. 9-2). Some manufacturers have special features that can save you slots, such as Zeos' instant SCSI upgrade—which requires only the addition of one chip. You can even order the system with the chip installed. In any case, you do not need a slot for a SCSI board.

It does not cost much for a manufacturer to add more expansion slots, so do not settle for a system with fewer slots than you will likely need. What type of slots will you need? To answer this question, we need to

Figure 9-2

Tower computer with lots of expansion space. Meridian Data

get a bit technical. If you are not interested or prepared to read technical details, just make sure you get several EISA slots and at least one PCMCIA-2 slot. The remainder can be ISA.

Now for the technical details for those interested or who need more information. Expansion slots in a computer are for installing new video (monitor) boards, SCSI adapters, fax-modems, video capture boards, network adapters, and other devices.

In the beginning, there was the S-100 bus, but it failed because the manufacturers could not compete with the PC. The PC came with 8-bit expansion slots, which was reasonable enough because it also came with 8-bit microprocessors. Then, the 286-based AT introduced 16-bit processing and an expansion of the PC bus (now called the industry standard architecture) that resulted in most computers having 8-bit and 16-bit expansion slots. You can put an 8-bit board in a 16-bit slot, but not vice versa.

The introduction of the 32-bit 386 microprocessor and even greater demands on processing capacity brought us 32-bit memory, along with a need for more expansion bus features and faster transfer speed. This need led to IBM's radical and noncompatible Micro Channel bus with its plethora of powerful features. Interestingly, according to the bus developers, the main design consideration for the Micro Channel was a need to reduce costs and customer complaints. They thus developed a bus system that did not require any switches or jumpers on the boards.

Before the Micro Channel (erroneously called the PS/2 bus by people who never noticed that some PS/2 machines used the old ISA bus), it was almost always simple to add one expansion board. Adding a second and third, however, led to highly complex bus-addressing problems and the need for users to play around with IRQs (interrupt signals) and other technical components that were better left to hardware hackers. This problem was similar in concept and result to the one encountered when you try to load several memory-resident utilities in your computer. In the early days, and TSR (which stands for *terminate and stay resident* and is another name for memory-resident) utility worked fine, as long as it was the last one loaded.

This method of loading a TSR last works fine for one TSR, but it causes problems if you have two or three because they all try to use the same area of memory. Similarly, only a few electronic locations or paths exist over which ISA expansion cards can be accessed by the rest of the computer. Setting two cards to the same hardware address worked about as well as having two city buses going in opposite directions but using the same bus lane.

The bus wars of the late 1980s featured two competing systems, the IBM proprietary system and an alternative EISA, or extended industry standard architecture. Both systems accepted old 8- and 16-bit ISA boards with their switches and jumpers but could also auto-configure new EISA-standard cards. No actual performance advantage existed with either system, but EISA has pretty much won out. We do not even need to discuss proprietary IBM Micro Channel multimedia systems. These systems are good and work well, but the architecture is just too restrictive, and future expansion is doubtful. When new devices are created, most will be available for ISA or EISA before Micro Channel, if they ever even get to Micro Channel.

The strange-looking Personal Computer Memory Card International Association (PCMCIA) slot is used for adding memory cards or peripherals, especially to laptop or notebook computers. It is not at all important, however, as of early 1994. Why then did I suggest you get one? Because while PCMCIA is not important to desktop users yet, it is already important to battery-operated computers. The chances are very, very good it will also be important for desktops in the near future.

A PCMCIA provides an external slot that enables you to slip a board the size of a thick credit card into your computer without opening the computer up. Currently, fax-modems, nonvolatile memory, network adapters, and even software for a satellite global positioning system can be plugged into that PCMCIA slot. Standards are still a bit questionable for this new technology, but if you have the choice between two equivalent systems, one with a PCMCIA slot and the other without, I recommend that you get the PCMCIA slot, even if it costs $50 to $100 more.

Another apparent bus type, VESA, is not really an expansion bus slot and is covered in the video section later in this chapter.

No disk drive is ever fast enough

I still have a PC-XT clone. It had a 10Mb hard drive and an average access time somewhere in the 30 ms range. I also have a caching disk controller operating a 345Mb hard drive that typically has a 15-ms access time, but actually has an access time of closer to 1 ms because of that hardware cache. Guess which system is faster?

What if I switched hard drives between the old 4.77-MHz 8088 and the new Zeos International 486DX-66? Which one would sort a massive database or spellcheck a very long document? Surprise! The old 8088 might actually be faster because the processing bottleneck (the slowest part of hardware) would be the hard drive, not the

microprocessor. In fact, in many cases, processor speed is not the bottleneck, especially with large files.

Hardware or software caches and data transfer speeds are crucial measures of how quickly information can get in and out of the system. Although integrated device electronics (IDE) hard drives are cheap and dependable, maximum data transfer speeds require the more expensive SCSI or EDSI drives.

Fortunately, large software or hardware caches can speed up even the inexpensive IDE drives enough for almost all uses. Unless you are building a platinum-plated production system, you can probably go with two 500Mb IDE drives for about the same price as a single 500Mb SCSI hard drive. Just ensure that the drive itself has at least a 15-ms access time (12 ms is even better). If you are serious about working on large multimedia projects, don't even consider a system without a caching hard disk controller and a minimum of 1Mb of dedicated memory. This configuration can bring your average access time to near 1 ms and can really make a difference in how quickly you can perform large editing tasks.

 # No video is ever too fast or too good

Video has two complete chapters all to itself. It is so important however, that I discuss it here as well. Also, in most cases, you can or even must order a video board when you purchase your basic system.

When I say video, I am talking about the video board that operates your display (monitor), not the video I/O board that captures and compresses video. Many manufacturers include a standard video board that is seldom fast enough for multimedia production, but they also typically offer accelerator boards that can provide enough speed to be practical for your system. If so, these boards are almost certainly less expensive when bundled with other hardware.

For more details, see the chapters on video. The simple rule, however, is get a Super VGA local bus video system with a minimum of 1Mb of video RAM (VRAM), and more is better.

No computer ever has enough total expansion capacity

Expansion capacity is related to the earlier sections on expansion bus slots and power supplies, but it also deserves separate mention because it can help you decide between a desktop and a tower configuration. Given sufficient reserve power and five to seven available expansion slots for new boards, the remaining hardware restriction is the number of available drive bays where you can mount various internal devices.

10

Macintosh-specific platforms

I F you selected Macintosh software, you should have read the last chapter, despite the fact that it focused on IBM-compatible PCs. In this chapter, I discuss basic Macintosh systems with the expectation that you already understand the basic concepts presented in Chapter 9.

The Macintosh computer is a good choice for multimedia production work because the computer itself is designed to be highly visual. In fact, the HyperCard authoring system supplied with the Macintosh was used for multimedia presentations before most people gave any thought to the term. As the power of Macintosh systems has grown and prices have plunged, the Macintosh has become ever more attractive to all computer users, and not just to those who were always sold on its easy-to-use interface. Prices have plunged because of the growing popularity of the Microsoft Windows graphical user interface, which has proven to be a strong rival in the ease-of-use arena.

Just as the Macintosh led the way to desktop publishing, it has also led the way to multimedia. Because the Macintosh was in the forefront, an array of good multimedia software runs on the Macintosh platform. Multimedia production software ranges in price from free, for those tools provided with the Macintosh operating system software, to $8,000 for MacroMedia's Authorware Professional.

Because a Macintosh comes with SCSI ports, Macs are easily expandable—even those models that lack more than one or two expansion bus slots. The standard SCSI port on a basic Macintosh is not very fast, though. Memory and processor power requirements are similar to those discussed in the last chapter. You will need a lot of power, plenty of memory, and a large hard disk.

The Classic Macintosh, with its closed architecture and built-in monitor, is not suitable for any but the most basic multimedia production. It should not be considered for serious production except to produce text.

 Storage

A multimedia producer needs high speed, low price, and high capacity in a Macintosh mass storage drive. No single product can yet meet those needs very well. Magneto-optical drives are inexpensive, but slow. Hard drives are fast, but large sizes are expensive. RAM disks are extremely fast, but are both small and expensive.

Most users mix several storage devices together in different proportions, depending on which need is paramount. For example, every minute of CD-quality sound you want to edit or patch into a multimedia production occupies about 10Mb of storage. Any processing involves loading chunks of that file into memory, so fast access and transfer are essential. If your archives contain hours of sound clips, you must use optical storage to contain the vast majority of your files.

Moving selected files to a fast hard disk allows you to edit and otherwise work with a few of the files without requiring your computer to spend most of its time loading files from slow optical drives. Companies supplying high-end audio and video subsystems for Macintosh users are well aware of the storage bottleneck and sometimes offer complete products that include their own storage. DigiDesign (1360 Willow Road, Suite 101, Menlo Park, CA 94025) builds high-end audio recording and editing systems with built-in magneto-optical and hard drives. Avid Technology uses fast hard disks combined with phase-change optical drives in its completely digital video-editing system.

SCSI confusion

Many people believe the inclusion of a SCSI port in the basic Macintosh to be a major advantage, but it is a mixed blessing. One major drawback of many Macintosh systems is the lack of a fast SCSI port, especially for highly demanding multimedia work. Of course, PCs do not typically come with a fast SCSI port either, but because they come with no SCSI port at all, you do not pay extra for one that must be upgraded, as happens with the Macintosh.

For a list of many SCSI-2 boards, see Appendix B. High-performance SCSI systems for Macintoshes are also listed.

 # Redundant arrays of inexpensive disks

Redundant arrays of inexpensive disks (RAID) systems use two or more PC-grade (as opposed to expensive mainframe- or minicomputer-type) drives running in parallel. These systems provide faster average access times and better data transfer rates than any of the individual drives alone could provide. Some versions of RAID work by splitting files between drives, allowing two or more drives to cue up data from the same file and transferring them as soon as the system or cache memory can accept them. RAID systems also offer data duplication across drives, providing extra security by copying files. Thus, if one drive fails, all data can be recovered.

The following is a listing of RAID systems, along with company names and addresses.

DayStar Digital
5556 Atlanta Highway
Flowery Branch, GA 30542

offers the PowerCard, which includes SCSI-2 Fast features and a memory bugger to provide maximum data transfer rates of up to 5Mb per second.

FWB
2040 Polk St.
Suite 215
San Francisco, CA 94109

sells the SledgeHammer RAID system for the Macintosh. SledgeHammer Array price ranges between $889 and $14,089.

Loviel Computer
5599 W. 78th St.
Edina, MN 55439

markets Loviel R1, a high-speed RAID system priced from $14,270 to $34,540.

MicroNet Technology
20 Mason
Irvine, CA 92718

sells NuPort, a high-speed SCSI-2 port that puts Quadra SCSI performance in any compatible system. NuPort SCSI-2 is only sold as part of the MicroNet system. The company's RAID system, the Raven-040 Disk Array, is priced between $3,990 and $17,890.

Newer Technology
7803 E. Osie St.
Suite 105
Wichita, KS 67207

claims up to 11Mb-per-second transfer speed for its DART. DART is a combination of a SCSI-2 controller and a RAM disk. A built-in battery backup system keeps the RAM disk memory intact during brief power outages. The SCSI-II Dart is priced from $4,700 to $34,920.

PLI
47421 Bayside Parkway
Fremont, CA 94538

sells the $399 QuickSCSI, an accelerator board with SCSI-2 capabilities similar to those found in the high-end Quadra systems. The company's $1,999 to $15,999 MiniArray is a RAID system.

Storage Dimensions
1656 McCarthy Blvd.
Milpitas, CA 95035

sells the MacinStor SpeedArray, a RAID system priced from $6,799 to $36,099.

Unbound
17951 Lyons Circle
Huntington Beach, CA 92647

makes the very high-end Raidstor RAID system, priced from $41,000 to $325,000.

⇨ Making the choice

The Quadra 900-series Macintosh comes with a faster SCSI chip and a way to connect several hard drives together in a RAID arrangement. This configuration serves the dual purpose of providing massive storage and, in some cases, automatically backing up data by duplicating them on more than one disk.

Backup capability is especially vital with multimedia hard drive systems because they work much harder than most systems. RAID is designed for this type of situation, where you can expect drive failures fairly regularly. Thus, the Quadra is a good choice as a multimedia platform, especially with the added advantage of great expandability. In some cases, however, a less-expensive base system is still acceptable for professional developers.

You need to evaluate all the available systems based on exactly what you intend to do with your Macintosh. Because you can only buy Apple brand and because you need the fastest processor available, the range of choices is not very large. It is not difficult to determine which system is most cost-effective for your particular needs.

The Apple PowerMac—which is Macintosh, MS-DOS, and Windows compatible—was discussed at the end of Chapter 9. Refer back to that chapter for more information on this subject. Remember, with Macintosh systems and PCs, no system is ever too fast—only too expensive.

11
Monitors

CHAPTER 11

BACK in the dim, distant past, computers were often hulking blue monsters fed by Hollerith cards (in fact, computers were IBM-blue, which is why the company is sometimes referred to as "Big Blue"). They were operated by typing at a console that looked and sounded just like a large, electric typewriter that had not been recently serviced.

If you were to substitute floppy diskettes for the old punch cards, then, except for the size (vastly smaller) and speed (much faster), computers might seem about the same today. One thing would be missing, however. You would not hear the loud clacking of a teletype, which was then the only way to get information back from a computer during job processing.

Sure, there were those rows of lights on the central processing unit (CPU), just like the ones seen in science-fiction movies. But they were only used to find what went wrong when the system crashed, which was fairly often, at least when I was at the console of an IBM 360. There were also chain printers as large as a small car (and they were more expensive and considerably noisier than a Corvette without a muffler). These printers were used to print out massive amounts of data, though, not control the computer.

No, the enormous difference between operating computers back then and operating them today is the monitors. Monitors can display 24 or more lines at a time rather than a single line printed out on paper. So few people remember the old days, that almost no one realizes you do not actually need a monitor to operate a PC unless you are running graphics-oriented programs. In fact, if you have a dot matrix or daisy-wheel printer, you can actually redirect your computer's output to the printer and operate from there, one line or character at a time. I have actually done this in an emergency when a monitor failed.

While you can use this method for input and output, no one would really try to work with a PC that way if a monitor is available. Today's graphics programs especially require larger and more sophisticated monitors. And certainly, multimedia production requires the most sophisticated video systems available.

For many reasons, the standard 14" screen (measured diagonally) is no longer big enough for many computer tasks and should not even be considered for multimedia production. I use a 19" Sampo monitor that lacks the very high resolution of much more expensive displays but is also perfectly suitable for long days of writing. The same monitor, or its current equivalent, is suitable for multimedia work. So are many smaller monitors. The real criterion is how good the monitor is and not how large.

A word about monitor sizes. Most monitors are advertised using the diagonal measure of the actual tube size, and sometimes even the outside diagonal measure of the case. My 14" IBM VGA monitor actually has a diagonal image size measuring only about 12.5 inches. A 19" Sampo TriSync actually supplies a 17.5" diagonal viewing size. The difference is caused by the bezel that surrounds the monitor's cathode ray tube (CRT) and blocks off the rounded corners. Because the text or images would be distorted in these corners anyway, they are never shown and are not used by the display.

Although we discuss PC monitors in particular in this chapter, most of the same quality considerations apply to Macintosh monitors. In fact, many monitors (such as the 19" Sampo TriSync I use) can be used on either Super VGA (SVGA) PC systems or Macintosh computers. So, once again, do not skip this chapter if you have a Macintosh.

⇨ Quality

Monitor quality is a broad category. For example, quality can refer to color purity, whether lines appear distorted, how many colors can be displayed, maximum resolution, dot pitch, or how long the monitor will last (its warranty). While you do not want the cheapest of the large monitors now available, you also do not really need the most expensive, highest-resolution, large-screen monitors with very low dot pitch. Remember that if you are producing multimedia for distribution to other systems, your maximum resolution need only match that of your lowest target system.

While some multimedia requires resolutions in the 1,024 pixel (image element) range or above, normal word processing tasks don't require or even use such expensive resolutions. Every monitor in my office is capable of a higher resolution than I typically use. If there had been a lower-priced option with standard VGA resolution available, I would probably have saved a few bucks and skipped the Super VGA option. But a Super VGA or higher-resolution monitor is not that expensive anyway and is essential for many multimedia tasks.

After physical size and price, dot pitch is the most important number to consider when buying a monitor. Dot pitch is essentially a measure of how clear text appears on a color monitor. The smaller the dot pitch measurement, the better. Virtually no user is satisfied with a monitor that has a dot pitch of more than 0.40 mm. The minimum acceptable dot pitch for a small monitor is probably 0.31 mm, with 0.28 mm being more satisfactory if the computer is used for extensive text processing.

Multimedia is even more demanding. Unless you plan to sit well away from the monitor, 0.28-mm dot pitch is the minimum for any multimedia workstation—regardless of monitor size. This dot pitch can make large-screen models pretty expensive, but choose fine dot pitch over monitor size to meet your budget.

What exactly is dot pitch? A bit of knowledge about monitor technology is required to understand this subject, but it is not very complex. It is, however, important to understand when selecting monitors. Color monitors work by having three color dots illuminated in different proportions for every pixel of the image. Basically, dot pitch is a measure of how close these three dots are and thus how sharp the picture is. Technically, dot pitch is defined as how far apart similarly color dots are in adjacent triads.

You sometimes see monitors listed with a dot pitch as large as 0.51 mm. The image on the screen with this dot pitch is similar to printing out a picture of a human face with a very low-resolution dot matrix printer, using a 9-pin printhead and making just a single pass. The results may appear impressive to a novice, but even a beginner will quickly tire of such poor quality long before the eyes complain.

A 0.40-mm dot pitch might be marginally acceptable for some users working with monitors larger than 20 inches. In general, however, you will not be happy with a monitor that has a dot pitch higher than 0.31 mm. A large monitor with a 0.31-mm dot pitch can be perfectly usable, even for long periods of time, if used mostly for nongraphics text with only occasional full-color-image work.

Generally, prices go up dramatically as the size of the screen increases and dot pitch goes down. Therefore, balancing size, precision, resolution, and dot pitch is important. Serious multimedia work, using complex high-resolution color images, requires a top-of-the-line monitor similar to CAD. But other tasks, including color graphics, are not too difficult using a less expensive display.

 Refresh rate

The refresh rate of a monitor is very important if you use your monitor for hours each day because it largely determines whether you develop the common "monitor-flicker" headache.

The vertical frequency indicates just how quickly the screen is rewritten with an image, whether the image has changed or not. The solid-seeming monitor image is more an illusion caused by persistence of vision than reality, just like television or motion picture images. The faster the screen is refreshed, the less likely you are to notice any flickering caused by the previous image fading in your visual memory before the next image is presented.

Standard VGA graphics call for a refresh rate of 60 Hz, which is the same as North American line current frequency. Because the power company chose this standard, however, it does not mean you are limited to it. A refresh rate lower than 60 Hz will cause annoying flicker for most users, but even one of the standard VGA refresh rates is slower and can cause problems.

There are three common refresh rates you will encounter in most current PCs: 56 Hz, 60 Hz, and 72 Hz. Do not accept anything less than 60 Hz.

⇨ Multiscan

To ensure that your expensive monitor fits not only your needs today but also when you purchase video card upgrades, choose a monitor that accepts a wide range of compatible input frequencies.

A *multiscan monitor* is one that can scan at more than one rate, making it compatible with a variety of video signals. (It is often referred to as multisync because of the popularity of NEC's MultiSync line of multiscan monitors.) The very popular NEC MultiSync 4FG, for instance, accepts signals from 27 kHz to 57 kHz horizontally and 55 Hz to 90 Hz vertically.

Both multiscan and multifrequency monitors are available. The terms are often used interchangeably, especially by advertisers who are not too careful about which ones are actually multifrequency. Some people now use the term *multifrequency* to describe monitors that work within narrow frequency bands, like a single-frequency monitor, but have several of these bands. No real standard terminology exists, so it is best to check the details if this difference is important to you.

For example, while the NEC MultiSync can handle any signal frequency in the advertised range, a multifrequency monitor, such as my Sampo TriSync, only works with frequencies within certain ranges. The TriSync works with VGA and SVGA, as well as some Macintosh video cards. This range is perfectly acceptable for those applications, but it is not multiscan. In my case, the manufacturer does not claim it to be, but some are not as careful.

A simple reason exists why you might buy a multifrequency monitor instead of a comparable-quality multiscan one—cost. It costs less to support only two or three narrow frequency bands than all of them. If your video signal falls within the supported band, the difference between multiscan and multifrequency does not really matter.

Interlacing

Another cause of monitor-induced eyestrain is *interlacing*. In an interlaced image, the electron beam makes two passes to completely paint a single frame. On the first pass, every other horizontal line is illuminated. On the second pass, the lines skipped in the first pass are hit. Television images are created this way.

Interlacing is an inexpensive way to produce very high resolutions. It was used in the IBM 8514/A video standard, bringing high resolution to standard IBM PCs by introducing the IBM PS/2 Micro Channel computer line.

Interlacing, however, is bad. Watch out for interlaced monitors if you do a lot of work at a computer, as any multimedia developer certainly will. Interlacing can be acceptable at very high scan rates, but those rates are not standard.

In your search for a quality monitor, you might see a very low-priced monitor advertising a fast vertical refresh rate or scan frequency. Watch out because monitor quality costs money. An advertisement like this is likely to be claiming a high scan rate based on an 8514/A standard, which can legitimately be said to scan at nearly 90 MHz. It is actually only half that fast as far as your eyes are concerned, however, because it is interlaced.

Convergence

Convergence is another technical term you should be aware of. Remember that dot pitch relates to the distance between similar color dots that make up adjacent color triads, which your eye translates as a full range of color. *Convergence* is a measure of how well the three electron beams (red, green, and blue) that illuminate those dots are focused. If they are poorly focused, each dot is a bit fuzzy, and white dots appear to have color fringes.

 # Controls

While you probably never alter the controls on your television, you almost certainly will want to adjust your computer monitor on a regular basis. Therefore, it is important that the contrast, brightness, and power switches are easy to reach.

The power switch might not be important if you use a surge-suppresser switching station for your components or if the monitor is plugged into the computer to go on and off with it. You might, however, need to reach that power switch more often than you think. For example, while you do not want to shut off your computer during lunch hour, you should turn the monitor off.

Your monitor should also provide other controls. Horizontal and vertical size, as well as centering controls, are important, no matter how well the monitor was adjusted at the factory. Linearity, or the tendency of long, straight horizontal lines to be slightly slanted, is a problem with all monitors but is not noticeable on small ones. Your expensive, large-screen monitor should have an adjustment for this defect.

Pincushioning, or barrel distortion, refers to the inward or outward bulging of images at the very edge of the screen. An expensive monitor should also have an adjustment for this condition.

Degaussing, either automatic or user-controlled, might be important, depending on the operating environment in which you place the monitor. Stray magnetic fields cause a buildup in your monitor and images can jump or blur. Degaussing will correct this problem.

Finally, some of the most sophisticated monitors used in desktop publishing (and in multimedia) might offer color adjustment to a specific standard (referred to as a *color temperature adjustment*). This option might be important to some high-end multimedia developers, but it is mostly intended for desktop publishers who work with standard color printing devices and need to match their onscreen images with hard copy.

Not all of these controls need regular attention. The only ones you need on the front panel are power, brightness, and contrast. Keep in mind when shopping that the more you spend for a monitor, however, the more adjustments you should be able to make.

⇨ **Standards**

Your video board must match the capabilities of your selected monitor and software, which still covers a wide range of possibilities. For multimedia work, you need a very fast video board because video display will be the bottleneck for many tasks if you followed earlier advice and have a fast processor and hard disk and large memory.

Because few applications software packages offer support for those higher resolutions, your video board will probably come with a special set of drivers to allow its use with the major applications programs. For example, the VidTech WinMax Graphics Adapter, made by

VidTech Microsystems
1701 93rd Lane N.E.
Minneapolis, MN 55434

relies on a Weitek W5186 Graphics Controller coprocessor to speed Windows operations. The coprocessor relieves the main processor of presenting complex graphics and comes with the following drivers:

> ➢ 16-, 256-, and 32,000-color drivers for Windows 3.x

> ➢ Autodesk (CAD) software support

> ➢ WordPerfect 5.x

> ➢ Microsoft Word 5.0

> ➢ Lotus 1-2-3 R 2.3

> ➢ GEM/Ventura Publisher 3.0

These drivers let the supported software display up to a maximum of 132 columns by 60 lines of text. Note that these very crowded screens are useless unless you are using a large, high-quality monitor. Many other enhanced video boards also come with a similar selection of

special drivers that let you take full advantage of a large monitor's extended capabilities without buying special software (Fig. 11-1).

Figure 11-1

L-TV Macintosh-to-TV video board. Lapis Technologies

This section discusses industry standards. Virtually all of them owe their creation to IBM. Notice that many monitors have higher resolutions listed. These are very commonly supported by after-market video boards, even those that come with many computers but are not really standards yet. Table 11-1 lists the common video standards and their resolutions. The standards are covered in the following paragraphs.

Monochrome display adapter (*MDA*) provides high-resolution text mode (no graphics) with 720 × 350 pixel resolution and 9 × 14 dot character group resolution.

Color graphics/adapter (*CGA*) was the first IBM PC graphics standard. It provides up to eight colors at 320 × 200 pixels or two colors at 640 × 200 resolution. Text is presented in the standard 80-character by 25-line format, with each character consisting of an 8 × 8 pixel group. CGA graphics adapters use RGB (red, green, blue) color monitors.

Enhanced graphics adapters (*EGA*) surpass the CGA standards. They provide up to 16 colors in their 640 × 350 pixel graphics mode and use 8 × 14 dot patterns to create characters in the 80-character by 25-line text mode.

Multicolor graphics array (*MCGA*) is used on the low-end IBM PS/2 computers and provides a modest enhancement of the CGA standard, as well as conforming to the EGA standard.

The above color standards are all digital. While the rest of computer technology uses increasingly specialized forms of digital encoding, monitor technology actually advanced when it moved from the limiting digital standard to analog. For example, a digital EGA monitor can display a maximum of 16 different colors. Analog monitors, however, can often show 32,000 different colors or even more and some could show as many as several million (if you can tell the difference between them).

Video graphics array (*VGA*) came in with the IBM PS/2 Micro Channel systems. It provides 16 colors in the 640 × 480 graphics mode. MDA, CGA, and EGA graphics programs are all included in VGA for downward compatibility.

Super VGA is a nonstandard developed by third parties to enhance the IBM VGA standard. It raised the 640 × 480 graphics mode to 256 colors and added an 800 × 600 graphics mode. Super VGA is generally downward compatible with VGA and other IBM standards.

8514/A or eXtended graphics array (*XGA*) is an IBM standard used by Micro Channel computers that provides 256 colors in a 1024 × 768 resolution graphics mode. It requires a special board having extra memory and a special video processor chip to provide enhanced graphics. XGA runs programs in MDA, CGA, EGA, and VGA modes, which is good because few 8514/A graphics programs are on the market.

Table 11-1

Video standard resolution

Standard	Resolution
CGA	320 × 200
Enhanced CGA	640 × 400
EGA	640 × 350
Hercules	720 × 348
VGA	640 × 480
Super VGA	800 × 600
8514/A (× GA)	1024 × 768

Resolution numbers used in monitor specifications refer to the number of lines displayed and the number of pixels or color dot triples along each line. Thus, 640 × 480 (VGA) means the monitor displays 480 horizontal lines, and each line has 640 dots. The numbers listed for each monitor refer to the maximum resolution of the display. All monitors are compatible with a range of lower resolutions.

VGA is the absolute minimum resolution suitable for PCs used in multimedia production, with higher quality being preferable in many circumstances. Remember two things regarding resolution: ultrahigh monitor resolution is no use if your software does not support it, and advanced graphics standards mean nothing if the target system is only VGA.

⇨ Making the selection

Seriously think about which monitor to buy. Once you have selected a computer that is fast enough to run your programs, two items determine, in large part, how happy you are with your system, because the computer itself is just a black box that you interact with via these two important peripherals: the keyboard and the monitor. These two items can determine your happiness. Keyboards are discussed in the next chapter; monitors are covered here.

The portion of your hardware budget that you allocate to the monitor is crucial. If you need to skimp on hardware by buying only the amount of memory you need initially and by getting a smaller hard drive, both of these can easily be upgraded later as more funds become available. You lose none of your original investment by upgrading these. New memory is easily added to the existing RAM. And when you need to upgrade your storage, you add a second drive, still retaining the first.

Upgrading a monitor and video card, however, means losing the one you already have. Keep in mind that, besides increasing the comfort of the operator, a big monitor is nearly essential for those who must demonstrate and train business users on any new software. Short of a projection system, nothing beats having a monitor big enough for four or five people to crowd around your workstation to comfortably see what you are doing. A larger monitor is also often required by visually impaired individuals.

Very high-priced, high-resolution CAD and other special purpose monitors are not needed for most multimedia production work, nor are extra-large monitors that cost as much as $5,000 or more.

 # Video cards

There are so many PC video cards on the market it might seem impossible to decipher their claims. Actually, the situation isn't very complex.

For multimedia work, you need the fastest video card you can afford with the largest amount of onboard video RAM (VRAM) memory. Don't get too carried away with claims about local-bus video performance. See Chapter 9 for more information on video cards for PCs.

 # Macintosh monitors & standards

Almost all of the same guidelines discussed so far in this chapter also apply to Macintosh monitors. Macintosh computers often use more

expensive monitors that are not generally compatible with those used on PCs but they are also usually of very high quality. Of course, we are talking only about the larger, free-standing Macintosh monitors, not those tiny ones built into the case of some low-end Macintosh computers. Some, however, such as my Sampo TriSync, can be used with both Macintosh and PC systems.

Like VGA and SVGA monitors for PCs, Macintosh monitors are analog-based, rather than digital—the standard used by EGA, CGA, and other early IBM PC-compatible systems. In analog systems, the display board handles the conversion from digital (bitmap) graphics images in the computer to the analog signal the monitor uses (Fig. 11-2). The digital systems use a conversion system installed in the monitor.

Figure 11-2

Typical video boards for the Macintosh. Lapis Technologies

The basic difference between monitors traditionally designed for the Macintosh and those for PC is that a text-mode never existed on Macintosh systems as there was on PCs. The Macintosh was always a graphics computer, just as Windows PCs are now. Macintosh monitors were always graphics-capable, even the tiny black-and-white screens on the early Macs.

The Macintosh also uses a different size 15-pin connector than the smaller VGA connector. If your monitor is analog and supports the frequencies your graphics board supplies, it can be used on either a Macintosh or PC (VGA or SVGA). All you need is a plug adapter to go from one size connector to the other.

A bewildering array of monitors are advertised for Macintosh systems, but you can quickly eliminate most of the specialized ones designed for desktop publishing. These include monochrome and dual-page monitors, which are of little or no use in multimedia development. As with a PC, you want as large and as high quality a monitor as your budget allows. Selecting a minimum display standard is done differently on a Macintosh, where you want to look for a 24-bit color card and compatible monitor, rather than a standard such as VGA. The 8-bit color standard for Macintosh is not acceptable for multimedia.

Some Macintosh systems cannot be upgraded to 24-bit color. These computers are not suitable for multimedia work, but they are also the slower systems and would be eliminated anyway. Eight-bit color is faster, however, than 24-bit. In many cases, you might want to use this advantage by switching a 24-bit card to an 8-bit mode, but you eventually need to look at the full range of colors and shades displayed by a 24-bit system. Some systems, notably the II, IIfx, IIcx, and SE/30, do not come with video capability. So you can thus add a 24-bit color card without having paid for an existing, but lower-quality, card. Unfortunately, none of these Macs is suitable for most multimedia because of speed restrictions.

An interesting alternative for some Macs is the development of external SCSI port video adapters. This alternative is mostly for PowerBooks, which lack external monitor attachments but might be used for portable multimedia presentations. The Radius PowerView (8-bit color or 1-bit monochrome), Outbound Outrigger Intelligent Monitor, and Sigma Power Portrait were the three best-known when this book was written. None is suitable for multimedia development but are useful in presenting multimedia.

The following companies also market video adapters for the portable Macintosh PowerBooks:

Aura Systems
P.O. Box 4578
Carlsbad, CA 92008

Lapis Technologies
1100 Marina Village Parkway
Suite 100
Alameda, CA 94501

SuperMac Technology
485 Potrero Ave.
Sunnyvale, CA 94086

The SuperMac SuperView even offers NTSC- or PAL-composite video output for television or projection screen use (Fig. 11-3).

Figure 11-3

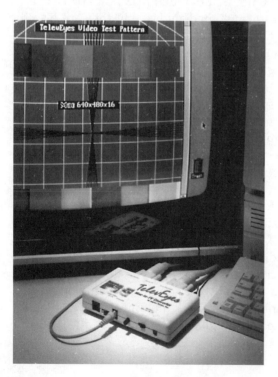

TelevEyes PC- or Mac-to-TV adapter. Digital Vision, Inc.

Envision
510 First Avenue N.
Suite 303
Minneapolis, MN 55403

markets the internal Envision ColorBook 16. Another 16-bit color board, the Computer Care BookView Imperial, comes from

Computer Care
420 N. 5th St.
Minneapolis, MN 55401

These are the only PowerBook adapters I know of that can support QuickTime video on a 16" monitor. These are display options, not suggestions for multimedia development platforms.

Multiscan or autosynchronous monitors are becoming popular for the Macintosh, mostly because they are far less expensive than the traditional single-frequency monitors sold by Apple and other suppliers. These monitors, however, do not offer the same quality as the more expensive Macintosh monitors. They are good, and improving, but multimedia developers should leave these bargains to their coworkers who work with spreadsheets and word processing tasks.

Finally, always specify what cable you need when ordering a monitor. Many cable types are available. Even if your monitor supports both SVGA and Macintosh color, you need the correct end on the monitor cable if you expect it to work. So tell the vendor whether you are going to use the monitor with a Macintosh or PC.

Radiation alert

Remember when your mother told you not to sit so close to the television set because it would make you go blind? Well, now you spend even more time at an even closer range to a computer monitor. Despite the known effects of electromagnetic radiation (EMF) on some organisms, it is only very recently that governments here in North America have followed the lead of Sweden's National Board for

Measurement and Testing and begun to require low-emission monitors in some locations.

Before ordering that giant monitor you will be sitting very close to for up to 10 hours per day during the next several years, remember that exposure to high levels of EMF might have some relationship to leukemia, lymphoma, and cancers of the nervous system in both children and adults. Understandably, industry groups ignore or discount such findings, but there is growing evidence that EMF could be harmful. Certainly, it is considered harmful in Sweden, which does not have a large television and monitor manufacturing industry.

If you think that this warning sounds reminiscent of the battle over the supposed dangers of tobacco, I won't argue with you. But I am a Certified Radiological Monitor for the Commonwealth of Pennsylvania. I personally (but not in any official capacity) am suggesting that you think about the dangers of EMF. You can buy MPR II radiation-standard-compliant monitors if you want.

12

Keyboards & pointers

NO matter how much of your multimedia presentation is derived from prerecorded sound and video clips, you will still need to perform a large amount of editing or other processing to create the final cut. Thus, you will use a keyboard and mouse or mouse-like control.

You might think that those touch screens where you touch your finger to the appropriate place on the screen and slide it around to relocate objects would be very useful for multimedia production. If so, you have never tried to work for several hours with your arm stretched out straight in front of you.

Touch screens and light pens, except in very special and limited uses, are total failures as input or control devices precisely because the inventors forgot how people actually work. Neither are included in this book because they are generally inappropriate for multimedia work, except possibly multimedia playback.

➡️ **Keyboards**

The traditional keyboard is the most familiar, and still the most common, input and control device used with computers. Even though it is not used for much input when working with multimedia projects, it is available on nearly every system. Although the mouse and menuing systems made so popular by Macintosh and Windows operating environments are widely used, shortcut command sequences using keyboard input are still the choice of many professionals. Keyboards provide faster and easier access to commands compared to the supposed simplicity of sliding the cursor around hunting for the correct menu command.

Multimedia production almost certainly requires using a mouse, even if the production is being done on software that operates in a nongraphics operating environment, because these programs create their own graphics working environment. You are not, however, constrained to shifting between keyboard and mouse control.

Alternative keyboards include touch pads, trackballs, and even joysticks. Many provide a better work environment than a separate keyboard and pointing device.

A trackball is essentially an upside-down mouse. You move the sensor ball with your fingers instead of moving the mouse housing. When using a mouse, the sensor ball within the housing then moves in contact with the mousepad or other surface on which the mouse is resting. The trackball can be either built into a keyboard, as shown in Fig. 12-1 and usually replacing the cursor pad or as a standalone device. Many people find the trackball offers better control than the mouse. In any case, the trackball always requires less space than a mouse, because it doesn't need to be moved around on a surface that must be smooth and clean.

Figure 12-1

Color screen 486-66 MHz notebook computer with built-in trackball. Micro Express

NOTE

Older PCs used a different keyboard port than that used on IBM PS/2 computers. Many newer PCs followed with IBM's improved keyboard port. Today, however, inexpensive converters are available that can connect one type of port to a different type of keyboard. Note that Macintosh keyboards use a different technology entirely and require more than just a different connector to operate with a PC, and vice versa.

Keyboards with built-in trackball devices include the following:

➤ The $100 *KB-5581*, a 101-key standard-size keyboard with integral trackball. Contact

Chicony America
53 Parker
Irvine, CA 92718
714-380-0928
714-380-9204 (F)

➤ The high-end $946 *Tracker Ball Keyboard* from Computer Keyboard Systems. Although using an old keyboard design, it still is available for both PC- and PS/2-compatible keyboard ports. Contact

Computer Keyboard Systems
1640 Fifth St.
Suite 224
Santa Monica, CA 90401
310-395-4639
310-393-6040 (F)

➤ The $100 *Trackball Keyboard*, which comes with a 200-dots-per-inch (dpi) trackball and the standard 101 keys. It includes software drivers to emulate a Microsoft mouse and is PC keyboard port-compatible. Contact

Electrone
1685 S. Colorado Blvd.
Suite 353
Denver, CO 80222
303-757-0335
303-758-3088 (F)

➤ The very inexpensive $50 *IDKbTrk*, a 101-key keyboard with trackball, from Identity Systems Technology. This keyboard connects to PC or PS/2 ports but is probably too low-priced to provide the quality a multimedia producer requires. Contact

Identity Systems Technology
1347 Exchange Dr.
Richardson, TX 75081
214-235-3330
214-907-9227 (F)

➤ The $249 *TrakPro*, a 101-key keyboard with 200 dpi trackball, from Key Tronic. This Macintosh-compatible keyboard is from a well-known keyboard maker. Contact

Key Tronic
N. 4424 Sullivan Rd.
Spokane, WA 99216
509-928-8000
509-927-5248 (F)

➤ The $150 *Enhanced 101 with Trackball*, a standard 101-key keyboard that includes a 25-mm or 16-mm trackball. It's IBM PS/2-compatible, provides Mouse 1 and Mouse 2 buttons with locks, and is made by Lexmark International—an IBM spinoff that also makes IBM LaserPrinters. Contact

Lexmark International
740 New Circle Rd. N.W.
Lexington, KY 40511
606-232-2000
606-232-2380 (F)

➤ The $75 *Keycat*, a 101-key keyboard that has a three-button, mouse-compatible, high-performance optomechanical trackball with 200-dpi resolution. Contact

Power Source Computer Systems
10020 San Pablo Ave.
El Cerrito, CA 94530
510-527-6908
510-527-3823 (F)

Pointing devices

Although keyboards with built-in pointing devices are useful, and some users find them very convenient, most multimedia and graphics-creation workers want a standalone pointing device, either a mouse or a trackball. In some cases, a joystick is useful, but joysticks are not generally used for graphics-related work. Its lack of precise control, combined with fast action, makes it more suitable for games.

Many computers, and virtually all that come with Microsoft Windows installed, also come with a mouse (and usually a two-button mouse). A professional multimedia or graphics worker, however, might not like the standard mouse, either for feel or precision. Fortunately, many alternatives are available, some more ergonomically friendly than the standard mouse. Although some companies, such as Microsoft, spend millions making their mice comfortable to the touch, others offer faster or more precise cursor movement.

Mice, joysticks, and graphics tablets are discussed in the following subsections. Appendix H also lists mice, trackballs, joysticks, and graphics tablets. Even more listings are included on the accompanying disk in the APPXH.TXT text file.

Mice

The mice listed in the appendix do not include the very inexpensive units, often priced less than $30 and sometimes offering very good value for occasional mouse users. Also not included are the weird ones, such as the MotorMouse Products MotorMouse. It is shaped like a Lamborghini Countach—a strange shape indeed because I personally cannot think of a less comfortable car to ride in or a less suitable shape for an ergonomic mouse. Listed in Appendix H are high-quality products of special interest, from major manufacturers, or offering higher-than-usual resolution. For example, cordless mice, which usually use a pair of infrared light beams to track the position of the mouse without the restriction of a hard-wired connection, are listed.

Mice are rated by dots per inch, but it is actually signals per inch. That establishes how sensitive the mouse is; that is, how much on-screen movement occurs for a small movement of the mouse. Some mice use software that dynamically adjusts their sensitivity according to how quickly you move the mouse. An inches-per-second or millimeters-per-second rating refers to how quickly the mouse can be moved without skipping.

⇨ Joysticks

Although not often used, joysticks can have an application in multimedia. They can be used in the control of 3-D, animation, and walkthrough demonstrations of virtual reality.

⇨ Graphics tablets

Digitizer, or graphics, tablets are especially useful for creating CAD images or paint-type drawings. Used as an electronic sketch pad, a digitizer tablet converts lines drawn on the surface into lines in the software. Some include special emulation software that lets them act as control devices or as a mouse, but the main purpose of a digitizer tablet is to generate a rough sketch that can then be manipulated in the software. They can also be used to trace a drawing or figure for input into the computer.

13

Video input & manipulation

CHAPTER 13

T HIS chapter discusses the hardware required to input both still and motion video images into your computer (Fig. 13-1).

Figure 13-1

Computer Eyes RT external SCSI video frame grabber for Macintosh. Digital Vision, Inc.

An exploding market exists in ready-to-use clip photo and clip video art, mostly on CD-ROM. But that does not mean a large amount of footage is actually available on an absolute basis. The chances of you finding just what you need for a particular task from the available stock footage are pretty slim—and nonexistent if you need a shot of your company's buildings or products. And, while some digital cameras produce graphics files, others produce standard video and must be connected to a video board.

For the foreseeable future, the only way you can guarantee access to the video you need for inclusion and editing in your multimedia project is to install your own video capture board. Using a video input board, you can pick up a video camera or use an existing video tape file, capture the images you need, and transfer them into your system (Fig. 13-2).

Figure 13-2

Video digitizer frame grabber for PC. Digital Vision, Inc.

Unfortunately, things just are not always that simple because of the massive processing requirements imposed by video capture. Getting a still image, even a full-color photo-realistic image, into your computer isn't difficult. Once you move up to video, however, and especially full-motion video, the situation changes dramatically.

Capturing a single video frame actually means recording two full interlaced screen scans. To capture the single frame, your video board must detect when the scan for a particular screen begins, synchronize its data capture process with the sequence of pixels, and stop exactly when the scan is completed. This video comes through the interface very rapidly and must be stored in memory before conversion and storage on the hard disk. Multiply this task by a factor of 30 frames per second (fps), and you can see that video capture is a formidable task. Even using video compression, such as Intel's Digital Video

Interactive (DVI), it takes about 500Mb of disk space to store even a compressed version of a 60-minute video.

Inexpensive solutions, such as the $500 VideoSpigot from SuperMac Technology, might make it seem as though the problems are solved. Remember that this board, however, can only capture full 30-fps video in a 160 × 120 pixel format (when installed in a 33-MHz 486), which only fills about a 2" window on a computer's monitor. At half-rate, this low-end video capture board can handle a window only two times as big. The program also requires Microsoft's Video for Windows or another program to enable it to show captured movies on a Windows system (rather than only a system with a VideoSpigot board). On the positive side, the board's compression technology can store several hours of audio and video on a single CD-ROM.

Video boards use a lot of dedicated onboard memory to capture and store video while it is being processed. The VideoSpigot board maps this onboard memory into the relatively unused space between 640K and 1Mb that somewhat reduces your available memory. Or, it might require you to reset various utilities that put TSRs and system drivers into high memory. It does not really reduce your operating memory significantly. Many video boards, however, do. The manufacturers of these apparently have not noticed that powerful multimedia machines require 16Mb or so of system memory.

WARNING

Some video capture boards map their onboard memory into addresses your computer system normally uses for memory increases from 8Mb to 16Mb. If your video capture board uses these addresses, you must lobotomize your systems to install the board, reducing your working memory to only 8Mb.

Video standards

Video comes in a variety of formats. For example, in broadcast television the video signal is transmitted in AM mode, but the audio is sent in FM. Fortunately, television tuners handle these different formats for you. As long as the tuner provides a standard RCA plug video output for a VCR, you can ignore everything except the video signal

when recording. Your VCR also has a built-in tuner with video-out, which can provide your signal without you needing to purchase a TV.

NTSC, the standard set by the National Television Standards Committee, specifies the 30-fps, 525-line television image throughout North America, Japan, Central America, and much of South America. Virtually all video boards accept standard NTSC video signals.

PAL (phase alternation by line) is the color television standard used in England, Holland, Australia, Germany, and some other countries. PAL images are also interlaced but are transmitted at only 25 fps, while the resolution is upped to 625 lines per frame. You must have a PAL-compatible capture board if you plan to use video from those sources. PAL-M is used in Brazil, the one country in this hemisphere where the people don't speak either Spanish or English. Brazil's TV standard is 525 lines and 25 fps.

SECAM (systeme electronique couleur avec memoire) is the television standard used in France, Eastern Europe, the former Soviet Union, and many African countries. Its 819-scan-line picture is a higher resolution than that provided by PAL.

If you are wondering why some countries use 30 fps and others 25 fps, remember that television receivers are not connected physically with the transmitters but need a common time reference to synchronize their activities. North American power grids operate at 60 cycles-per-second (or hertz), while the PAL countries use 50-Hz power.

To summarize, systems that adhere to U.S., French, and British standard TV signals, whether broadcast or on videotape, are totally incompatible. Brazil's system is unique.

Other standards include S-VHS, which provides higher-quality video and requires yet another compatibility jack. CIF (common intermediate format) is an integrated services digital network (ISDN) videophone standard that forms a portion of the international CCITT H.261 standard. This standard is not important now, but if and when videophones become common, it could become important. CIF specifies a 352 × 288 pixel color image.

H.261 (pronounced "h-dot-261"), also known as Px64, is a powerful but expensive-to-implement scheme for transmitting video at rates from 64 kbps to 2 Mbps. Included are several video and still-image formats. QCIF (quarter CIF), for example, is a part of H.261 specifying a 176 × 144 pixel window.

Captain Crunch, from Media Vision, covers video playback, video conferencing, and CD-ROM. MotiVE (motion video engine), also from Media Vision, has been adopted by Microsoft for video playback, conferencing, and CD-ROM. Cirrus Logic and Weitek have both signed on with Media Vision.

M-VTS (Marconi video telephone standard) is another videophone standard (implemented by the MCI Video Phone) and providing 10 fps at 128 × 96 pixel resolution.

While you might need to output video in these video standards, the chances are that you will not need to capture such low-grade video.

Compression standards

With full-color broadcast-standard television requiring between 45Mb and 90Mb of storage per second of data, even today's large hard drives are incapable of storing the minimum of 20 or 30 hours of stock video a professional multimedia producer needs to have available.

You can avoid the data storage problem in one of two ways: either reduce the image quality or reduce the file size. Greatly reducing the quality of the image by removing some of the color, skipping every other frame, or limiting the size of the displayed image to only a tiny portion of the full screen is unacceptable for most professional applications. The typical solution is to drop some of the quality from the original image and then compress the resulting file as much as possible. Compression saves storage space and transmission times, but it requires processor power—and a lot if you are using full-motion 30-fps video. Specific compression standards are discussed in the following subsections.

 JPEG

Joint Photographic Experts Group (JPEG) might become a world
standard for video compression. The digitized image is broken into 16
× 16 pixel blocks. Every other pixel is then removed from the block,
converting it to an 8 × 8 pixel block. After further information
processing that further reduces the size of the file, the data are stored.
They can be later reproduced by reversing the process.

JPEG is highly computation-intensive. Although some JPEG software
is available for use by standard processors, the technique is usually
implemented with a dedicated microprocessor. The JPEG compression
technique is applied only to single frame or still video, but you can
string these together to form standard video. Look for about a 10:1 to
20:1 compression ratio.

MPEG

The Motion Picture Experts Group ISO/CCITT standard is a full-
motion video standard that offers even greater compression than
JPEG. Because MPEG handles multiple frames, this compression
system saves tremendous storage space by storing just a single frame,
then recording only the changes to subsequent frames. This method
results in about a 3:1 compression benefit for most video sequences,
as compared to frame-at-a-time JPEG compression, or a maximum
compression ratio of about 100:1 in extremely advantageous
situations.

QuickTime

QuickTime is the time-based Macintosh standard for displaying image
and sound data. Although designed for video, it was also designed
with the Macintosh's limitations in mind. Thus, QuickTime video is
displayed in a 160 × 120 pixel window that requires only 57K of data
per frame—not the 900K of data for a full-screen 640 × 480 image.
Compression rates vary, depending on the content of the video clip
and particularly on how much the image changes from scene to scene.

A major advantage for low-end presentations, QuickTime ensures that sound and images are reasonably well-synchronized, no matter what the speed of the particular Macintosh system the file is played back on. QuickTime makes certain that audio and video playback start and finish at the same time. This synchronization could cause a very choppy video display on slower systems because of the way QuickTime makes adjustments: it plays the sounds and chops out video frames as necessary.

Cinepak

This SuperMac Technologies compression system is the basis of QuickTime's video compression but has also been licensed by Microsoft (Video for Windows), Sega, Atari, and 3DO for their video games. Compression rates vary from about 20:1 to 200:1.

Microsoft Video 1

This technology, licensed from Media Vision, is also used in Video for Windows and offers compression ratios from 10:1 to 100:1.

Other standards & nonstandards

Run-Length Encoded is a simple compression technique used by Microsoft. A string of identical data is represented by a symbol, and a multiplier decodes to a string of identical data the length the multiplier specifies.

Indeo is Intel's video compression algorithm released in conjunction with Microsoft's late-1992 announcement of Video for Windows ($199). Indeo is based on the Intel i750 microchip but can also be decoded by software, automatically adjusting its quality to the video display available. Indeo's compression rate is only about 10:1.

MMPM/2 (MultiMedia Presentation Manager/2), IBM's OS/2 video extension, is compatible with Indeo and IBM's own UltiMotion compression algorithm and PhotoMotion.

AVC (Audio Visual Connection) often is used as if it were a standard, but it is actually a multimedia program from IBM. It works with IBM audio and video capture boards that are installed in Micro Channel computers.

CD-ROM XA is a standard, but not a video standard. Rather, it is a sophisticated specification for interleaving audio with data onto a CD-ROM.

CD-V (compact disc video) places a five-minute video segment, such as a music video, on a 3" optical disc. Its time has come and gone, so you can ignore this specification.

Captain Crunch, which was mentioned previously, is a video playback and video conferencing compression system from Media Vision. *MovtiVE*, also from Media Vision, is another video playback and conferencing compression scheme. A version of it was licensed to Microsoft as Video 1.

Video boards

In 1992, C-Cube Microsystems lowered the price of JPEG compression with a $500 ISA board that offered four stages of compression, ranging from 8:1 to 100:1. The highest compression rates produce unacceptable quality loss for most multimedia, but even at 10:1 compression, this board is very useful and that can handle about 1Mb of bit-mapped video per second. Creative Lab's $500 Video Blaster included JPEG compression and even shipped with Mathematica's Tempra image-editing software. For the professional multimedia producer, however, neither of these low-end boards cuts it. Appropriate video boards are listed in Appendix D.

Because the technology is changing so rapidly, there is no need to provide details about any other boards that were available when this book was written. The only advice I can offer is to check with the companies listed in the appendix to learn which boards are currently available. In general, a professional-grade multimedia production system requires a relatively expensive video capture board (Fig. 13-3).

Figure 13-3

Parallel port video frame grabber. Digital Vision, Inc.

Look for a board with built-in support for JPEG or MPEG and ensure that the image resolution you need is supported at the correct capture speed for your applications. Input signal compatibility is also critical. You might want to consider a board that includes audio input capabilities; most boards don't.

⇨ Video problems

Controls for correcting contrast, color, and brightness are included with many cards. They are needed, perhaps every time the scene changes! This problem is worse with the less-expensive boards, which also suffer greatly because of their inability to smoothly digitize at high enough rates to capture each of the 30 frames displayed each second.

I won't mention specific problems encountered with current cards because most will have been modified by the time you read this book. It is important for you to know, however, that not all video capture boards are created equal—some wash out colors because of brightness-setting problems, others have a predominant hue regardless of adjustments. Still others just cannot capture a very good image. Some boards tested in 1993 even had the very annoying habit of defaulting to PAL, requiring regular resetting.

Few boards, and none of the inexpensive ones, can capture full 30-fps video at 24-bit color, even on the fastest Macintosh systems with very fast hard drives (the system processor is involved in video capture). A board such as the SuperMac VideoSpigot only captures 30 fps when installed on the fastest Macintosh computers and even then only in a tiny 160 × 120 pixel frame.

Because apparent video quality depends more on the smoothness of the image than anything else, most boards require you to cut color fidelity by reducing the capture file to 16-bit color. Unfortunately, this strategy cannot help you unless your target systems are also quite fast. If the images will eventually be played back on slower machines, they won't be able to process the large 30-fps files fast enough for a smooth display, no matter how much work went into tweaking the capture/production machine for peak performance.

Digital cameras

Gen-lock video boards can capture usable still video images from various sources. To get any degree of quality, however, you need to use a specially designed digital still camera to capture the real-world image in electronic form. Some of these cameras require a video capture board in your system, while others can exchange ready-to-edit files through the serial port of your Macintosh or IBM PC.

There are two general categories of digital still cameras—those below $2,000, and those above. Not surprisingly, there is also a world of difference between the two.

Low-end cameras have lower resolution, poorer quality optics, and other limitations. Logitech's FotoMan Plus, a low-end camera, can deliver what you need—it all just depends on your particular production. Low-resolution is, after all, a relative thing; FotoMan Plus offers 376 × 240 pixel resolution at 8-bit (256-level) gray-scale, which is more than enough for many applications.

A high-end camera, such as Eastman Kodak's $9,995 DCS 200ci, offers capture and storage of 50 1524 × 1012 digital images.

FotoMan Plus

This useful low-end camera weighs well under one pound and measures only 6.75" × 3.25" × 1.25", small enough to fit in a large pocket. If you are accustomed to using single-lens reflexes (SLRs), you might have to readjust a bit to using a separate viewfinder with an f/4.5-rated lens. The field of view, however, is similar to that of a normal 50-mm lens on a 35-mm camera and its sensitivity is about equal to a film speed of 200.

Because the lens does not have an adjustable iris, you cannot adjust depth of field. All light control comes from the variable shutter speed, which is an electronic equivalent of about 1/30 to 1/1000 of a second. A neutral density filter reduces the amount of light in bright situations such as full daylight. Two optional lenses provide telephoto and wide-angle capabilities. A serial port interface is provided to transfer data that can be stored in TIFF format for manipulation by its supplied software or any other program.

The camera is battery-powered, with a battery life of 100 hours on a single charge, and stores up to 32 images on a memory chip.

For more information, contact

Logitech
6505 Kaiser Dr.
Fremont, CA 94555
510-795-8500
510-792-8901 (F)

Dycam 1

Dycam offers an identical-looking camera, the Dycam 1, with identical features as the FotoMan Plus, but uses different software. The Dycam Model 4 is a $1,300 color version of the same camera that records 32 256-color images. For more information, contact

Dycam
9588 Topanga Canyon Blvd.
Chatsworth, CA 91311
818-998-8008
818-998-7951 (F)

 # Canon RC-250 Xapshot

Unlike the Logitech and Dycam cameras, the $900 Xapshot uses a removable floppy disk to store images, making it bulkier and about 8 ounces heavier. The disk also gives the camera an unlimited storage capacity at 50 images per $10 diskette. Again, the lens offers about the same viewing angle as a standard lens on a 33-mm camera, and the company offers a telephoto lens.

Both the sophistication of controls, including an auto-adjustment for backlit scenes, a self-timer, and choice of single or continuous exposure mode (3 fps), and the resolution, 640 × 480 pixels, make this a higher-end product. The battery is good for more than 500 shots on a single charge.

The camera includes NTSC video output, so you need a digitizer board if you want to import the images into your computer. You can also feed the images directly into any standard VCR or the video-in port on television/monitor combinations.

 # Kodak DCS 200ci

This high-end digital still camera, based on the well-known Nikon 8008 35-mm SLR, has a camera-sized extension that extends from the bottom of the camera body. This electronic package makes the

camera lens see the digitizer just as if it were a roll of standard color film capable of 1524 × 1012 pixel resolution. This resolution is high by digital image standards, but poor for film.

Because this camera is based on an actual Nikon camera body, you have the full range of compatible Nikon and third-party lenses available, as well as special attachments for photographing through microscopes or telescopes. You do lose the 8008's most powerful feature—a special high-quality automatic exposure mode—because the charge couple device's (CCD's) image surface is considerably smaller than that of a piece of 35-mm film.

The black-and-white model lists for about $8,500, and the color version sells for $10,000; both use a standard serial port to transfer images to the computer. The low-priced versions can store only a single image, but more expensive models have built-in hard drives. Because the resolution is so high, it can take five seconds or more to transfer data from the CCD to the hard drive, so you cannot take a number of images quickly.

The Digital Camera System is priced at $19,995 to $24,995. For more information, contact

Eastman Kodak
343 State St.
Rochester, NY 14650
716-724-4000

⇨ Ektron (Kodak) 1412

This high-end, $20,000 CCD 1412 digital imaging camera system captures 4096 × 4096 pixel images and transfers them through an IEEE-488 interface. Ektron Applied Imaging, 23 Crosby Drive, Bedford, MA 01730.

⇨ Sony MVC-7000

This $9,000 Sony camera uses an unusual recording method that captures digital images from a CCD (actually, three separate ones for

color) but stores them in analog form. Image quality is extremely high, but so is the cost of accessories. The Sony is not based on a standard SLR body, as the Kodak camera is. Instead, it is a custom design, which means paying several thousand dollars for a different lens.

The floppy diskette used can store 25 images per disk. Because of the video format of the data, the camera can capture 2.5 images per second, which makes it just about essential for sports photographers.

Sony
Sony Dr.
Park Ridge, NJ 07656

also offers other still-video models.

14

Audio hardware

CHAPTER 14

C HAPTER 7 discussed audio software as well as the different types of audio signals and files you need to handle, so they are not discussed again here. This chapter focuses on audio hardware.

With the exception of some Tandy computers, many Macintosh systems, and, more recently, new systems from different vendors, personal computers never had any audio input capability—nor much output capability. For multimedia playback capabilities in most computers, you need to add an audio board.

The most basic computer audio is analog sound, which is converted into a digital signal, stored in the PC, and then converted back to audio. This sound is the type you get through the tiny speakers supplied with most computers. These speakers were intended to vocalize clicks and beeps that signaled software or hardware errors. This sound capability should only be used if you intend to rely mostly on images and text and use only basic beeps to alert users to make selections or such. Otherwise, the multimedia producer can totally ignore this sort sound capability. Note that when considering the advantages of sound to enhance presentations, remember that only about 10 percent of existing personal computers actually have any real sound output capabilities.

The MPC standard, which is about the lowest level of computer a multimedia developer should target, requires that compatible systems have a CD-ROM and thus audio playback through headphones in most cases and an 8-bit digital sound board. The 8-bit designation refers to the size of the file used to store each sample, not the bus connector the board uses to interface with the computer.

The minimum acceptable audio board for a multimedia production system can record 16 bits per sample, in stereo, at a 44-kHz sample rate with MIDI interface. You might want to make less sophisticated recordings, but you need this board as a minimum for better-quality productions. CD-quality audio (and you will be surprised how quickly users will demand this level of sound quality) generates about a 10Mb file for every minute recorded in full stereo in 16 bits at 44-kHz sampling rate. If you don't believe the size of that file, consider that an audio CD stores about 60 minutes of sound on a disc that could be used to store 600Mb of data. The math is simple.

Of course you do not want to record everything at that quality. Any voice annotation does just fine in mono at about an 11-kHz sampling rate. You need to decide which parts of your presentation need the highest quality and balance those needs with your hardware limitations.

The higher level of audio cards for a high-end multimedia studio will mostly come with a MIDI interface included as well as a MIDI synthesizer. You can thus play back MIDI files without an external synthesizer.

There is a sharp division in the quality of digital audio boards, below which are the FM-synthesized systems that produce good-quality playback and above, which are the high-end sampled audio synthesizers that use prerecorded samples of high-quality sounds to produce very high-quality synthesized music.

Audio input boards

Remember that you don't need to be too concerned with audio playback. You need to worry about audio capture or input instead. Thus, make sure you do not get a board that only produces .WAV sound files. You need a board that offers both line and microphone input. You also want as many sampling rates as possible, more than just one or two, so you can store as much quality as you need without generating larger files than necessary. If a microphone is supplied it could be carefully matched to the board, or it could just be thrown in and not supply very acceptable quality, even for voice.

Perhaps more than with any other PC accessory, you get what you pay for with an audio board. Cheap quality does not exist. If you are getting a sound board complete with CD-ROM interface (which is probably not a good idea for a multimedia studio, anyway, because of the low performance of these interfaces), at least be sure you are getting a SCSI interface and not a less-expensive proprietary one.

Of course, if you are specifying a number of multimedia upgrades for the basic computers used to play back your multimedia production,

then the least-expensive soundboard might be just what you want, and a proprietary CD-ROM interface probably will not be a problem.

Audio boards are listed in Appendix C, and some of the more popular ones are discussed next.

 # SoundBlaster

Because of the wide support for this hardware and its relatively good quality, the $350 SoundBlaster 16 ASP board is a good choice for many PCs, especially with the optional $300 MIDI daughterboard. Better-quality boards are available, but unless the playback system you are designing for is very sophisticated, your sound files will not sound as good to your viewers and listeners as they did to you when they were created. This situation can lead you to create sophisticated sounds that waste time and disk space but then cannot be properly reproduced on the PCs that play it back.

 # Audiomedia II

This sound board comes with the powerful Sound Designer II software and the two make a powerful sound upgrade for NuBus Macintosh systems. Audiomedia II offers CD-quality 44-kHz and digital audio tape (DAT)-quality 48-kHz sampling rates and a direct connection for DAT devices. The board also comes with two stereo input and output ports. This company also offers high-end Macintosh-based audio recording and editing equipment for those with even more sophisticated needs.

Because this equipment is really in the realm of audio engineers, I do not need to go into it in this book. For more information, contact

DigiDesign
1360 Willow Rd.
Suite 101
Menlo Park, CA 94025

MIDI hardware

MIDI hardware comes in several types. First, there is the interface board that lets your computer communicate with the MIDI device (Fig. 14-1). You also have a device that used to generate MIDI signals such as a keyboard like the one shown in Fig. 14-2. Finally, you have synthesizers. A MIDI device might or might not include its own synthesizer. You do need a MIDI-OUT and MIDI-OUT port on your adapter card.

Figure 14-1

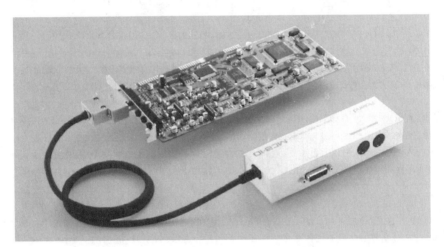

Roland Super MPU dual-port (32-in/out channels) MIDI interface for PCs. Roland Corporation, U.S.

Figure 14-2

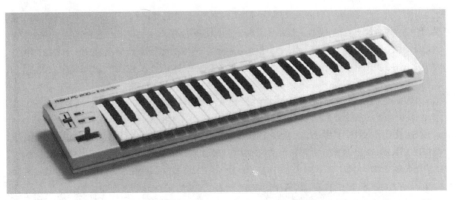

Roland PC 200mkII MIDI keyboard, providing 49-key MIDI-out signal. Roland Corporation, U.S.

Generally, there is no major advantage to an expensive separate MIDI interface board unless you plan to produce professional-quality audio, which is not the same as producing professional-quality multimedia. Remember, you don't need a MIDI keyboard device to play back MIDI sounds.

MIDI devices can have MIDI-IN or MIDI-OUT ports. A MIDI-OUT port lets you generate MIDI signals as well as play them. Many devices also have a MIDI-THRU port that lets you daisy-chain MIDI devices, similar to the way SCSI devices can be strung from a single port.

Any MIDI board can support 16 channels or devices. Some even go beyond this. For example, the Roland Super MPU provides dual-port, 32 MIDI channels (both in and out) and SMPTE synchronization for multitrack recorders.

When looking at MIDI devices, get one with velocity-sensitive keys—so that the loudness of the sound will depend on how hard you strike the key. Velocity-sensitivity does not work for all instruments, such as a carillon, but it is essential for those that do recognize the speed and force of a keypress.

Even a relatively inexpensive MIDI keyboard provides most multimedia workers with the tools they need to produce MIDI sounds, but a real musician will want to look at dozens of factors well beyond the scope of this book. Professional musicians should visit a local music store to see what is available.

Many boards offer low- to high-quality MIDI synthesis onboard, so all you need to add is amplified speakers. Advanced users will probably want a separate synthesizer that does not have a keyboard attached.

For those who might be interested in MIDI composing but lack a musical education, Software Toolworks offers a combination MIDI synthesizer with full-sized velocity-sensitive keys and a complete music instruction program that can teach you to play the piano. You do not even need to buy a MIDI adapter board to use this system because the piano lessons are played through a special serial port cable. (Of course, you do need a MIDI board to use the MIDI capabilities.) The Miracle Piano system costs about $400 but has been available at a

street price of $200; at that price it is about the least-expensive MIDI keyboard device on the market and is actually of respectable quality.

⇨ Conclusions

Even the most basic multimedia hardware and software probably offers capabilities beyond the needs of anyone without specialized musical training to make full use of the audio features. Those MIDI-experienced musicians reading this book already know more about audio processor technology than would really be appropriate to this book. Thus, the chapters on audio are rather generalized.

Finally, your choice of sophisticated audio components should be greatly affected by the audio capabilities of the playback system you are targeting. If your users do not have MIDI capabilities in their systems and you are producing computer-based multimedia, all the advantages of MIDI are lost anyway.

On the other hand, if you are producing videodiscs, videotapes, or publishing your own movies on CD-ROM or any of its variations, you need the highest-quality audio. You also need a musician on your team, one who is already familiar with MIDI and able to advise you on the proper equipment. Fortunately, most sophisticated musicians either work with or are familiar with MIDI tools.

15

Selecting & installing scanners

CHAPTER 15

A multimedia presentation would not be much without fancy images—it would just be scrolling text, charts, and background sound. While the paint-and-draw software described previously can produce some remarkable images, most multimedia projects either require or are greatly improved by scanned images, especially color images or photographs.

An artist could produce an excellent rendering of your company's headquarters or new product if given a week and some expensive software. For about the same amount of money, however, you could purchase a Polaroid camera and an inexpensive scanner to capture a dozen such images. These images could then be used for direct inclusion in the final production or as input for morphing or other manipulation in the computer.

A few years ago, scanners were a desktop machine the size of a modern laser printer and cost almost $2,000—and that was just for black-and-white scanners! Prices for color scanners started at $4,000. Fortunately, increasing demand and improved technology caused a dramatic decrease in price. Color scanners are now in the budget range of even home-based desktop publishers, let alone professional multimedia producers.

Types of scanners

Scanners, whether color or gray-scale, flatbed or handheld, all work basically the same. Light reflected from the surface of the image is focused on an array of charged coupled device (CCD) sensors that convert the image into an array of digital signals. The scanner itself physically shades the image from extraneous light, so virtually all scanners include a built-in light source.

The number of signals recorded for each square inch of the image is the resolution, described as dots per inch (dpi). The minimum resolution for multimedia is typically 300 dpi, but that is definitely the bare minimum. In fact, only listed scanners with higher maximum resolutions are listed in Appendix F because, as multimedia matures, low-resolution images will be used less and less.

If you classify scanners by the type of documents or objects they can scan, there are six basic types:

> ➤ handheld, which are moved across the image by hand

> ➤ flatbed, which operate like the familiar copier

> ➤ page-feed, which move the pages past the scan head

> ➤ 3-D or overhead, which scan an object placed on a platform

> ➤ slide

> ➤ drum

Scanners can also be classified by the types of files they generate:

> ➤ black-and-white (line image)

> ➤ gray-scale

> ➤ color

Gray-scale and black-and-white (B&W) files are essentially the same in most cases. Software controls the contrast and records the number of gray scales in the image.

We discuss all these various combinations, but gray-scale flatbed and handheld scanners are the most useful for desktop publishing as well as multimedia production.

 Handheld scanners

Because the price of semiconductor components is constantly dropping, the most expensive part of a scanner is the scanning mechanism. This mechanism is the hardware that moves the image past the CCD array (or the CCD array past the image).

For many users, the handheld scanner is the answer to high prices and limited desk space. The electronics and image quality of handheld scanners are similar to the low-end (less than $1,000) flatbed scanners. The major savings in cost are from the lack of mechanism that holds the document and moves the scanner.

Handheld scanners offer the following advantages:

> low price

> small size

> hand control

> ability to scan bound images

Even on a very limited budget, you can afford an image scanner or a color handheld scanner. A gray-scale flatbed also fits the budget.

Unlike page-feed scanners, you can scan an image that is part of a bound document without cutting pages or otherwise damaging the original. A handheld scanner is about three times the size of a mouse. Their small size means you can put one right on a small desk or even hang it up and bring it down only for scanning jobs.

Hand control means that you can easily scan just a portion of an image. Using special software, other scanners can be set to scan just image segments, but nothing can beat the speed and convenience of just pressing a button, moving the scanner a few inches, and then stopping the scan.

The limitations of handheld scanners are the following:

> small size

> hand control

> skilled operator required

> alignment problems

While small size is a major benefit of a handheld scanner, it is also a major drawback because it can only scan an image that is about four inches wide. Software allows you to scan larger documents by pasting the image together, but this takes time and is generally less satisfactory than what a full-page scanner can do.

Hand-scanned images also can suffer from several image impairments. These impairments are not because of the quality of the optics or electronics but rather because they are recorded by hand. Hand

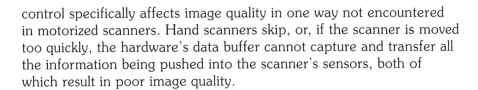

control specifically affects image quality in one way not encountered in motorized scanners. Hand scanners skip, or, if the scanner is moved too quickly, the hardware's data buffer cannot capture and transfer all the information being pushed into the scanner's sensors, both of which result in poor image quality.

The speed with which you move the handheld scanner across an image is, if not crucial, then certainly important. It is not difficult to get a good image with no skips, but it does take practice and good physical control, which brings us to our next problem. Handheld scanners require training and definite operator skill in positioning and moving the scanner. This process does not require the sort of control needed by an Olympic marksman, but it also is not something you want to sneeze at—at least not during a scan.

You can often re-scan again if you get a bad image, but it is sometimes difficult to see minor errors until you start the detailed editing of the scanned images. At that point, it might be too late to go back to the scanning task—images could have been misplaced, the operator might have been under short-term contract, deadlines might be close, etc.

If the scanner is not aligned perfectly parallel to the image, the scanner will produce a skewed image. Poor alignment can occur with both hand-scanned images and motorized scanners, but they are far more likely to occur with a handheld scanner. Unlike flatbed scans, skewed images can occur during scanning, even if the image was aligned perfectly.

Flatbed scanners

Flatbed scanners look and operate like most desktop copiers (Fig. 15-1). You place the document or object to be scanned on a flat glass screen, and the scanner's mechanism moves the CCD array and light source underneath the glass.

Flatbed scanners have the following advantages:

> ➢ easy alignment
> ➢ ability to scan bound images

➤ higher-quality scans

➤ ability to scan larger images in one pass

➤ limited operator training required

Figure 15-1

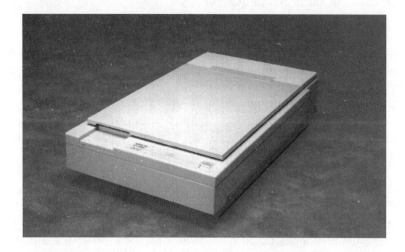

Epson flatbed color scanner. Epson

As mentioned in the previous section, a major cause of problems with images produced by handheld scanners is the initial alignment of the image with the scanner. Unless the image is almost perfectly parallel to the scan head, a "jaggie" or sudden break at one or more places

along the length of the image will occur. The image will be shifted slightly to one side or the other, thus shifting an entire portion of the scanned image out of alignment. A similar-quality flatbed scanner almost always produces higher-quality scans than a handheld scanner, if only because of the handheld scanner's alignment problems, which are nearly eliminated with a flatbed.

Flatbed scanners consist of a flat piece of glass on which the item to be scanned is placed and, typically, a two-sided alignment grid similar to two rulers placed at a right angle. If you want to scan a single sheet of square-edged paper or photograph, all you do is lay it securely against both of these edges, then carefully hold it in place while lowering the cover.

Just as a handheld scanner does, a flatbed scanner can usually scan bound images. The only limitations are those related to the physical size of the document and the type of binding. Obviously, if a bound page cannot be laid flat or nearly flat (to the margin of the area to be scanned) cannot be scanned properly on a flatbed scanner. The only choice when scanning bound images, however, is a flatbed or a handheld scanner. The other types of scanners are completely unsuitable for any bound material, unless the binding can be removed.

Another major cause of poor-quality scans when using handheld scanners is irregularities caused by changes in scan speed. This problem is eliminated entirely when using a powered scanner. Because the scanner is designed to operate more slowly than the buffer and interface transfer the data, there will never be any lost lines from scanning too quickly or repeated lines from moving the scanner too slowly or jittery.

A flatbed scanner can also scan a larger image in one pass than a handheld scanner can. The minimum capacity of a flatbed is the standard 8.5" × 11" page, but some scanners are much larger and can be used to scan maps or large drawings. Most common flatbed scanners easily accommodate legal-sized pages at a minimum but can also be set by the control software to limit scanning to a small portion of the total available area.

The amount of operator training and practice required to produce good-quality scans is much less than for a handheld scanner. Alignment is usually as simple as pushing two 90-degree edges up against the sides of the scan bed's glass, and scan speed is entirely controlled by the internal mechanism. Both types of scanners do require operator training in setting and running the associated control software. The software is very similar for all scanners and is not any more or less complex for any one physical type. Of course, the software is usually more complex for color image software than gray-scale.

Multiple single-sheet document pages can be scanned by most flatbed scanners using a special optional power feeder mechanism. This type of attachment is more commonly required by scanners used to gather images processed by optical character recognition (OCR) software that converts text images into ASCII computer files. Power feeders are not very useful to those who primarily capture high-quality images. Even if you have a large number of images to capture, page-feed mechanisms, whether attached to a flatbed scanner or part of a different kind of scanner entirely, introduce new alignment problems that can degrade the images.

Another accessory for some flatbed scanners is an attachment for scanning slides. If you only have a limited need for transparency scans and top-quality is not required, your flatbed scanner can also scan slides without this attachment. You just need to add a mask (to exclude extraneous light) and additional light to back-illuminate either the slide or film negative. This method, however, only works with scanners designed to be used this way because the scanner must shut off the normal front light and be able to scan a relatively tiny area. Results will not equal to those that even the least-expensive dedicated slide scanner can provide, but, in some cases, this dual-use capability can be practical. Slide scanners are discussed in more detail in their own subsection.

Page-feed scanners

Page-feed scanners move the pages past the scan head, as opposed to the flatbed scanners that move the scan mechanism past a fixed page. Flatbed scanners do often have page-feed mechanisms available as an option, but these only move pages onto the flatbed scan screen, where it is then scanned by the mechanism that moves the scan head while the page remains motionless.

In contrast, page-feed scanners operate as do laser printers or fax machines, where a page is pulled through the mechanism at a steady rate. In this case, the CCD array and light source remain fixed while the document itself moves.

Because of obvious problems involving in page slippage and feed mechanism irregularities, page-feed scanners typically suffer minor alignment problems and, in the worst cases, can produce wrinkled documents. They are not suitable for multimedia image scanning but are highly efficient for large-scale OCR.

 # 3-D or overhead scanners

Only a few 3-D scanners are on the market, which is probably enough. These scanners scan a solid object that is placed on a platform underneath a fixed scan head, which pans to scan the object.

Some distortion is introduced by the changing angular relationship of the scan head to the object, but these 3-D scanners are actually quite effective and produce very good results. But, although some multimedia projects might use this type of scanner, most multimedia productions do not involve this sort of image. If quality 3-D images are required, they will almost certainly need to be produced using the powerful 3-D graphics programs instead of scanners.

 # Slide scanners

Slide scanners are very specialized scanners designed to do only one thing—very accurately digitize high-quality images from a piece of film (Fig. 15-2). All other scanners scan from a nontransparent document. Typically used to scan color slides, the image is placed into a holder and slid between a carefully calibrated light source and CCD array. Because of the high cost of these scanners ($5,000 and up is common for a quality slide scanner) and very high resolution, these scanners are used for desktop publishing rather than multimedia productions. They

Figure 15-2

CI-3000S color film or slide scanner/film recorder with 2,000 line resolution. Polaroid Corporation

are, however, perfectly suitable for multimedia. Look for a minimum of 600-dpi resolution in a slide scanner.

A decent-quality 35mm slide scanner can cost as little as $2,000. Once you have one as part of your basic system, it will prove useful on many occasions and will be used a lot.

The 600-dpi minimum limit I specified for professional slide scanners will probably be fine for most multimedia applications if you do little or no cropping of a 35mm image. A higher resolution is needed if the slide must be enlarged further than full-screen VGA or Super VGA.

Optical resolutions for slide scanners range from 600 dpi to 4,000 dpi or even more. The highest-end machines are not necessary for even the most demanding multimedia productions unless a great deal of enlargement is required—computer monitors do not have very good resolution. All the slide scanner needs to do is match that resolution when the slide is blown up to full-screen.

Monitor size used for output is not important either because resolution is based on the specific standard (EGA, VGA, Super VGA, etc.), rather than size of the monitor.

 # Drum scanners

There is still another kind of scanner, but you are unlikely to run into it except in a shop doing top-end publishing. This is the drum scanner, and it can only scan with flexible flat images.

In the drum scanner, the image is wrapped around a drum and spun at high speed while a light beam and pick-up scan along the axis. It produces an extremely high-quality scan that is far too precise to be useful in most multimedia or desktop publishing projects. Of course, if your business is already a full-service publishing operation, one or more drum scanners might already be available. If so, there is no reason not to use them for scanning appropriate images.

 # Resolution

For standard scanned images, minimum resolution for a scanner to produce quality multimedia images is 300 dpi. That 300 dpi is horizontally *and* 300 dpi vertically, which is a total of 90,000 dots for an area the size of a postage stamp. (Slides need 600 dpi, or 360,000 dots.) Beware of manufacturer claims that state that their scanners have a resolution of 300 dpi or greater when they really do not. The problem is especially common when the claimed resolution is said to be higher than 300 dpi. The reason for this false advertising is because of the leeway that exists in the technology. Unscrupulous advertisers take advantage of a process called interpolation to hype their products as meeting a higher standard than can actually be delivered. Basically, interpolation involves taking a 300 or lower dpi

resolution and using software to double that resolution by taking the average value of each pair of dots and inserting a software-created dot in the middle with the average value.

Interpolation is not quite that simple, but it is pretty close. Just as you might suspect, the result of interpolation creates larger files but adds no additional information, so you do not actually get any better results. Often, the scanned and dithered image is a bit lower quality than a straight scanned image of the original resolution because interpolation often causes blurring.

The situation is even worse when a true 100-dpi image is used to create a 300-dpi image through more interpolation. Don't misunderstand; interpolation itself isn't bad and can even be useful when you need to enlarge an image without getting too blocky. It is especially useful when scanning line art that would otherwise generate jagged lines. You just need to ensure that the scanner you choose produces a resolution of 300-dpi (and preferably better) before any software interpolation and that the software does not impose unwanted interpolation that can affect image quality.

Sometimes, you see interpolated resolutions described instead as nonproportional resolution, indicating that the vertical scan has a higher resolution than the horizontal resolution. Interpolation in this case produces better results, making the two resolutions equal rather than increasing resolution on both sides. Nonproportional resolution, however, still is not the same as real resolution. Look for optical resolution, which is basic resolution before any software manipulation.

Color vs. gray-scale

After determining which type of scanner you need, you need to consider either color or gray-scale.

Because the quality of the final digitized image almost entirely depends on the cost of the scanner (unless you are paying for some feature that you don't need, such as powerful OCR software), it is important to decide whether you really need high-quality scanned

color images in your final projects. The cost of color scanners has dropped dramatically, but you can still get a better-quality image from a $2,000 gray-scale scanner than from a $2,000 color scanner. Because of the way the human brain processes images, however, the color image might seem better.

The choice for a high-end multimedia shop is simple: you almost certainly want the capability of scanning color images, so a gray-scale scanner will not be acceptable alone. A high-quality gray-scale scanner can be very useful for line art and working with B&W photographs, but a high-quality color scanner can be used for the same tasks. Only a little more work is necessary because of complexity of the software.

You have probably heard horror stories about color-matching and other problems with scanned color images. These problems, however, while very common, are not important for most multimedia producers. Color matching, registration, and other printing problems are encountered when trying to reproduce fine-quality color images, such as the covers of a glossy magazine, onto paper. These problems are especially apparent when several separate images have been edited together and the final result must be a highly faithful reproduction of the original. For multimedia productions, however, we are only trying to put fleeting individual images on a computer screen, which is not a very demanding reproduction medium.

Color scanners are essentially three gray-scale scanners built into the same unit. Each one produces a file containing data representing 256 shades of gray, ranging from black to white. Because each set of images is either made through a color filter or when the image is illuminated by one of three different color lights, the resulting file actually represents the true color of the image.

In some scanners, the three color images are recorded in three passes. In others, a single pass is used to collect all three sets of images. To record full color in one pass, the image must be illuminated by three different lights—red, blue, and green—that are rapidly switched on and off to create three images for each line scanned. A three-pass scanner uses three passes of the CCD detector but only one light, which is covered by a different color filter on each of the passes.

⇨ **What to buy**

Because their applications do not totally overlap, it is a good idea to have both a flatbed and handheld scanner. Each should have as high of quality that fits the budget, but you don't need extremely high-resolution—it just isn't needed for multimedia. Color is probably essential for multimedia publishers because, unlike desktop publishers who often work only with laser printer output, any multimedia production involves color. B&W (gray-scale) images are suitable only for line drawings or special effects.

Virtually all scanners, except for low-end handheld scanners, are SCSI devices, so connection to the computer usually poses no problem. Those that support the scanner interface provided with Windows can integrate with any Windows software and thus allow scanner control directly from Windows.

16

Main storage

CHAPTER 16

THIS chapter provides additional information if you want more details selecting your main hard drives. It repeats some of the information covered in Chapter 9, which described basic system hardware, but focuses on file types and data compression, both of which are important when specifying how much storage is actually needed. It is particularly intended for you if you are a sophisticated user to help you determine just how much storage space you need and what drives you should choose.

While the multimedia developer is probably anxious to explore all the video, audio, and sound components and options that constitute the multimedia system, the less glamorous and almost invisible, details of planning an advanced production system are at least as important as the "whiz-bang" production software with all its bells and whistles. Next to computer speed, and sometimes more important than the sophistication of applications software, is a basic hardware component—storage.

If this statement seems drastic, consider a powerful production system capable of producing 3-D color animation, but crippled by an inability to store parts of the production. Or consider being unable to store a good selection of stock files online so they are ready for instant use.

Computer users who typically work with text or numbers, as well as graphic artists who are familiar with film images or videotapes but not computers are unlikely to really be aware of just how much storage sound and graphics files use. This chapter explains the storage you need for various applications and shows how you can manage this vast amount of data in a cost-effective yet efficient manner.

Before we discuss storage in detail, let me remind you about the difference between memory and storage. This topic has been covered previously in Chapter 1, but I feel it is important to mention the difference once again. Memory, often referred to as RAM (random-access memory), is where programs are run and data are stored. Anything placed in memory disappears when the power is turned off or when another program is run. Storage is a permanent but usually erasable area where programs and data are kept until needed. Something placed in storage is available any time the computer is

turned on unless it is intentionally or accidentally erased, written over, or lost due to a disk crash.

Text & numbers

Computers were originally designed to work with text and simple numeric files and are therefore stored in a very compact and efficient manner. The entire text of this book only occupies about 700K of hard or floppy disk space in straight ASCII (text) files, and less than 400K in standard compressed format (ZIP). By way of comparison, the cover image alone takes about 700K by itself. It is good for multimedia producers that a picture is worth 1,000 words because that picture takes about that much more space!

Because a book requires a large amount of research data, a single 250-page book might, when stored with a reasonable amount of research text, fit on a single high-density floppy diskette. Several books can fit on such a disk if stored compressed. Numbers occupy a similar amount of space unless formatted in some special way, such as being stored as part of a spreadsheet. Compression is even more effective in spreadsheets because the average spreadsheet is actually empty of formulas, data, and formatting information.

What this all means is that, as a professional writer, I would not hesitate to begin writing a book on a computer with only 10Mb or so of free hard disk space. I could comfortably work even just from floppy diskettes. Remember, though, that my documents are sent to editors, who don't want any formatting, integrated graphics, or even common business text elements as underlines.

The situation becomes radically different for desktop-published documents, which have a variety of special formatting commands and different type sizes. These files also even have special headers that define printers and print quality. Desktop-published documents can take up 20 times as much space as a simple text file. For example, a simple template I use to generate business letters in WordPerfect 5.1 places a 1"-high graphic of my company's name at the top of the page, includes a business closing in simple text, and contains three

lines of small-type contact information. This 74-word template occupies a 16,174-byte file and is still larger than 15K when the graphic is removed. With the graphic and special type instructions removed, the same text becomes a 750-byte (0.75K) file. Thus, adding formatting instructions causes even a simple text file to become very large. The reason the graphic only takes about 1K to store is that it is really only a special WordPerfect formula, not a regular image file.

 # Graphics

Similar to formatted text, graphics images can also result in a very wide range of file sizes, depending on the file format and the amount of information contained in the image. For example, a simple black-and-white bar chart that fills an entire page in the finished document, or a complete video screen, might only require a file $\frac{1}{100}$ as large as a full-color half-screen VGA image. On the other hand, a 24- or 32-bit color single-screen image in Macintosh format (or similarly precise PC file) can occupy more than 10Mb of disk space.

 # Video

The situation with video is, of course, a lot worse than either graphics or formatted text. Even very limited QuickTime video clips occupy between 15Mb and 20Mb of disk space for a 30-second clip. And that is for a 160×120 pixel image! A full screen 640×480 pixel image requires about 1Mb of storage space per frame! For smooth full-motion video you certainly want 30 frames per second, increasing the size of a single 30-second video clip file to 900Mb. A multimedia producer working on a three- or four-minute production might need to look at an hour of clips to select the segments necessary for the final cut. Is it any wonder that I keep talking about the necessity of using CD-ROM storage and of buying the largest hard drive capacity you can afford?

Those file sizes are for uncompressed full-screen video, of course. But we also only looked at a single, relatively small production project. Although compression can reduce video file sizes by as much a factor of 100, you do lose some quality with any compression technique. The greater the compression, the more information you lose. Video compression is not the same as a file compressor, such as PKzip, which does not lose any data. Video compression means reducing the amount of information on the stored image. At a minimum, you need to keep most images on videotape and digitize them only as needed. You also, however, need to have many video images available online and ready to edit.

 # Audio

Two types of audio files are normally encountered in multimedia productions. Both are digital, but one occupies vastly more space than the other and might even produce lower-quality sound.

Analog sounds can be converted to digital format by a sound board or supplied already in digital format as a stock sound file. They can occupy a varying amount of storage space depending entirely on the quality of the recording. The better the fidelity, the larger the file size.

MIDI files, which were discussed in detail in Chapter 7, are actually computer programs that pass instructions to music synthesizers. They contain no actual sound elements or representations of analog sounds, so they take up very little space.

 # Hard disk specifications

The hard disk drive, also known as a Winchester drive or fixed drive (IBM terminology), is the most familiar online storage device. (*Online* means available for near-instant access, as opposed to data stored on backup tapes, floppy diskettes, or other removable media.) Virtually all computers sold these days have hard drives because boot files, system files, and certain applications programs are almost always used every time the computer is started.

Removable drive systems can be substituted for a hard drive, but none offer the speed and cost-effectiveness of a traditional hard drive. With

data storage costs hovering in the $1-per-megabyte range as of early 1994, there is no reason not to have a hard drive-based multimedia system. The few exceptions are either sold as network workstations, or purchased by users who wish to install a hard drive they already own on the newly purchased computer.

The first hard drives held a whopping 5 to 10Mb of storage space and offered access times comparable to today's floppy diskettes rather than modern hard drives. I had one of those early systems and can report from experience that those of us who owned IBM PC-XTs with 4.77-MHz clock speeds and 10Mb hard drives felt the same way a buyer of a Pentium-based system with 1.2Gb drives feels today.

We had state-of-the-art technology and knew it. Even after loading the system with every useful program and file we had collected on floppy diskettes, most of us still looked with amazement at the bottom line of the screen after entering the DIR command. We saw an amazing 6 or more megabytes of free disk space still available. We couldn't understand how anyone could ever need that much space. Needless to say, within a year we were all frantically learning about file compression techniques and buying boxes of floppy diskettes to store files that we wanted to access but did not have room for on that once-large hard drive.

In discussing hard drives today, three specifications are important: capacity, performance, and cache memory. Each is discussed in the subsections below.

⇨ Capacity

No matter how large your hard drive is, if you really use your computer, it will fill up far more quickly than you expect. This situation is especially true for multimedia developers, who need to access both stock files and previously generated presentations to use ready-made sounds and graphic elements.

Prices might drop enough in the next few years to change my recommendation, but as of mid-1994 I suggest that a serious basic multimedia production system be initially equipped with a hard drive in

the 500Mb range, or preferably two similarly sized drives, each 300 to 500Mb in capacity. With gigabyte (1,000Mb) drives commonly available, buying two smaller drives instead of one large one might seem like a waste of money. Not, however, when you think about reliability.

Despite their highly reliable nature, while your desktop PC is running, your hard drive spins constantly at about 3,000 revolutions per minute. Mechanical and magnetic wear eventually affect the drive, resulting in failure. If you have two drives, you can keep your most vital files on both drives and be ready to swap out a bad drive and continue running the system without any data or time being lost.

Of course, that 500Mb recommendation is only for a basic production system. Serious developers need one or more gigabyte-size drives, but the basic premise remains: you are safer if you divide your hard drive needs between two smaller drives.

An alternative to two drives is to use one of the removable media drives described in the next chapter as one of the two or more drives in your system. This alternative is particularly attractive for users who work in an office where it might be desirable to move data or entire drives between different computers.

You might also want to consider hard drive insurance in the form of a program named Disk Technician. This software can make you feel and actually be far more secure in your computing, whether you have one or multiple drives.

Disk Technician constantly watches your drives and marks any disk sectors that appear to be going bad. Disks can be marked in this way because operating systems do not make just one attempt to read data. They try a number of times, and the data are considered lost only if they cannot be read after a set number of attempts. Disk Technician watches all sectors that need several read attempts. If the sectors start to get worse, the software moves the data to another area and attempts to repair the bad sector. If the repair is successful, the sector is again available for use. If it remains questionable, the section is marked as bad and not used again. Disk Technician is discussed in more detail in Chapter 17.

⇨ Performance & caches

Hard drive speed is probably the most important factor to consider when choosing a drive. Size is important, but once you have enough space to contain your software and files, extra space has no immediate impact on system performance. As drives get larger, however, the time required for your computer to locate and download to memory specific data or a program from storage becomes more important.

Loading a single file or program from a hard disk takes very little time, even on the slowest drives in common use today that offer an average access time of 30 milliseconds, or 0.03 seconds. The time you spend waiting for that program or file to be copied into working memory might be fairly long, but the time it took to locate it was not noticeable. Transferring the data is what takes time, which is referred to as the *data transfer rate*. Performance that is acceptable for a single event can become a major system performance bottleneck as files are searched, loaded, and stored 1,000 times per second.

The minimum acceptable average access time for a modern PC is about 15 ms. Multimedia producers will not find that very fast, so aim for a base average access time of 12 ms or less. Access times below 10 ms require a special caching hard drive controller, which can act as a buffer when writing to the drive. The controller often is able to also store the next needed piece of data when copying information from the drive. Hardware caches can provide an effective average access time below 1 ms.

These controllers are relatively expensive, and upgrading an existing system can result in discarding a perfectly good, but noncaching, controller. The solution is to use a software cache, which performs nearly as well and can easily be adjusted in size to maximize performance while minimizing the amount of system memory used. Some newer cache software can even speed up CD-ROM drive performance. A good software cache can reduce a 10-ms hard drive to a 5-ms drive, depending on the size of the cache and the sort of data being moved around.

Cached hard drives are very fast. In fact, the only thing faster than even a relatively slow hard drive is actual memory. While some applications benefit from loading files into a RAM disk, RAM is just a segment of memory set aside to act as if it were a very fast hard drive. A cache can do almost the same thing and is less cumbersome to set up and properly tune for peak performance.

⇨ Disadvantages

While a hard drive is usually the basis of all storage systems for PCs and most larger computers, hard drives do have their disadvantages. Limited capacity, data vulnerability, and the inability to remove the drive or data to secure or transport large amounts of data are significant and must be considered when selecting fixed storage and removable drives.

To achieve its extreme performance characteristics, a hard drive must combine ruggedness with an essential delicacy of construction. Too robust of components increases the weight of moving parts and thus reduces performance. Drive heads traveling next to the delicate, fast-moving disk surfaces ride on an air cushion so thin that a smoke particle could actually cause a crash. The mechanism that moves the read/write heads must be moved very quickly and precisely if it is to locate a particular data sector in an average of only 0.012 seconds. The platters themselves must be light so they can be spun up to high speed quickly and thin so many can be stacked on top of one another in a small space.

For increased performance, speed and reliability are given priority in the design and construction of most drives. To achieve this, builders assume that the drive is in a location carefully isolated from dirt, excessive heat or cold, and vibration—in other words, the environment of the average desktop or tower computer.

Merely bumping a desk where a hard drive-based computer is running is sometimes enough to cause permanent damage to the hard disk's medium, as well as loss of data. And the failure of any component inside a hard drive is disastrous. Besides physical damage, data stored on a hard drive can be lost through carelessness when a user erases

the wrong data, or through software error when a bug in a program causes the program to damage data. Data can also be lost due to the intentional vandalism of a computer virus infection.

Another disadvantage of a fixed hard drive is transfer rates across computers. Very large files, such as those used to publish a CD-ROM, cannot be transferred to a publisher or other office over telephone lines in a reasonable time, even using the latest techniques. Removing and shipping delicate hard drives is not a good idea for all the above-mentioned reasons involving data integrity.

Various secondary storage systems compensate for or entirely eliminate these disadvantages. Any professional-grade multimedia system must use some sort of secondary working storage in addition to the primary hard drive; that topic is covered further in the next chapter.

 # Selecting a hard drive

The most sophisticated systems require hard drives with the fastest access times and optimum data transfer times. The vast majority of users, however, (even those operating professional multimedia production shops) do not require the ultimate in hard drive performance, especially when drives only slightly less powerful cost less than half as much.

Besides performance, one other important feature of hard drives must be taken into consideration the interface that connects the drive to the computer. If you already have a computer and are upgrading it to multimedia, you either must add a new drive using the same interface or add a new interface card, perhaps even removing the existing drive and adapter. Consider the following three important factors when selecting the drive interface:

➤ performance

➤ expandability

➤ cost

The interfaces you will encounter are ESDI, SCSI, and IDE, each of which is discussed in the following subsections. SCSI and IDE are the most common.

IDE

IDE (integrated drive electronics) is the newest of the systems and trades a bit of performance for ease of installation, compatibility, and inexpensive construction. The electronics integrated in IDE include most of the interface control electronics. By putting most of the interface electronics on the drive itself rather than the interface card, computers that only use floppy drives (operated from the same card) are less expensive to build.

IDE drives are highly compatible because each drive essentially contains its own interface. Adding a second drive to an existing IDE-equipped system therefore is usually very easy.

SCSI

SCSI (small computer system interface) drives are far more sophisticated than IDE drive interfaces and are not limited to connecting only hard or floppy drives. Performance depends somewhat on the drive and somewhat on the particular interface card used, but SCSI drives typically offer faster data transfer speeds than IDE drives. SCSI drives are also easy to install as external or portable drives.

An IDE interface can easily accommodate two hard drives and two floppies, but that is their limit. SCSI ports, on the other hand, can string a number of different I/O devices onto the same interface, and more than one SCSI port can be installed in a single system.

 ESDI

ESDI drives are generally the highest-performance hard drives available, but they are only marginally better than SCSI drives,

which is not usually worth the extra cost or lack of expandability of ESDI drives.

How to add hard drives

Users who can open a computer and upgrade or add a hard drive can easily manage hard disk capacity. They can start with a single 500Mb drive and later add a similar or even much larger disk drive to supplement the first.

Although you can simply replace an existing drive with a larger or faster one, you will be wasting your money unless you install the removed drive in another system. Fortunately, even small desktop computers have two or more drive bays (empty spaces designed to hold hard, floppy, tape, or CD-ROM drives). Adding a second drive is about the simplest task you can attempt inside your computer.

IDE drives are particularly easy to add, requiring only that you purchase a bare drive, bolt it in place inside an empty bay, and then plug in the available power leads and spare ribbon connector. Completing the installation consists of running the configuration program that is already in most computers. The program can be accessed on startup and tells the computer you have installed a new drive. The computer then makes the drive available for access after you enter the next sequential drive letter.

If your PC (not Macintosh) system already has a C drive (A and B are always floppy drives), the new drive will be designated D. If, however, you have the instruction LASTDRIVE=C in your CONFIG.SYS file, it is impossible for your computer to access another drive. You must change any such entry so that all your drives can be recognized, including CD-ROMs and additional hard drives.

To correct this problem, change the drive letter in that instruction from C to E or F. It is best to leave one or two spare drive letters in the LASTDRIVE environment, but do not set the drive too far down the alphabet because those empty spaces take up DOS memory every time you start the computer.

IDE drives are highly compatible. If you already have one IDE drive, you can probably add a second without any trouble or extra expense beyond buying that bare drive. Drives sold with an interface card are for computers that lack an existing hard drive or if you want to change drive types.

High-performance ESDI drives are used on some sophisticated systems, but differences exist between some makes of drives (notably IBM PS/2 ESDI drives) and others. Adding a second ESDI drive might not be the trivial task that adding a second IDE drive usually is. Because ESDI drives are being surpassed in performance by SCSI drives, you should probably avoid them anyway.

You might also have trouble with SCSI drives that should be standard but are not. Here, however, the effort to get various devices to operate from the same SCSI port is well worth the trouble because, unlike the IDE interface, many drives or even other kinds of devices can be daisy-chained to other SCSI devices. Not only can you string four or five internal or external hard drives on a single port, you can also add CD-ROM drives or image scanners, both of which are essential to a multimedia production system.

Secondary storage

CHAPTER 17

DESPITE all the advantages of hard drives and the drastic price drops in recent years, experienced users know that no hard drive is ever large enough to store everything. Especially for multimedia developers, it is important to have a secondary storage system, preferably one with unlimited storage capacity and one that is relatively immune to data loss.

Secondary storage is online or archival storage where information that is less frequently used is stored but still easily available (as opposed to ¼" backup tape cartridges). Ideally, everything would be instantly available all the time, but as files grow that ideal becomes impractical.

In this chapter, we first compare which types of file goes in primary and secondary storage. The actual mix varies with installations (depending on the speed of secondary storage) and actual use patterns, but the basic idea is that information used most often should be in the fastest storage device.

Use primary storage (a hard drive) for the following:

> ➤ operating systems

> ➤ often-used utilities

> ➤ regularly used applications programs

> ➤ regularly accessed databases of text, images, or sounds, including boilerplate, company logos, or signature sounds

Use secondary storage for the following:

> ➤ massive image and sound archives

> ➤ infrequently used applications programs

> ➤ archives of earlier productions

⇨ Magnetic

The most expensive but fastest secondary storage is a second or third hard drive. Your primary storage drive should be large enough to

contain everything you access on a regular basis, but if you added massive additional drives, you could access everything as fast as possible.

The major problems with using a standard hard drive as secondary storage are the following:

> limited capacity

> cost

> less security

No matter how large your hard drive (and relatively inexpensive gigabyte-sized hard drives are becoming common), you will always need to store more information than your drive can handle. Prices of hard drives are dropping, but so are the prices of other storage devices. After 1-2Gb, alternative storage devices become more cost-effective than hard disks.

Hard drives also provide much lower levels of data security. If a disk crashes or is infected with a virus, you could lose all your critical files. If the files are on CD-ROMs, they are still perfectly okay. All you need is a new drive to access them.

Bernoulli and others offer magnetic hard drives with replaceable platters, which provide both fast magnetic storage and a solution to the capacity problem because you can have an unlimited number of disks. These disks are still susceptible to physical damage, however, including being susceptible to the effects of stray magnetic fields while stored offline. They aren't cost-effective either, because the cartridges are relatively expensive compared to their capacity.

⇨ Optical

Optical storage refers to technology incorporating laser-based recording and playback techniques.

Floptical disks are not included in any discussion of optical storage devices because, while the formatting of the disk is optically based, the

actual storage method is traditional magnetic. These 3.5" floppy drives use magnetic read/write technology to store from 11 to 50Mb of data on a single floppy disk. They only offer the access times associated with floppy disk drives, however, and properly belong in the same classification as other magnetic-based drives, falling between floppy disks and hard drives in capacity, cost, and speed.

The rest of this section is devoted to true optical storage, which might use magnetic fields, but the data are recorded and written using laser light.

WORMs

The creation of more powerful solid-state lasers in the 1980s allowed the development of WORM (write once read many) drives. These are losing their once-prominent place in the secondary storage market, however, mostly because of CD-ROM recording and erasable drives, which are now available. WORMs still have a large installed base, so they need to be mentioned.

In the 1980s, CD-ROM was a mass storage or publishing medium that required extensive manufacturing facilities, including clean-room environments and injection-molding machines to mold permanent information onto a disc. WORM drives, which could write to discs as well as read them, attached directly to computers and recorded data totally transparently. They function just like very large, very slow, hard disks that slowly fill up because you cannot erase the information once it is "burned" into the surface by the intense laser beam.

A WORM disc contains only formatting, or at most, about 150Mb of data impressed during manufacturing. When writing to the disc, the optical characteristics of the disc are permanently changed by a powerful laser pulse, while a weaker laser beam can then read the digitally encoded information.

WORMs come in many sizes, including 12", 8", and 5.25". An ISO standard exists for the 5.25" size. Unlike CD-ROM drives, which use a constant linear velocity (CLV) scan method where the drive speed varies with the read head's distance from the center of the disc, some

WORM drives use constant angular velocity (CAV). Thus, WORM drives turn at a constant speed, making their drive and control mechanisms simpler, although other factors make them more expensive than CD-ROM drives.

Data can be recorded on a WORM disc using several methods. In one, the laser beam heats the metal film until a bubble forms in the film. Another method is to melt a hole in the metal surface. A third recording technology bursts a bubble preformed when the disc was originally pressed. These recording methods make WORMs ideal for archival storage but not much else. Because WORMs cannot be erased and reused (the software just renames the older files when you write an update to a file to the disc), WORM drives offer an excellent way to maintain a complete audit trail of all your files, essentially backing themselves up.

WORM drives are inherently slow, in both recording and reading data. One early drive did overcome many of the speed problems by buffering all read/write activities with a fast hard disk, the presence of which was transparent to the user.

Erasable discs

Magneto-optical (MO) or thermo-optical discs take advantage of the pinpoint heating ability of lasers and that some materials change reflectivity after exposure to intense light. These discs produce WORM-like storage that can be erased and reused almost indefinitely.

MO drives use a powerful magnetic field to impose a different light-reflecting polarity on the disc surface. Even the strong internal magnetic field has no effect on the polarity until the area is heated by a strong laser beam, so MO discs are highly stable when stored. They are not affected by either normal magnetic fields or reasonable heat or cold. They are a bit slower than WORM drives during the write cycle because the track about to be recorded is erased in the first pass and recorded on in a second. Reading data, however, is a one-step process. A certain amount of compatibility is available between different drives, so MO discs are more interchangeable than WORM discs.

Larger 5.25" MO drives are quite heavy and expensive, costing about $3,000 for a drive that records between 600Mb and 1,000Mb on a single $100 disc (Fig. 17-1). Many users prefer the more compact 3.5" MO drives, such as the Fujitsu DynaMO 128. It's a better choice because of the low initial cost (less than $1,000) and smaller size; you can install them in a standard desktop PC's drive bay. The same drive and disc operate with both PCs and Macs. Each cartridge costs about $30 and is the size of two 3.5" floppies stacked together.

Figure 17-1

128Mb magneto-optical drive and removable cartridge. Plasmon Data Systems

Although the 3.5" discs only store 128Mb of data on a single cartridge (Fig. 17-2), many databases used in multimedia production are smaller than this. For example, you could store all animal images on a single disc, or if you access a lot of such images, you could further subdivide animals and store all birds on one, and so forth.

Because the smaller drives cost only about one-third as much as the larger MO drives, the 128Mb MO drives are better for smaller operations. Several computers can be equipped to share the same files for the same cost as installing a single 600Mb MO drive.

Figure 17-2

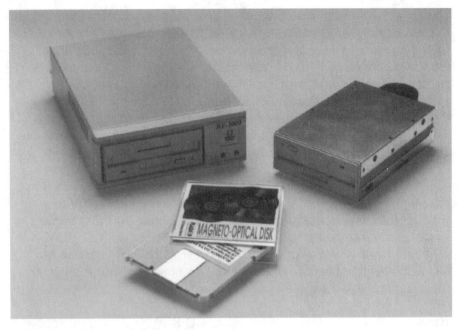

1GB magneto-optical drive. Plasmon Data Systems

⇨ CD-ROM

CD-ROM (compact disc-read only memory) is the secondary storage device of choice for many users. This statement is even more true now than just a few years ago because of recent developments that allow users to record their own CD-ROMs on a special $4,000 drive. Today, CD-ROM provides a very inexpensive way to publish or archive data and programs whereas it was once only suitable for publishing.

CD-ROM isn't actually memory, according to the computer-oriented definition in which memory is the working area where programs are run and data processed, but the name has stuck. This is yet another case where novices can become confused by the sometimes inconsistent terminology used in the computer field.

According to the standard, a CD-ROM disk is a 12cm plastic disk sandwich. It is created on a large, vacuum-forming machine by pressing soft plastic against a master disc mold. The disk is then

coated with a very thin aluminum or gold reflective coating that follows the same bumps and flat data areas on the base plastic. The disk is then overcoated with a tough, clear polycarbonate plastic coating. Now it becomes a CD-ROM disc (with a c). These discs can only be produced by the same large replication facilities that produce the physically identical CD audio discs. As a mass publishing media, CD-ROM is unequaled in cost and capacity. Large production runs of 10,000 or so discs (each with about 550Mb of data or programs) only cost about $2 each to produce.

CD-ROM players are all compatible, from the slow 500 to 1,000 ms, (one-half to one-second) under-$200 drives to the latest high-tech marvels that have average access times well under 300 ms. Some newer recording formats such as CD-I (CD-Interactive), CD-ROM XA (eXtended Architecture) or PhotoCD, which is Kodak's version of CD-ROM XA, require additional hardware only built into the newer, more expensive drives.

Because the drives are so inexpensive, CD-ROM is also an attractive self-publishing media for many companies; publishing only 12 or so discs is less expensive than using MO drives. This fact is especially true with the recent availability of $2,500 to $6,000 CD-R (CD-Recordable) drives. These can record (and in some cases also play back) a special $30 CD-R disc that is fully compatible with standard CD-ROM players.

Multimedia producers can use CD-R to publish small quantities of titles, but CD-R discs are more commonly used to archive important files, publish databases for in-house use, or function as test-beds for CD-ROM titles, where you test the titles before you commit to the thousands of dollars base cost to produce a master and begin mass replication.

Even if you don't use CD-R, you should certainly have one or more CD-ROM players attached to every multimedia production system. Many important databases containing stock photos, sounds, and even type fonts, are published on CD-ROMs. Some applications programs and operating systems are now so large that companies are even beginning to offer them on CD-ROM.

Which type and how many CD-ROM drives you want depends on what you publish. If your multimedia productions are mostly text with some simple, self-generated images that serve as backgrounds, CD-ROM will not prove very important to you. You need only one inexpensive, low-performance drive. The interface doesn't matter in this case, so you can use the one that probably came with your low-end sound card. As explained in the next subsection, however, you will need a separate SCSI card if you intend to install any scanners and do not have a SCSI CD-ROM adapter.

If, on the other hand, you want to add photo-realistic stock images or listen to different sound clips, you probably want to have one or more of the stock CD-ROMs published by Aries Entertainment or other companies available online. You can either daisy-chain several fast CD-ROM drives together or add a multidisc jukebox that can automatically switch between six CD-ROM discs (Fig. 17-3). Even more massive online storage is available by daisy-chaining five or more of these multidisc players.

Figure 17-3

Multi-gigabyte magneto-optical storage jukebox. Plasmon Data Systems

Whether you use separate single drives or multidisc players depends on how often you need to swap discs. The multidisc players have good average access times (300 ms or so) for the already loaded disc but take several seconds to unload one disc and *mount* (old-time mainframe computer term) a new volume. The need for multiple and higher-performance drives also requires that you use a SCSI interface to daisy-chain several devices together.

Because you are building a multimedia production system, you probably already need SCSI to attach a scanner or perhaps an MO drive. If so, you can use the same port for CD-ROM, attaching different types of devices together. Macintosh users can automatically turn to SCSI because it is built into their computers. For PC users, a good SCSI board only costs about $200, and SCSI is a good investment to increase the expandability and versatility of your system.

Installing a CD-ROM drive is usually very simple. You first need to add a SCSI port, if your computer lacks one, by opening up the case and inserting the board. Next, you attach all SCSI drives and other devices to each other and the port. Be certain that only the last one on the chain has a terminating resistor.

Some devices require that they be installed at the end of the daisy-chain. If you have two of these type of devices, you either need two SCSI ports or have the terminating resistor removed from one of the devices. Because of this possible problem, ensure that all your SCSI devices are compatible; that is, all (or at least all but one) have both SCSI-IN and SCSI-OUT connectors and use external terminators.

Manufacturers' SCSI cards are notorious for being slightly incompatible with the standard and thus might not work with all of your devices. Therefore, it is best to buy a universal SCSI interface, such as a board from Trantor. These universal SCSI interfaces come with drivers and installation software that can detect and automatically install most SCSI devices. You thus need to have them all connected before you complete the installation process.

The very least expensive CD-ROM drives (and many multimedia kit drives) come with custom interfaces that offer lower performance and also cannot be daisy-chained. If they can, they only work with a

second identical drive. This situation is acceptable for low-end multimedia players where the upgrade kits often include the CD-ROM interface right on the sound board, but it is not suitable for a multimedia production station.

Comparison of storage devices

The following information is based on list prices and common capacities as of early 1994. The products listed are those commonly used with desktop PC and Mac systems or workstations. Left out are such exotic items as 9-track tape, which can be used with PCs but is normally reserved for mainframe or minicomputer use. The speed provided is average access time.

Larger hard drives

Cost	$1/Mb
Capacity	300Mb to 1.2Gb, 2 to 3 drives maximum
Speed	1 ms to 14 ms (lowest uses caching controller)
Drive cost	$350 (300Mb average performance) to $1,100 (1.2Gb average performance) to $2,000 (high-quality/high-performance)

Floptical (3.5")

Cost	$2/Mb
Capacity	720K, 1.44Mb, and 20Mb (floptical format)
Speed	35 ms to 100 ms
Drive cost	$300+
Media cost	$1 for 1.44Mb (standard high-density) to $25 for 20Mb floptical formatted diskettes

WORM

Cost	50 cents/Mb total (counting drive and discs)
Capacity	200Mb to 600Mb each, unlimited number of discs
Speed	50 ms
Drive cost	$1,800
Media cost	$150

MO drives

Cost   50 cents/Mb or less
Capacity   128Mb to 1Gb/disc
Speed   30 ms to 120 ms
Drive cost $1,000 (3.5" 128Mb) to $3,000 (5.25" 600Mb to 1Gb)
Media cost $30 (128Mb) to $250 (600Mb)

CD-ROM

Cost   less than 1 cent/Mb (using mass replication)
Capacity   550Mb each
Speed   250 ms to 1,000 ms
Drive cost $150 to $1,500

CD-R

Cost   50 cents/Mb (media cost only)
Capacity   550Mb each
Speed   20 minutes to one hour to record full disc; partial disc
                recording proportionately faster
Drive cost $3,000 to $6,000
Media cost $40 each

⇨ Backing up your files

It is difficult to overemphasize the need for performing regular
backups on all computers used to produce multimedia. Considerable
work goes into every file, much more than word processor files or
even spreadsheets, because the multimedia file goes through numerous
stages of processing and editing and is interrelated to all the other
files. Therefore, any lost multimedia file represents a bigger blow to
the project's finances than do most working files in a business, except
for customer lists and accounting information. These types of files,
however, can usually be restored much more easily, using older
versions from backups, than multimedia files can be, simply because
these files are mostly raw data.

Disk mirroring

One way to avoid any chance of a file being lost (other than through an accidental overwrite) is to have software that makes two copies of every file you save and have additional hard drives to store those data. This procedure is called *disk mirroring* and is similar to the much more sophisticated RAID systems but does not speed file access or data transfer like RAID.

BlackCurrant Technology
575 Anton Blvd.
No. 300
Costa Mesa, CA 92626

provides a totally transparent mirror system called BlackMirror. A 240Mb BlackMirror system costs $1,500. It works very simply by intercepting every file written to your main drive and sending a copy to the external BlackMirror drive.

Software disk mirroring systems are also available. They can mirror to existing internal or external drives and can even make mirror duplicates of files on different partitions on the same drive. Using different partitions is obviously the least safe backup because mechanical failure in the drive still causes a catastrophic crash and file loss. Your only hope is to ship the drive off to be repaired and, with any luck, get the files recovered at the same time.

 # Tape drives

As a multimedia producer, you already have about half of a basic backup system already installed—that SCSI port. Standard ¼" SCSI-port backup tape drives are inexpensive, fast ways to archive large amounts of data in a short time.

Drawbacks of tape drives include the inability to work directly with the files without first loading them back into the computer and the vulnerability of the tapes themselves to physical damage.

⇨ Optical devices

All the secondary storage devices described earlier in this chapter are candidates for backing up files. Because you will almost certainly require a large amount of secondary storage anyway, it makes sense to standardize backing up your important working files as well. Optical storage in particular is an excellent backup medium because of its relatively low cost and virtual invulnerability to common physical threats, such as stray magnetic fields and normal aging.

⇨ Backup application software

Numerous backup programs are available, but most of the standalone software, such as Fastback, is intended for use with floppy diskettes. Therefore, they are not a practical backup method for the size and quantity of files in multimedia work.

The backup utilities built into MS-DOS, and those programs intended to expand the usefulness of the latest versions such as DOS 6, are just not useful for multimedia backup despite the fact that they work well for word processing and other backup tasks. High-end network backup software is beyond the scope of this book and probably not of interest to multimedia producers. Although many might work in a networked environment, it is almost certain that they are not the network administrator (the person or staff responsible for maintaining the network and keeping backups).

The majority of tape backup systems come with their own backup software. Even some universal SCSI adapter boards such as Trantor's come with general backup software for whatever tape drive you attach to them.

⇨ Disk Technician—hard drive insurance

A different type of file and hard disk security is provided by a $150 program called Disk Technician Gold, shown in Fig. 17-4. For more information, contact

Disk Technician
1940 Garnet Ave.
San Diego, CA 92109
619-272-5000
619-272-4008 (F)

Figure 17-4

*Disk Technician
Gold.* Disk Technician, Inc.

Instead of backing up your files, this software actually tries to eliminate disk crashes. Disk Technician Gold monitors hard disk reads using artificial intelligence to watch for deteriorating media. This software uses only 14K of RAM while you work, constantly monitoring each hard drive access. When a data access problem occurs, the software notifies you and then copies recovered data to the 120K to 150K data bank reserve—a hidden file it creates on the drive.

Installation takes some time because the software repeatedly tests each part of your disk(s) looking for potential problems in what is

designated *media certification*. This process also includes a cleanup step, where it tries to recover any damaged files, and moves files from questionable segments before marking those segments as bad. Once the program performs the media certification, it settles down to its routine, almost invisible daily work. You will only notice it if a problem occurs or during bootup when it displays the tests it is conducting.

Disk Technician Gold also watches for and alerts the user to potential hardware failures. These hardware failures include defective power supply, read/write misalignment, or even a bad bearing that can cause the platter to wobble slightly. Disk Technician is not a replacement for a backup system, but it may ensure that you never need to learn whether your backup procedure really works. Multimedia users especially need this software because the hard drives used in multimedia production get a harder workout than those performing most other tasks.

I highly recommend that you install Disk Technician Gold on any hard drive, especially any boot drive carrying important data or working files and programs. As a side benefit, it also automatically cleans up lost clusters and cross-linked files every time you boot the computer. These will multiply each time you run Windows, or if you use automatic disk compression software, such as Stacker from Stac Electronics in Carlsbad, California.

18

Putting your system together

CHAPTER 18

A FTER reading the first 17 chapters, you should now have assembled a pile of boxes containing hardware, software, and a stack of manuals. Now you must put everything together. Even if you ordered a basic system with all the memory and hard disk space you need, you still need to connect a lot of separate components to your system. Because you might be upgrading an old computer, we also quickly look at how to make basic changes to your present hardware configuration. Lastly, we look at where to put your computer and additional hardware you should consider adding, regardless of the type of computer you purchased.

Despite all the well-advertised claims by Apple Computer about ease of use and simple upgrades, Macintosh users will find that they face almost as many problems as PC owners when assembling a final system. Fortunately, PCs themselves are not nearly as difficult to upgrade as some advertisers have tried to make users think.

Assembly is when you discover if everything you have selected actually works together. You should have informed all vendors of what other hardware and software you intend to use. But even the most conscientious vendor cannot know if absolutely everything will be compatible.

One hint before you start: always install and test the hardware before trying to install software in the new system. Modern programs are quite sophisticated and can often configure themselves for any hardware they locate during installation. You can always update software configurations, but this sometimes requires a two- or three-step operation, first updating one program and then another that takes its clues from how the first was configured.

⇨ Assembly

First the basics. Unless you bought a powerful computer with all the video, memory, hard drive capacity, and ports you need, you must open your PC to add hardware, even if only a SCSI-2 port. This statement is also true for Macintoshes, most of which do not have a fast SCSI port and require an immediate upgrade. (You might not

need to open your computer initially, but the chances are you eventually will need to, so I want you to be comfortable with what is involved.) It really is not very difficult.

The first thing to do is buy a few basic tools at the nearest Radio Shack if you don't already have what you need. Your most important tool is usually a Phillips (X-shaped end) screwdriver and a ¼" hex wrench. In most cases, these tools are all you need to remove the cover from your computer and make any changes to the hardware inside. If your system uses separate memory chips, you also need a special chip insertion tool so you can easily insert additional memory. The common single inline memory modules (SIMM) require no special tool.

Some computers (most notably Compaq) require special tools to remove Torx-head screws, but these computers usually provide the correct tool right in the box. If you do you need a special tool, Radio Shack probably has it. Many of you will have tools already, and the Shack isn't the only place to buy appropriate tools. I only mention that store because almost everyone knows where to find one, and they are more likely than a hardware store to carry an inexpensive tool that can do the job.

If you already have one of those magnetic screwdrivers with replaceable bits, get it away from your computer now! I have several, and they are very useful, but floppy disks are quite susceptible to stray magnetic fields. As a matter of policy, I never allow any magnet near any computer. I suggest you adopt the same practice because it is just too easy to forget and lay a diskette down on a magnetic screwdriver or vice versa, damaging the programs or data contained on that disk.

If you are replacing the CPU or central processor chip with a faster one, or adding a math coprocessor to upgrade a marginal 486SX system, most likely you will either not need a special tool or that tool is supplied with the new chip. You will probably upgrade one of the systems that are specifically designed to have faster CPUs added as needs change, such as those from Zeos International. These come with a tiny daughterboard that contains the already-mounted CPU and another support chip or two and plug into a socket after you remove the old CPU board.

Once you have the correct tools, it is time to open up the computer. You will probably have instructions about how to do so with your new system, but some general directions apply to most computers. For example, ALWAYS remember to unplug the computer completely before beginning any physical modification, including work on the monitor or any existing peripherals (such as a CD-ROM drive) plugged into an outside power source.

Now to the installation. The case of your computer probably is held in place with a series of ¼" sheet metal screws on the back. Be sure to just remove the ones that hold the cover, not ones that support internal components. You can easily determine which screws are which because the correct screws are at the extreme outside edges and are obviously attaching the cover to something underneath (the main chassis).

After the screws are removed, the case usually comes off by lifting the back end slightly and sliding it backwards. It might take a bit of force to get a well-fitted metal case loose, so be prepared to apply a small amount of pressure, but only if you are certain that all the retaining screws are removed. Now you will be presented with a confusing array of components (Fig. 18-1). You will also see wires bundled into small cables that attach floppy and hard drives to their power and I/O connections at the separate controller board or motherboard. Unless you are adding or changing a drive, you probably need to locate the bus, which is where you insert a new accessory board.

STOP! At this point, look but don't touch anything! At the moment, your body is probably carrying a relatively large static charge. You know, the static electricity that gives you a tiny (or not so tiny) shock when you touch a door knob after walking across a rug.

Even if you have not built up enough charge to feel even a tiny tingle (about 50 volts), you could cause permanent physical damage to the 5-volt components inside your computer. What you need to do (remember, your computer must be unplugged, including any telephone connection to a fax/modem) is first touch a bare metal piece of the chassis to make certain you are at the same potential as the computer and all its internal parts. To really be safe, you actually need to wear a grounding strap and have both it and the computer attached to a safe ground. This step is seldom necessary, however, and

Figure 18-1

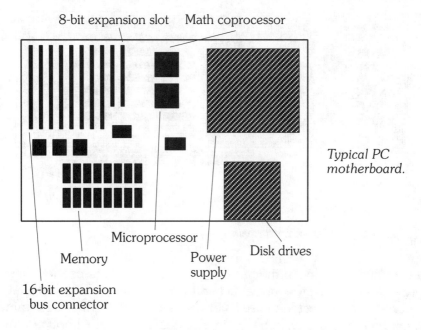

8-bit expansion slot   Math coprocessor

Microprocessor

Memory

16-bit expansion
bus connector

Power
supply

Disk drives

*Typical PC
motherboard.*

most people would not be able to locate a safe ground anyway.
Because you just had the computer plugged in (and assuming the
building is built to code) your computer probably was safely grounded
and remained at a safe potential after you unplugged it.

Adding expansion boards

The expansion boards you will most likely add are a SCSI-2 board, a
sound board, and a video capture board. The board will come in a
static-safe protective plastic package. All you have to do is remove it
and insert it in the computer's bus connector. But first you need to
decide just where to put it.

For a high-performance multimedia system, you should have chosen
16-bit boards. Thus, you need to locate an available 16-bit bus
connector. Just look at the connector on your board (the connector is
the rectangular projections on the edge of the board with the tiny
electrical contacts and shown in Fig. 18-2). Compare this connector to
the available sockets, and it should be very obvious which of those in
the computer are the correct length.

Figure 18-2

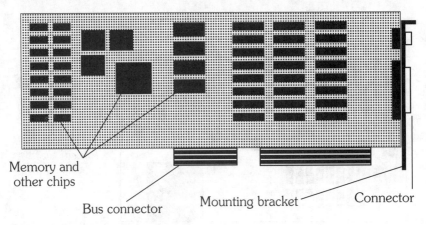

Memory and
other chips

Bus connector

Mounting bracket

Connector

Typical PC expansion card design.

You next need to remove the back chassis cover that closes the holes
where outside connectors are attached to some boards, but where, at
the moment, the selected unused slots are located. But first, determine
whether your board physically fits in a particular space. Although most
16-bit slots are *full-length*, meaning that the longest boards can fit
without touching any other computer component, some 16-bit and
many 8-bit slots are partially blocked by the power supply or some
other component. These slots are then only usable for shorter boards,
usually designated ¾-length or ½-length. The full-length board simply
won't fit.

Once you have located a suitable slot, or slots if you are installing two
or more boards during the same session, remove the appropriate
chassis covers (Fig. 18-3). These are flat (usually) metal strips that
measure about ¾" wide and 5" long, tapered at the bottom and having
a ½"-wide bend at the top that is usually secured to the chassis with
another ¼" sheet metal screw.

These covers protect the computer from foreign objects, maintain
radio-frequency shielding, and ensure proper air flow for cooling. Do
not throw away the ones you remove because they will have to be
replaced if you ever remove the boards taking their place. Occasionally,
one bracket overlaps another slightly; if this is the case you might need
to loosen the offending bracket to remove the one you want.

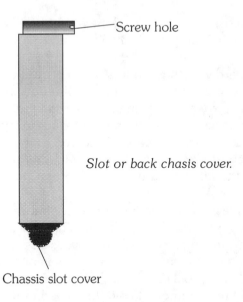

Screw hole

Slot or back chasis cover.

Chassis slot cover

Figure 18-3

Now, carefully slide the new board into the selected slot. Be sure that the bottom connectors seat firmly and fully in the bus connector (Fig. 18-4). A slight rocking motion while gently pressing downward is sometimes helpful. If you inserted the board correctly, the new cover plate, which now contains outside connectors, will fit where the old one did. Replace the retaining screw you previously removed.

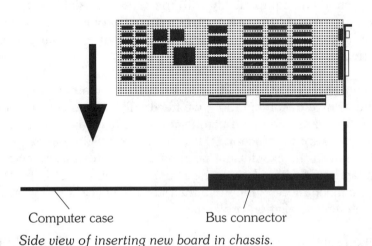

Figure 18-4

Computer case   Bus connector

Side view of inserting new board in chassis.

That's it! In most cases you are done, except for replacing the cover and connecting all the external cables.

Sometimes, hardware (bus) address conflicts will occur, but the best bet is to just install the hardware and try it. If it does not work correctly, then you can worry about changing bus addresses. That problem is not covered here because those changes depend on the particular board. They should be covered in detail, however, in the installation documentation. If not, you need to contact the place you purchased the board or the manufacturer for further assistance.

Although this task might seem complex at first reading, it really is just removing a few screws, sliding off one big cover and another small metal cover designed to be easily removed, inserting the new board, and closing the case again. It ain't as easy as pumping your own gas, but it certainly isn't rocket science, and it isn't nearly as difficult as making good bread. I know; I bake the bread in this house.

 # Board compatibility

Compatibility involves compatibility of the new board with the computer itself (those bus addresses I mentioned earlier), compatibility with external devices (microphones, speakers, video sources, SCSI devices, etc.), and compatibility with the software. As for software, you should have planned things so it will not be a problem. There's no point in buying the latest, most sophisticated video or sound board if the software you selected does not support it.

Because we leave changing bus addresses to the manufacturer's help line and printed documentation, we need only discuss compatibility between the expansion card you have just installed and whatever devices you want to attach to it. If you choose a SCSI-based system, you are now in the exact same position as Macintosh users whose computers came with a built-in SCSI port. Although SCSI devices and ports are much more compatible than just a few years ago, you still face potential installation problems.

The first problem is with the cables. There are several kinds of SCSI connectors, and you have to make certain that the cables you buy fit

the devices you have. Some cables are the common DB pin-type connectors that look like the ones used by serial and parallel ports on the computer. These are the ones that you are likely to find on the SCSI board's bracket. Actual SCSI device connectors, on the other hand, look like larger versions of the familiar Centronics printer connector.

Cables won't be any real problem—unless you forgot to ask whether they are included with the device or which kind you need to buy if they were not. What you need is a single SCSI cable to connect the board port to the first SCSI device and a series of cables that can then connect each subsequent device to the others in the daisy-chain.

Another concern is the SCSI device number, which is an address set on each device. Some devices need to be set to a specific number. If you have two devices that need to be set to the same number, you have a problem that could require you to install a second SCSI port, but this is relatively rare.

Much more common is a drive that needs to be placed at the end of the daisy-chain because it contains an internal terminating resistor. If you only have one of these, just put it at the end. If you have several, you need to open up all but one and remove those extra terminators. You also need to be sure the final device does have a terminator. Most devices do, either having an internal terminator or a simple external terminator that just plugs into the last device's SCSI out port (the one not attached to a cable).

Now we just have to worry about SCSI software compatibility—whether your SCSI board comes with the drivers needed by all of the devices you want to attach to it. In the past, a manufacturer of a scanner or hard drive supplied a SCSI interface designed to work with that one device. Manufacturers paid little attention to the fact that a major reason people bought SCSI was so they could install five or six different devices to the single port.

For example, if you installed a Trantor SCSI-2 board, you need to connect all the devices you expect to use before running the SCSI installation software. Trantor software comes with dozens of drivers and is ready to recognize most SCSI devices ranging from CD-ROM drives to hard drives and scanners. Reconfiguring the software after the fact usually is not difficult, but it does mean lost time and the need to read even more of the manual than if you just connected everything at the beginning.

Multimedia work area

Now we go into a vague area that involves ergonomics. The average office has furniture and lighting designed to make it easy to type, answer the phone, and perform traditional filing. Today we no longer have typewriters or nearly as many file cabinets, and the traditional office is not at all suitable for intensive computer use (Fig. 18-5).

Figure 18-5

Hergo Ergonomic Support System. Hertz Corporation

Take lighting, for example. You need a lot of general lighting to see documents on your desk and read text on paper as you type. The easiest way to provide this lighting is using overhead fluorescent lights. Computer screens do not need light for you to read what is on them.

In fact, most lights make computer screens harder to read. Where you do need light is on the desk where you have paper documents. This means you need a light fixture right on the desk that can be positioned so its glare does not interfere with seeing the screen. Overhead lighting is not desirable for computer workers.

Something else you need to give up is that nice window. If the window is behind the computer, the light will almost certainly be too bright at some times during the day, making it difficult to see subtle images on the monitor. If that window is behind you, it will almost certainly produce glare on the screen.

Of course, you might be stuck with a particular office configuration and not even be able to remove any fluorescent bulbs to make the area more computer-friendly. Still, you need to be aware of problems so you can either plan to have your workstation in a better location or add a glare shield into your hardware budget.

⇨ Reliable power

You might think you are finished with hardware, but there are some other items you should consider adding to your quite-expensive system.

Line power, as supplied by the power company and the wiring in your building, is not particularly reliable or well-regulated. You have seen lights dim when a window air conditioner kicks on, or when a brownout strikes. Power is not perfect. No place offers really good power for your sensitive computer unless it is especially regulated very near to your system.

The most basic addition to any computer system (and home stereo, television, and other electronic appliances) is a quality power strip that includes a surge suppression system. Power surges can be introduced into the power line by nearby lightning strikes or other environmental events. Even a large appliance shutting off can feed a surge of power back into the same line you are using to operate a computer.

Probably the best way to get quality surge suppression, along with simple power filtering to remove any radio frequency signals picked up by the wiring and fed into your computer, is to get a switching system that costs $100. This system includes a master power switch along with several separate switches for devices such as your printer, modem, CD-ROM drive, computer, and monitor. You should also have a socket for your modem and telephone line. Even if the power line is fully protected by an expensive power filtering system, the telephone can carry similar surges and your modem can transfer this voltage surge right into your computer's components.

While surge suppressors are useful, they are far from foolproof and do not condition the line power as well as it can and should be controlled. A relatively inexpensive power conditioner can remove some of the peaks and valleys of line voltage. Once you go this far, it makes little sense not to go one step further and install a full uninterruptible power supply (UPS).

Your computer's power supply was not designed for brownouts or other fluctuations in the power supply. System operation can become erratic when running on less than the standard 120 volts. A good power conditioner can automatically raise or lower the incoming voltage to a constant value, greatly reducing the strain on your computer's components. A UPS goes one step further by adding a battery supply and electronics to generate alternating current that duplicates line current.

When the line voltage drops too far or goes off entirely, the UPS takes over and either adds more power from its battery reserve or cuts out of the line completely and generates power itself for the computer. Many power outages last only a fraction of a second, so any UPS, even a very-low-capacity unit, can prevent many otherwise unexplained computer crashes. A good UPS or power conditioner can also extend the life of your computer's expensive components.

Many UPS systems are available, but I am only going to list one manufacturer—the one who makes the UPS I use in my office: Best Power Technology. This company's units have performed very well, and they come in a very wide range of prices and capabilities. Best Power

also publishes a very useful booklet on UPS technology, and I urge you to write for it, even if you intend to use another vendor's system.

For more information, contact

Best Power Technology
P.O. Box 280
Route 1
Necedah, WI 54646
800-356-5794
608-565-7200
608-565-2929 (F)

Software installation

Installing software is detailed in each program's documentation. There is little I can add beyond reminding you to install all the available hardware before starting the software. Most programs today have sophisticated installation systems that copy and decompress files to the appropriate directory on your hard drive. Windows applications in particular are so sensitive to the presence or absence of required hardware that they sometimes refuse to install when a required component is missing. Performance can also be affected if the software thinks you are running with a certain configuration and sets its startup parameters to compensate for small memory or such, when you are actually going to increase memory.

Remember to keep your original diskettes, even after you have installed the software and made backups of the working copy. Many specialized drivers are shipped with programs and you need those when you upgrade your hardware.

You should also watch out for programs that modify CONFIG.SYS and AUTOEXEC.BAT files without notifying you. Many programs pay little attention to what is already installed, and new commands could cause previously installed software to stop working. At the very least, protect yourself during software installation by making a backup of both of those files before adding any new software. Some programs do this for you automatically, but don't depend on the good intentions of

some programmer, who might have left the installation process as the next-to-last step before shipping the program.

Finally, if you are new to computers, I should point out that the very last task given to programmers is writing the documentation. This statement goes a long way toward explaining the large amount of terrible documentation that has flooded the software market in the past 15 years.

⇨ Testing your assembly

Your computer is closed up, all the hardware is plugged in, and your first program is installed. Test it out now as thoroughly as you can. All software comes with bugs, or programming mistakes. Some bugs are real program-killers while others are relatively minor, but they are there. Determine now whether your main application program has any major bugs and then contact the company to learn about any fixes already available or in development.

For example, when Microsoft and WordPerfect battled to come out with new versions of their word processors for Windows (versions 6.0 in both cases) back in late 1993, there were so many bugs it was impossible to count them all. Windows 3.0 itself was so prone to unexplained crashes that many users gave up in disgust until the much-more-stable 3.1 version came along.

Now install your second program and repeat the effort, but also go back and do a quick test on the major features of the first program— especially the critical features such as importing and exporting files or saving and retrieving them from storage. The reason you test each program in turn, rather than loading everything at once, is because each new program might introduce system bugs that affect others in a way that makes it appear that a properly operating program is at fault. You won't know where the bugs are unless you have already tested the preceding software and know that it works properly.

 # Getting help

If you need help, first read the manual. When I began my long-running "Power User" column in *Government Computer News*, the basic guideline my editor gave me was "Real power users don't read manuals." Because I had not read a computer manual thoroughly for about 10 years, I knew I had found my editorial home! This philosophy, however, only works when you have a lot of experience with computers (I ran my first computer program on an IBM 1401 back in 1963). You should also know enough to go back to the manual when you have problems.

If you don't find the answer in the documentation, look at the README or READ.ME file supplied with most programs. These, or similarly named files, contain the latest information on bugs or changes to the printed documentation. Although power users don't read printed documentation, we do read this file—before beginning the installation if possible, although the file is often packed into others and can't be accessed until the program is loaded.

If there is nothing helpful in the README file or the printed documentation, it is time to do battle with the company's help line. But, before you pick up the telephone, you need to write down and have available certain information. It often takes a long time to get through to the correct person to ask for help, so don't compound this delay by having to call back because you do not have basic information.

Write down the following before you call:

> ➤ A description of every component plugged into your computer, along with numbers displayed when you query the system for memory, extended memory, expanded memory, and disk space.

> ➤ Exactly what happens. This includes any strange messages you encounter during system bootup, and any error messages you get when the problem occurs.

> ➤ Exactly what programs were installed after the one that used to work but doesn't now (if that is the situation).

➤ Any error messages displayed during installation.

➤ Any other information you think might be helpful, depending on the problem, the software, and your knowledge of computers.

➤ What is in your AUTOEXEC.BAT and CONFIG.SYS files. You will almost certainly be asked for this information.

Now put that help line on autodial and get ready to really listen to the person who answers.

Some companies, especially those that sell very high-end programs, are very easy to contact for help. That is part of what you are paying for. These programs also generally have fewer bugs (due to fewer updates and more thorough testing) and better documentation. Other companies have a lot of very well-trained customer support staffers, but they also sell a lot of copies of their programs and therefore get a lot of help calls, many of which would have been unnecessary if the frustrated callers had only read the documentation.

Very, very few companies want to incur the ire of their customers by providing poor support, but there are only so many qualified software and hardware support workers.

⇨ **Online help**

If you don't have a modem and an account on one of the major commercial electronic bulletin board systems (BBSs) such as GEnie, BIX, CompuServe, America Online, Prodigy, or AppleLink, this is the time to remedy that fault.

Multimedia is very complex, and it will prove very difficult to keep up with this field unless you have access to the various vendor-specific and general news forums on these BBSs. When you can't reach a help line, or they can't give you the answer you need, you can almost always post a question in the appropriate forum on one of these systems and get help from someone with a similar problem. Many vendors not only maintain direct help on these systems, they even pack discount coupons in with their programs to encourage new users to join up and get better service. The very latest bug reports, hints,

tips, and even software fixes and new hardware drivers are posted in these interactive forums, often days or weeks before the information filters down to users via mailed bulletins.

Even more useful for many professionals are the vendor-neutral forums on multimedia and other topics also found on these BBSs. You can download demo programs, shareware software, and even image or sound files from many BBSs, as well as share your experiences with other users.

If you are really serious about advancing your professional expertise and not just looking for help, you probably want to join BIX, a technical BBS that includes full access to the gigantic academic-government-commercial Internet network that has more than 10 million users. Other systems allow you to download files from the Internet, but as of press time BIX offered the only direct access that allowed users to actually log onto remote systems.

Have you heard of the Information Superhighway? The Internet is that highway—carrying many thousands of specialized news groups that share information on virtually everything.

BIX, the Internet, and all the other BBSs mentioned above also carry the latest computer and telecommunications news from Newsbytes News Network. This network is the oldest and largest independent international news source for the computer industry and carries everything from news about conferences to new product announcements. Although it doesn't specifically cover multimedia, Newsbytes covers the entire field of computers and telecommunications, from video games to supercomputer software and from local phone service to international video conferencing. About 30 new stories are provided every day.

Other news services are available on many of these systems. They are mostly provided by computer industry newspapers and magazines that might or might not have a particular bias (a bias you might appreciate if a publication covers just the topics you are interested in), but Newsbytes is the source of hard news on new products and events in the industry.

Almost every computer magazine contains advertisements for these online services, often including free introductory subscriptions. I urge you to be aware of this wealth of up-to-the-minute information and to take advantage of the expertise you can find there.

19

Electronic publishing

CHAPTER 19

L ONG before you begin actual production of a multimedia presentation, you need to decide just how individuals will view your finished work. You can distribute multimedia four ways:

➢ diskette

➢ CD-ROM

➢ videotape

➢ videodisc

Which methods you decide to use depends on several factors:

➢ total size of presentation

➢ whether it is interactive

➢ audience

⇨ Diskettes

We begin our discussion with diskettes because they are the least expensive initial investment. If your finished project is anywhere from a megabyte or two in size to about 20Mb and your target audience is business or home computer users, just copying your product onto floppy diskettes, either in compressed or uncompressed formats, is a viable option.

Advantages of a floppy-based presentation include the following:

➢ everyone with a computer already has a floppy drive

➢ inexpensive low-quantity replication

➢ reusable media if you made a mistake or change something

➢ easy in-house replication of small quantities

➢ ease of changing presentation

Disadvantages of floppy distribution, however, are the following:

➢ the user usually needs a hard drive

➢ the user must install the program in a tedious, multistep process

> multiple drive sizes require that you exclude some potential users or offer a minimum of two different sized diskettes

> diskettes are inherently subject to virus infection, and duplication requires special care

> very limited presentation sophistication and size

Despite their disadvantages, floppy distribution is a very attractive choice for many business presentations precisely because it allows the producer to create individualized presentations for different clients without major replication costs. Very small quantities can be published using the computer's standard formatting and copy commands.

If up to 100 or so copies are to be made (the number depends on how many disks constitute each set and how often you publish new material), a fast integrated utility for testing, formatting, and copying is what you want. Duplicator Toolkit PRO, made by

Copy Technologies
14252 Culver Dr.
Suite 323
Irvine, CA 92714
714-975-1477

is a good example. Duplicator Toolkit manages quality testing, formatting, copying, and copy verification of disks in one step. You can have a completely finished disk in about the same time it typically takes to format a single floppy disk. It also manages a two-floppy drive system, speeding the process further. Copying two disks at once isn't as fast as just making one copy, but it is faster than making two sequentially using a single drive.

Buying preformatted diskettes and copying from a RAM disk, or using a very large disk cache setting, makes duplication nearly as fast for smaller-quantity publishers. But a duplicator utility is very useful for those who either publish a lot of disks at one time or publish small quantities on a regular basis. If you need a minimum of 1,000 or so copies of each disk, companies such as

Micro Media International
23372 Madero Rd.
Suite K
Mission Viejo, CA 92691
714-588-9882
714-588-9767 (F)

which sells preformatted diskettes, will also copy your software while formatting the disks. Copying charges are only a penny or two extra.

For in-house production without tying up a computer or employee, look into a standalone, self-feeding disk duplicator, such as one from

Copymaster
31 Waterloo Ave.
Second Floor
Berwin, PA 19312

Systems like the ones marketed by this company are either attached to a PC or operate entirely on their own. They copy up to 250 diskettes per hour in any of a number of formats.

If you do use a floppy distribution system and your publication is fairly large, you should obtain a license to use one of the dependable disk compression utilities, which is cheaper than buying extra disks. PKzip is a popular compression program. You might be tempted to use one of the self-extracting versions to compress your program, but PKWARE software is not public domain—it is shareware or commercial, depending on the version. For-profit and large nonprofit users must obtain a license to use it. Contact

PKWARE
9025 N. Deerwood Dr.
Brown Deer, WI 53223

for further information.

Because compression software saves both disks and copying time, the use of compression/extraction software will be cost-effective for most publishers. This software is especially useful if it includes a self-prompting utility that helps users install the software. All publishers

targeting PCs need to either develop or purchase an installation utility to manage directory creation. The utility should also prompt users to change disks when installing a multidisk program onto a hard drive and then verify that the correct disk was inserted. How well this installation process goes is crucial in how well the presentation itself is received. This is especially true when you send it to journalists for review or want a busy business person to install your catalog or multimedia sales presentation. If your product does not install flawlessly and fairly quickly on the first try, you have lost your chance. Then it won't matter how good the presentation was because no one will ever see it!

⇨ CD-ROMs

CD-ROM, the computer data sibling of the CD audio discs, is the near-ideal multimedia distribution medium. This fact is especially true now that multimedia is becoming more popular and a CD-ROM player is considered common in many PCs as well as all MPC computers.

CD-ROM drives cost as little as $200 to $300 if ordered with a new computer. Even the fastest players cost less than $1,000, so many computer systems are now equipped with CD-ROM drives and are thus capable of some multimedia playback. Many multimedia productions are so large that, despite the massive size of CD-ROMs and the use of file compression utilities (not video compression), multimedia games often come on several CD-ROM discs. It is easy to see that such productions would be impossible on floppy diskettes.

Advantages of CD-ROM are the following:

- ➢ massive storage capacity (550Mb average)
- ➢ inexpensive mass replication ($2/disc in quantities)
- ➢ hard drive often is not required
- ➢ high security—you cannot modify an existing CD-ROM
- ➢ easy installation

The disadvantages of CD-ROM publication include the following:

➤ requires expensive new hardware for small-quantity production ($5,000 minimum)

➤ small quantities are expensive (raw media costs of $20/disc)

➤ requires special formatting and publishing software

➤ requires the user to have CD-ROM drive

➤ nonerasable (if you make a mistake during copying, the bad CD-ROMs are unusable—except to turn into tacky clocks)

You can produce CD-ROMs in two ways: either use a mass replication facility that produces hundreds or thousands of discs in a few days at a cost between $2 and $10 each, depending on quantity, or use a desktop CD-R recorder that uses special $35 to $50 discs that can be written to once and then played in standard CD-ROM drives.

CD-ROM is by far the most important publishing medium for multimedia. For those interested in exploring in-house CD-ROM publication, or who wish to make use of service bureaus, Appendix A provides considerable detail about costs and the various steps involved. More information about CD-ROM and other optical storage devices is also available in my book, The New Optical Storage Technology (McCormick, Business-ONE Irwin, July 1993, $30, ISBN 1-55623-907-6).

CD-ROM standards

Multiple data format standards exist for CD-ROM technology, although none bypasses or eliminates the High-Sierra or ISO 9660 CD-ROM Directory Standard. Other standards are mostly for multimedia discs, where binary (program code) and text data are stored on the same disc with audio and even video (image) data. The basic CD-ROM standard does not provide for the ability to add compressed sound and images to data in a way for computers to access them simultaneously. Thus, these other standards (all upwardly compatible with CD-ROM) have been developed to define standard ways of adding sound and pictures to a CD-ROM disc.

The other CD-ROM standards are the following:

➤ CD-ROM XA

➤ Kodak Photo CD

➤ Intel's DV-I

➤ CD-I

➤ Kaleida

These formats offer technically superior ways to produce multimedia. As the base of installed CD-ROM drives grew, however, Microsoft developed the MPC standard discussed previously, which based multimedia production and presentation on a combination of Windows and CD-ROM drives. Although MPC does not set a new hardware standard for CD-ROM storage, it is definitely in competition with the XA, CD-I, and PCTV multimedia alternatives, because if MPC becomes universally accepted the others will not be needed.

It might be surprising, but storing audio information is actually more difficult than storing video on CD-ROM, regardless of the standard. This fact seems especially ironic because the CD-ROM came from the development of the CD audio disc. Remember though that all the information on the CD-ROM is digital, and thus no difference exists between any data, audio, text, or video. It is all just 1s and 0s. The problem is because of the difference between how people hear and see.

As discussed earlier, persistence of vision lets us view a series of still pictures as one moving image. Both television and movies function this way, and the same applies to computer-generated or displayed images. Using persistence of vision, a video image changed 30 times per second is perfectly adequate for high-quality images. And 15 frames-per-second (fps) is acceptable for industrial applications.

Sound is another matter. There is no equivalent persistence of hearing. The slightest interruption in a continuous sound is easily detectable. With the DV-I standard, for example, the audio information is systematically laid down on the disc, but the video data are just stuck into the empty spaces.

⇨ CD-ROM XA

If your application requires graphics and especially audio as well as text, CD-ROM XA (eXtended Architecture) could provide sufficient quality without the added overhead of DV-I. XA's extension to the CD-ROM Yellow Book Standard is the added ability to interleave sound, images, and text data on the same track. The XA standard currently consists of protocols defining how audio data are compressed and how the various types of data are interleaved on the disc. The XA standard for audio was established by Philips, Sony, and Microsoft, but the graphics standard is still being developed. The first major CD-ROM XA system to hit the market was the IBM PS/2 Ultimedia M57 SLC multimedia microcomputer.

The XA standard does not require major new hardware, although it does require the addition of a small sound processor chip, the ADaptive Pulse Code Modulation (ADPCM) sound chip. This chip can be added on to any CD-ROM player now installed as long as the player has built-in audio capability. The ADPCM sound chip can also be added to the PC interface board used to connect the CD-ROM player to the computer.

CD-ROM XA provides a superset of the CD-ROM specifications that uses the ADPCM chip to compress digital audio, allowing real-time interleaving of text, graphics, animation, and audio signals. XA also allows the simultaneous, multichannel presentation of digitized information with sound, text, and graphics using existing CD-ROM players and computers.

The CD-ROM XA standard transfers audio and data blocks, each 2.26K in size and lasting one 75th of a second. The blocks are transferred from the disc to the computer/workstation at a rate of 170K per second (kbps), whereas the normal data transfer speed for CD-ROM discs is only 157 kbps, using the highest-level Mode 1 error correction protocol necessary for computer data. (An interesting development, however, is double- and triple-speed CD-ROM drives which, along with faster interfaces, have greatly increased the data transfer speed of CD-ROM data.)

The XA standard can accomplish the faster data transfer by bypassing much of the error correction. Data blocks are split into audio and data segments with the audio portion sent to a digital-to-audio converter to provide sound. The rest of the data, including text, programs, and various graphics, are stored using Mode 1 error-correction and processed as digital data.

The real strength of the CD-ROM XA standard is the ability to mix various sound qualities along with text and graphics. Applications can thus switch between narration at low-quality, which takes up little space on the disc, and very high-quality stereo audio. Applications can thus provide narration in different languages, while sharing the same graphics and high-quality music.

Although a CD audio disc can only hold about one hour of high-fidelity stereo sound, much more information can be contained on a digital disc if lower sound quality is acceptable. Level C, or monophonic, audio can be stored on a CD-ROM disc in 16 channels, providing up to 16 hours of audio on one disc if nothing else is stored on that disc.

For example, these audio channels or tracks could be multilingual, providing 16 different translations of information. Alternatively, they could contain a continuous recording up to 16 hours long by switching between tracks. Stereo audio can be recorded as eight separate pairs of tracks, allowing up to eight hours of low-quality stereo sound. Both of these recording techniques are perfectly adequate for narration, but neither are music-quality.

Level B is the next higher level of audio storage. It provides very good music-quality audio storage and reproduction, but still falls short of the superb quality available under the full CD audio standard. XA can mix both levels.

XA's shortcoming is restricted graphics size. There just is not enough space for high-resolution graphics that fill the entire screen. Partial screen graphics are used instead because current computer processors are not fast enough to decompress large graphics quickly enough to provide the full-screen images.

Graphic data can be stored interleaved with other information or can be placed at the end of the other data on the disc (CD-ROM standard). How data are placed determines how smoothly images can be retrieved to accompany sound or text. If they are interleaved (as permitted using the extended XA standard), the relatively slow drive does not need to access some data in one part of the disc and then switch to another position to capture the images. Multimedia productions would naturally tend to interleave the images, sound, and text to make transitions smoother.

Kodak Photo CD

In September 1990, Eastman Kodak unveiled Photo CD, a future product concept previewed in the 1982 science fiction movie, *Blade Runner*.

Photo CD, which finally appeared in 1992, uses a compact disc to store 35-mm film images. The images can be retrieved and enlarged through a special viewer that attaches to a standard television. Positioned as a competitor to the slide projector, Photo CD can do more than just show photographs. It can also enlarge or crop the image.

Photo CD discs cannot be run on standard CD-ROM players but are not restricted to Kodak Photo CD-only players. They are compatible with both Philips CD-I and CD-ROM XA players. This compatibility is not surprising when you realize that Photo CD is just CD-ROM XA restricted to images and noninterleaved audio. The Photo CD player does lack the capability to play XA's interleaved sound and graphics, so Photo CDs are produced with sound tracks containing pointers to images and vice versa. Because this is a still photograph medium, there is no problem with having the sounds located in a different part of the disc from the images.

For a cost of about $20 per 24-picture-roll, photographers can have up to 100 images stored on a single disc. The cost of the disc is additional, but you can continue adding photos to an existing disc until it is full; it does not have to be filled the first time you purchase it.

Original specifications called for the use of a $100,000 Sun Microsystems' SPARCStation Unix workstation as the basic Photo CD production system. By March 1992, however, Philips had introduced a $6,000 CD Recorder that could produce CD-ROM, XA, CD-I, and Photo CD format discs at a much lower cost. Finally, in 1993, Apple Computer purchased Kodak color printer technology to add to future Macintosh systems. With this partnership, retail photo store imaging workstations could produce Photo CDs with a Macintosh rather than using the very expensive Sun Microsystems units.

When Eastman Kodak first introduced its set of professional Photo CD tools and applications, Kay Whitmore, then chairman and chief executive officer of Eastman Kodak, stated that any major success for the product would ultimately only come when the players become popular with home users. In interviews, Mr. Whitmore indicated that, while it might take time for the new Photo CD product to gain a foothold in the market place, Kodak expected people to use and become familiar with these tools in the workplace. They would then want similar capabilities at home, similar to the migration of personal computers to the home. Photo CD was to compete with VCRs and video cameras, allowing viewers to interact with the images by zooming in on isolated portions of the image.

Among the professional photo products announced was the Kodak Picture Exchange, a global images transmission network. Millions of CD images would be available from the Exchange to commercial users via telephone data links. Acting as a massive catalog order system for stock photos, PCs and Macintosh systems could download and view selected low-resolution images from the Picture Exchange. Purchased photos could then be ordered from Kodak for inclusion in magazines or books.

Also unveiled were several new CD formats, including Pro Photo CD Master disk. This format extended photographic electronic imaging beyond 35-mm film size to encompass the images from the larger film formats used by commercial photographers. Uses for professional Photo CD included medical applications, such as storing X-rays, and real estate, with national networks that real estate sales companies could use to show images of distant properties to local clients.

New software for Photo CD included the following:

➤ PhotoEdge, a photo-editing system for business users

➤ Shoebox, a search and retrieval system for pictures on Photo CD

➤ Browser, a scaled-down version of Shoebox for use with the catalog disk

➤ Renaissance, a page layout software system

At the introduction of Photo CD, many industry observers believed that while Photo CD might have potential in business, especially in desktop publishing, it would be a long, difficult battle to convince home photographers to pay $400 for a machine to view their photographs on television, especially when those photos then could not be put in a wallet or mailed to friends and relatives. Experts were also skeptical about the home market for Photo CD because Polaroid cameras, despite the high cost and limited quality of the pictures, are so immensely popular entirely because they provide instant gratification—exactly opposite of what Photo CD provides.

The commercial outlook is much more promising. For example, Aldus, the company that developed desktop publishing software for the Macintosh platform, immediately announced its support for Photo CD technology as an image delivery system for publishers. PageMaker, the Aldus page layout software, and the graphics program FreeHand both support Photo CD in Macintosh file format. A new mixed media text, sound, and graphics file storage and retrieval system called Fetch also supports Photo CD, and Aldus said that future desktop publishing-related products from the company would support the image delivery standard.

The Image Bank, a stock photo supplier in Dallas, Texas, also announced early support for Photo CD, releasing its first Photo CD image catalog in 1992. This catalog included both photographs and illustrations that can be searched by keyword or browsed. The images are stored only as low-quality television views rather than the high quality required for reproduction.

Other early interest in Photo CD was expressed by such diverse publishers as the clothing mail-order company L. L. Bean and the Smithsonian Institution.

✳ **Multimedia with Photo CD**   Because it is so easy to put images and sound on Photo CD discs, many businesses could use it as the basis for their initial multimedia productions. In fact, it should be economically feasible for companies to use Photo CD to create custom presentations or catalogues for individual customers interested in high-end products. By taking an audio tape recording and a set of images to a Photo CD publisher, you could easily generate a simple multimedia presentation with very little effort.

Having some color images put on a disc with narration is a very attractive alternative to purchasing and learning to use a $5,000 CD-R recorder, especially considering that the CD-R disc itself will cost about $40. Although Photo CD does not run on older CD-ROM drives, many newer units include CD-ROM XA (and thus Photo CD) compatibility. This trend is expected to continue.

Photo CD is a small-volume production option because it is less expensive to mass-replicate discs after a certain volume is reached. Remember, however, that a single Photo CD can be produced and then sent to a replicator.

 Intel's DV-I

CD-ROM Digital Video-Interactive (DV-I) was initially developed at the General Electric (RCA) Sarnoff Laboratory in the early 1980s and later acquired by microchip-maker Intel. It is supported by powerful industry leaders such as Microsoft's chairman, Bill Gates, and, like CD-ROM XA, was originally intended for business and industrial rather than consumer use.

DV-I can compress up to 72 minutes of video information onto a standard CD-ROM disc, about the same amount of playing time as the high-quality CD audio discs. Video decompression at the user's

computer is a massive proposition, however, requiring two separate processor boards. Intel is currently developing a single board to perform video compression, though, and the board is expected to be available very soon.

DV-I's development was long held back because of the expense involved in the image data compression—the expense of three separate boards to interpret the data for the end user, as well as a less than TV-quality image. Even after Intel succeeded in putting all this hardware into a few chips so the controller could fit on one board, the board remained expensive, and probably too expensive to sell to average consumers. Part of the reason for this expense is the amount of computing power required to process the images.

The video processor board runs at 12.5 MIPS (million instructions per second), a speed that pushes the edge of current desktop technology. In addition, the board also needs at least 1Mb of dedicated video RAM or random access memory. The audio capability involves standard compression techniques that put four channels of audio on the disc. Four channels allow two separate stereo channels or extended monophonic play (up to 40 hours of AM quality sound).

The video can be uncompressed for display using the special video board installed on a standard PC, but the massive computing power needed to compress the 30 fps DV-I quality video requires a mainframe and special software. For developers, an edit-level video (ELV) can be run on a microcomputer that compresses lower-quality video at a 10 fps rate, suitable for development tests.

Video signals can be obtained from a standard NTSC analog video source (used in U.S. television) such as a VCR or from a video camera to be digitized and compressed. Still pictures can be stored and reproduced in even greater detail by using specialized digitizing scanners to provide a digital signal of higher quality than the standard NTSC/TV image contains. Any normal analog audio signal can be captured and digitized by the DV-I audio processor board. Both the video and audio signals are stored as data, along with synchronizing information to combine the two signals together.

The DV-I system is especially useful for developing training simulations for general business, academic, and military applications. In education, DV-I is being tested by everyone from The Children's Television Workshop (Sesame Street) to Virginia Polytechnic Institute and MIT's Media Lab. Another potential application involves mapping surfaces onto wire-frame models for drafting and design departments. No such 3-D standard has yet been set, but several companies are currently working on the concept.

As an information storage and retrieval system, the DV-I multimedia approach is far more suited to a sales or marketing environment than the straight text available with CD-ROM. One application already being tested by VideoDisk Publishing in New York lets customers design a complete living room, using wire-frame furniture which is then displayed with a variety of texture-mapped fabrics. The video furniture catalog could be used by potential customers or designers to see how the new furniture appears from any angle. Other similar uses include landscaping, travel, and real estate applications.

The same features that make DV-I perfect for interactive educational and simulator use make it ideal for adventure games and flight simulators. Such computer/arcade games are very popular today, but the addition of TV-quality color images and detail can bring even greater acceptance.

Once the high cost of reproduction hardware is overcome by the economies of mass production and once all the processing power is in a few dedicated microprocessor chips, DV-I has a tremendous potential for home entertainment, either as part of a home computer or hooked directly to a TV/entertainment center. But this application is years away.

CD-I

Compact Disk-Interactive (CD-I) is a new consumer-oriented multimedia standard that requires a separate player connected directly to a TV and a home audio system. Because CD-I does not require a separate computer, it is appropriate for home or business training centers, but not where data need to be accessed.

CD-I is backed by Philips International (The Netherlands) and Sony (Japan) and has been informally named the Green Book Standard. The CD-I specification allows for the mixing of CD audio music and CD-I video and data on the same disc, providing an alternative to the CD-ROM XA and DV-I multimedia standards. A major advantage of this proposed international standard is that it defines three video definition levels. Data are stored so that any CD-I disc produced can be used with U.S.-, Japanese-, or European-standard TV sets. The complex way in which this compatibility is accomplished is beyond the scope of this book, but the important thing to realize is that this standard has the potential for becoming a true international multimedia standard for home users.

A wide variety of multimedia applications, ranging from interactive maps in automobiles to talking books and reference materials, could be published in CD-I format. And, because a personal computer is not required, CD-I provides a far lower entry-level cost.

Kaleida

In the fall of 1991, IBM and Apple announced Kaleida (as in kaleidoscope), their second major cooperative venture. Many observers saw this joint venture as another way to attempt to combat Microsoft's growing dominance of the entire microcomputer world. Kaleida, with a 50-50 mix of IBM and Apple executives on the board, was envisioned as a developmental think tank for multimedia.

Most people want Kaleida to provide a sophisticated new multimedia development language. Whether Kaleida will also adopt Taligent, the other IBM/Apple joint venture's RISC computer as a hardware platform for multimedia, or just stick to software, is not clear.

The two companies' multimedia efforts had, until the Kaleida announcement, been as incompatible as their microcomputer hardware platforms. Apple concentrated on the small-shop or home development of multimedia, providing sophisticated computers and inexpensive development tools. IBM stuck to its traditional high-end industrial grade development platform, encouraging the production of point-of-sale and training applications for business.

As of early 1994 no Kaleida products were available to discuss.

 # Video cassette recorders

Video cassette recorders (VCRs) are common in publishing multimedia productions, as long as the productions are not interactive. Professional-grade VCRs are also used as input devices controlled by multimedia production software to feed video into a computer's video digitizer board.

The publishing capabilities of VCRs are severely limited by the fact that they are serial devices. They can be used to play a program from beginning to end, but, except when special professional hardware and computer control is used, videotape cannot skip around to display the desired information or provide a further explanation of some confusing topic using a hypertext link. Videotape is not interactive.

One example of a professional-grade VCR is the $3,000 GVR-S950 S-VHS from Sanyo Industrial Video. The special controls required are available through RS-232 (standard serial port), RS-422 (industrial), SMPTE drop-frame and non-drop-frame time-code generator and reader, and a single-frame animation controller. The drivers that come with this and similar professional multimedia recorders are compatible with most computers. Sony products for similar applications include the Betacam SP family of videotape recorders: the UVW-1800 editing recorder, UVW-1600 editing player, UVW-1400 recorder/player, and UVW-1200 player.

These VCRs are especially designed for offline editing, animation, and computer-controlled presentations. Standard RS-232 and RS-422 ports are provided for control.

 # Laserdiscs

Large laserdisc players, such as those used in schools or advanced home/office theaters to provide high-quality movies, do have interactive capabilities. In most ways, they can be viewed by multimedia producers as large CD-ROMs.

The differences, of course, are that these players do not require a computer to operate, although they can be linked to one. They are much less common than CD-ROM, so multimedia productions published on laserdisc format must be targeted to a limited market that already has the correct hardware. Laserdiscs must also be produced by special service bureaus. They cannot be produced the same way CD-R allows you to publish small quantities of CD-ROM-compatible discs.

A

CD-ROM publishing

APPENDIX A

THIS appendix explores the basic costs and steps involved in producing a CD-ROM for internal use in a company or for sale to the public. Replication costs and the basic process are the same whether you produce a data-only disc or a multimedia presentation. Costs are the determining factor in publishing a CD-ROM. For more details on CD-ROM publishing than provided here, read one of my other books, *The New Optical Storage Technology* (McCormick, Business-ONE Irwin, July 1993, $30, ISBN 1-55623-907-6).

CD-ROM discs provide vast amounts of data at low cost if for the mass market or at high cost if for a relatively limited universe of potential users. Even publishing a relatively small amount of data on CD-ROM can be very cost-effective.

Until the early 1990s, the base cost of publishing a CD-ROM was substantial, but it has recently become so low that even the smallest companies can easily absorb the costs of having a CD-ROM disc mastered and pressed.

⇨ Producing a CD-ROM

If you want to produce a CD-ROM, you need to work with an expert who is familiar with all the variables and options involved. This appendix, however, gives you a good understanding of the basic process. This section discusses the tasks involved in the approximate order in which they need to be finished. After reading this, you are less likely to want to do jobs towards the end of the process yourself because they require very specialized software tools, skills, and hardware. Likewise, you are less likely to have a service bureau perform any of the early stages of the work because you can easily accomplish them.

For in-house desktop CD-R (CD-Recordable) publishing, the steps are virtually the same, except the discs are produced individually, rather than replicated at a mass production facility.

The basic steps in producing a CD-ROM are the following:

❶ Acquire the data in machine-usable form.

❷ Edit the data.

❸ Author and index the data.

❹ Premaster the data.

❺ Master, replicate, and package the disc.

The mastering, pressing, and packaging of the discs are usually the least expensive and the easiest to determine in advance. They are also the factors that you, as the CD-ROM developer, will be least able to change. CD-ROM discs produced in quantity are made under strict clean-room conditions in a vacuum chamber. The manufacturing involves producing a flawlessly machined master disc, using plastic molding machines, and coating the disc with a perfect mirror surface. Meeting clean-room specifications are beyond the capabilities of most companies and should usually be left to large CD-ROM and CD audio disc manufacturers, such as Nimbus Information Systems.

In any CD-ROM project for which you hire a manufacturer, be sure you have a clear idea of what you are contracting for and what responsibility the reproduction facility assumes for producing a usable disc. You must also be very clear about your responsibilities and what you need to do to the data before sending them anywhere.

Although you do not need to learn all the details about producing CD-ROM discs, it is important to understand the basic process so you know what replicators are talking about when you shop for their services. While the following information is correct, some software packages or suppliers combine certain steps, blurring the distinction between stages of data preparation. Remember, when storing and retrieving 500Mb or more of data, details are everything, and this section is just a brief overview.

⇨ Acquiring data

Acquiring data is the very first step in producing a CD-ROM disc, but it is the most difficult to cost because it depends on so many factors. Data acquisition, along with editing, is the core of multimedia production.

⇨ Editing data

Almost as many variables are in editing data as in acquiring data. Once you have all the data in computer files, you must edit them to conform to one format or data structure. This step is also known as the *markup* stage.

If you have text files, they might have been created and stored using different margins, page lengths, or embedded characters used by various word processors. Control characters that specify italics, bold, underlining, and such must all be removed or put in a special format. Graphics can be added to a CD-ROM to accompany the text. Whether hand-drawn illustrations or digitized photographs, they must all have the exact same format in the final publication. Sounds can also be used on a CD-ROM—everything from 74 minutes of full-stereo CD audio music to hours of speech-quality sound. You can even have multiple tracks of different languages.

As part of either the editing or authoring step, you must add special *tags*, or formatting information. These tags specify to the data preparation software where paragraphs, pages, chapters, and documents begin and end.

Multimedia productions that use little text face other problems with getting images into the proper format. That will actually be much simpler than cleaning and marking large quantities of text.

⇨ Authoring

After the data are all in the same format, they must be merged into one very large file suitable for reproduction on a CD-ROM disc—this step is referred to as authoring, or data preparation.

A multimedia production probably already has the entire presentation integrated, but additional processing might be needed before the final cut can be transferred to CD-ROM. This processing is done using special authoring software that creates an exact duplicate of the final database except for the error-correction data, which are added during the

mastering or premastering step. A full multimedia production authored as a self-contained program needs very little authoring, or simply can be copied to a CD-ROM disc in proper ISO or Macintosh format.

Once authored and stored on a large hard disk, the file can then be either transferred to a selected storage medium and sent to the mastering facility or published directly on a CD-R disc. Low-cost desktop CD-R systems and inexpensive large hard drives have made it practical to build a virtual CD-ROM on a hard disk. You can also publish a CD-R disc for testing and evaluation and then send the drive or CD-R disc to the replication facility. If you plan to distribute just a few copies, produced in-house on CD-R drives, you can publish as soon as you have evaluated the test run for errors.

Authoring software is available for a number of different computer systems, including micros. Any computer fast enough to develop multimedia presentations is quite sufficient to preprocess a CD-ROM file. A CD-ROM publishing workstation needs a minimum of a 1-gigabyte (Gb) hard disk and an acceptable method of recording completed data in a portable form so they can be sent to a service bureau or replication facility.

Generally acceptable output media include the following:

> 4-mm DSS or DATA digital audio tape

> 8-mm Exabyte tape

> 9-track tape

> ¾" U-Matic tape

> WORM, Magneto-Optical, removable Iomega or SyQuest disc

> CD-R disc

> SCSI or other hard drives of sufficient capacity

If an index is required for the disc and is not provided for in your multimedia authoring system, you can create one using a program called a *build engine*. The build engine takes data that have been rough-formatted and creates both an index and a logically formatted file. Indexing is of interest mostly to those developers who publish text data, but images might also need to be indexed.

Image indexes are usually quite simple. While a CD-ROM can easily contain tens of millions of words that need to be indexed, you can only fit a few hundred images on most CD-format discs. If your CD-ROM consists of a set of images or computer programs, you cannot index anything but the titles and brief descriptions, along with a cross-reference menu to help select the proper files. This indexing takes planning, but it is far smaller and easier to produce than a full-text database that lists the location of every word except for specified null words such as *a*, *the*, *and*, *but*, and so forth.

Premastering

After all data are edited, checked for errors, tagged, indexed, and file-formatted in standard ISO 9660 or Macintosh format, they are premastered. In premastering, the data have error-correction and other codes added. They are then ready to be copied onto a CD-ROM disc.

Just what constitutes premastering depends on the service bureau and your software. If mastering is just the physical preparation of the mechanical device used to make the final discs, premastering can cover several tasks. Understanding just which tasks a salesperson at a service bureau is talking about is important when comparing prices and determining final costs.

The premastering process adds error-correction encoding to your completed files. This error-correction step is necessary to ensure that your presentation can be retrieved from the CD-ROM correctly. Error-correction information is part of the definition of a CD-ROM. It is therefore meaningless to discuss how much data could be stored on a "perfect" CD-ROM that did not require the addition of error-correction data.

The original data, along with the newly added error-correction codes, are converted from the original 8-bit signal into 14-bit signals. This process spaces data physically further apart on the disc to make them easier to write to the disc and easier for the drive to read. This processed information is the master file, which is used to create the master disc. How the master file is formatted depends on who is doing the next step.

Mastering

In mastering, a 10mm-thick, 20cm-diameter glass disc is polished and cleaned until perfectly flat, then covered with a photosensitive coating. This prepared disc is then exposed to a blue argon laser beam, which is modulated to cut an image of the data played from the U-matic master tape. After developing the photosensitive coating on the disc's surface, the portions exposed to the laser's light are dissolved, leaving an image of the final CD-ROM's surface. A metal coating is then applied to the master's surface.

The master disc is checked for accuracy, then placed in a heavy plating bath for several hours to apply a heavy nickel plating about $\frac{1}{16}$" thick. The two parts are then carefully separated, and the plating becomes the final metal master that, in turn, is used to produce *stampers*.

At this stage, hard costs can be discussed. The mastering step will cost between $600 and $3,000, depending on a number of factors described in the section on cost.

Replication

Replication is the step where the actual CD-ROM discs are created, using the stampers to form soft plastic in an injection-molding machine. The clear plastic disc is then coated with either evaporated aluminum or another shiny metal, sometimes even gold. The final step then overcoats the now-shiny disc with a clear, protective plastic coating. It might surprise you to learn that this final step is most crucial for disc longevity. If the clear top coating is done properly, covering even the edge to completely seal in the metallic layer, the disc will last for many years. If air can penetrate the disc, however, the disc will deteriorate rapidly (sometimes in only a few years) because the aluminum will oxidize and become dull.

Although both sides of a CD-ROM disc are shiny and look alike, data are recorded on only one side. Final production steps involve printing a label on the unused side of the disc. This final step might seem

unworthy of consideration by anyone but the company's art designer. Yet, in the early days of CD-ROM development, inexperienced printers silk-screened fancy labels on the discs, using paint that reacted with the plastic of the CD-ROMs, eventually dissolving them.

In quantity, replication costs are as low as $2 per disc.

Packaging

Because the discs are relatively strong, tough, and immune to most careless handling, they do not need to be packaged in any special manner. The well-known "jewel" cases have become popular for storing CD audio discs and are now considered a standard packaging technique and usually specified for the finished CD-ROMs.

A brochure or label is usually printed for insertion in the jewel case, but many discs are sold with blank cases. Companies find that the information printed on each disc is sufficient for anything but flashy consumer productions. Some companies just slip CD-ROMs into cardboard holders or drop them into the same paper or plastic sleeves used to protect 5.25" floppy diskettes.

In general, packaging CD-ROMs cost about 30 cents each.

Costs

You can have as much or as little of the above steps done by outside companies as you can afford.

Depending on the size of your business, you might have only the steps from mastering done outside, while performing the rest in-house. Or you might contract someone to take a stack of paper and return to you a completed CD-ROM. These variables are why costs are so hard to discuss. Licensing fees for search software are another variable to consider if your production needs it.

The cost of getting a single master made from your already prepared data can cost from about $500 (during specials or for special customers) to about $2,500. Pressing each disc drops to about $2 each in large quantities. Thus, if you are selling a commercial product, it is perfectly feasible to produce and sell CD-ROMs for less than $20, depending on the cost of the original data, the amount of work involved in premastering, and the volume of sales. Even back in 1989, companies were making a bundle of money selling CD-ROM discs for less than $100. That market included only a relatively small number of users who then had a CD-ROM drive, too.

The following volume pricing information was in effect in early 1994. If history is any guide, costs will probably drop slightly over the next few years, but not by much. So, the prices listed here should provide a good guide for readers. Very big price cuts occurred in the late 1980s, but CD-ROM publishing prices have generally stabilized.

Although detailed pricing schedules are provided only for a few replicators, this field is very competitive. Total costs for producing 10,000 discs were the same to within a couple of pennies per disc for six surveyed producers. The total costs shown might include other miscellaneous charges not listed. The prices are for turnaround times of three to seven days.

Turnaround time is the most important factor in determining price. Customers who can wait a week or two to see a finished product will see total prices down around $1.50 per title in 10,000 quantities. On the other hand, those who demand 24-hour turnaround will pay substantially more for the rush service.

Onsite CD Services

Combined mastering/premastering services	$1,000
Replication per disc cost (for 5,000)	$1.70
Total cost	$9,500 ($1.90 per disc)

Sony

Premastering	$125 per hour
Mastering	$860
Replication per disc cost (for 5,000)	$1.63
Total cost	$9,260 ($1.85 per disc)

3M Corporation

Premastering	$300
Mastering	$1,400
Replication per disc cost (for 5,000)	$1.85
Total cost	$10,950 ($2.19 per disc)

Optical Media International

Premastering	$250
Mastering	$1,300
Replication per disc cost (for 5,000)	$2.00
Total cost	$11,550 ($2.31 per disc)

A detailed listing of Optical Media International's (OMI's) pricing is listed next as supplied by the company in August 1992. It is typical of other service bureaus and replication facilities and, for comparison, includes audio CD prices. The prices are for a three-day turnaround. A CD premastering surcharge of $300 is added for 24-hour turnaround. None of the prices includes the cost of any special search software used for most datasets.

Apple SCSI hard drive one-off special (CD-recordable)	$299 (1 disc)
System operator time (ISO 9660 file origination, XA or CD-I file interleaving, etc.)	$200 per hour
CD-ROM encoding/premastering (adds error-correction code)	$250
Audio processing (editing digital audio tape for CD master)	$299
Sampling rate conversion (converting 48-kHz DAT to 44.1-kHz CD sample rate)	$100
CD-ROM one-off (test CD-ROM created by CD-recordable)	$250 (1 disc)

CD-ROM Mastering (creating a glass master andstamper set)

15-day turnaround	$800
3-day turnaround	$1,800
1-day turnaround	$2,900

CD-ROM Production (includes two-color label on disc, insertion of printed material, jewel case, and shrink-wrapping)

100 to 250 discs	$3.50 per disc
10,000 discs	$2.00 per disc

CD Audio Prices (includes glass master, replication, two-color label on disc, insertion of printed material, jewel case, and shrink-wrapping)

100 discs	$9.95 per disc
1,000 discs	$2.00 per disc
10,000 discs	$1.70 per disc

 CD-R

A CD recorder, or CD-R, is the base of a desktop CD publishing system that can produce between 7 and 14 full CD-ROM-compatible discs each work day per drive. Multiple drives can increase that production rate through a daisy-chain SCSI connection. The recorders cost from $2,800 up.

The economics of such small-scale production are not much different from the costs for low-volume CD-ROM production using regular replication facilities. The ability to produce discs in-house, along with the speed, convenience, and security in-house production entails, makes this a very attractive option for many businesses.

Sony, Philips, Yamaha, and JVC all make CD recorders that comply with the Orange Book Part II Write-Once CD format. The Philips CDD521 Double-Speed Desktop CD Recorder, which measures only 4.7" high by 16" wide by 13" long, produces a 600Mb CD-ROM driven through a SCSI port at data transfer rates of either 307.2 kbps (Mode 1) or 352.8 kbps (Mode 2).

CD small volume publication costs

After data are premastered, they can be fed to the CD recorder to be written to a special CD-WO (CD-R) disc that costs about $50 (prices are currently dropping and will probably be about $30 each by mid-1995). Because the disc is recorded serially instead of being pressed all at once as in a replication facility, the time needed to

record the data depends on how much data are being stored. Thus, a CD-recordable drive can produce about 10 CD-ROM compatible discs in an hour if they contain only about 90Mb of data each.

This production rate results in a cost of about $500 (plus time) for 10 CD-ROMs (the same base cost applies whether a full disc is produced or only a few megabytes are used on the disc). One hundred discs produced using CD-R would cost $5,000 counting raw materials alone. If the 100 discs were full of data, they would need a minimum of 50 hours to record, or about seven standard work days. Newer multispeed drives operate at recording rates of 2 to 4 times faster.

In comparison, a CD-ROM master can be produced and 100 replicas made in five days at a mastering cost of $1,100 and replication cost of $3.50 per disc (because of the small quantity), resulting in a total price of $1,650.

Obviously, CD-recordables have very limited applications for mass-producing CD-ROM discs, but they do offer important new uses for the publishing media. The breakeven costs for CD-recordable versus standard service bureau production comes at about 40 discs that could be produced in 20 to 40 hours, or about four working days at a material cost of about $2,000. Three-day mastering costs about $1,800, and 40 discs could be replicated for about $170. Of course, those costs and the breakeven comparison were valid at the time this book was written and the cost of blank CD-recordable discs is currently dropping.

One major international service bureau and publishing software producer (CD/Author),

Dataware Technologies
222 3rd St.
Suite 3300
Cambridge, MA 02142

predicts that disc prices will soon drop to about $10, drastically changing the economics of CD-recordable in-house self-publishing. One example of CD-recordable use cited by Dataware Technologies in its "CD-Recordable Applications Guide" white paper (available on

request from the company) is custom database publishing being done by the A M Best insurance industry analysis company. Eastman Kodak publishes inventory and production statistics on CD-ROM and uses CD-recordable to produce overnight updates to its international locations. Another company uses CD-ROM to publish employee identification information for its far-flung multinational staff. CD-recordable produces quick updates used by the traveling executives.

SCSI-2 adapter boards

THIS appendix lists products and companies that supply high-performance SCSI port expansion boards for various computers. Because of the number of boards on the market, the list included here is only a selection. These boards and many more are included on the disk that accompanies this book. The listings are in standard ASCII format, and the file is named APPXB.TXT. This file can be loaded into any word processor and searched for specific names, printed out, or read on screen. Eight-bit PC boards are not included because their relatively poor performance makes them unacceptable for multimedia production systems.

In the listing, ISA is the acronym for industry standard architecture, which signifies that the board is compatible with the old IBM PC/XT/AT bus style. Compatible boards also can be installed in EISA (extended industry standard architecture) systems.

MCA and Micro Channel indicate the special non-ISA compatible bus created by IBM for many of its PS/2 systems. Please note that some low-end PS/2s use the old ISA bus.

Macintosh SCSI-2 boards are listed separately at the end of this appendix. Although Mac systems come with SCSI ports, these are often low-performance ports and Multimedia users will want to add a high-performance SCSI-2 board to their systems.

The address of the company appears first, followed by one or more of the products that company offers.

⇨ PC boards

Adaptec
691 S. Milpitas Blvd.
Milpitas, CA 95035
408-945-8600
408-262-2533 (F)

AHA-1510/20, $110. ½-length 16-bit ISA board.

AHA-1744, $650. Bus-master, full-length EISA board.

BusLogic
4151 Burton Dr.
Santa Clara, CA 95054
408-492-9090
408-492-1542 (F)

BT-445S, $499. VESA Local Bus, includes 80188 microprocessor, supports dual floppy drives.

BT-646D, $589. Full-length MCA board, bus-master.

Ciprico
2800 Campus Dr.
Plymouth, MN 55441
612-551-4000
612-551-4002 (F)

RimFire 5500, $695. Full-length 16-bit ISA board, includes floppy disk controller.

CMS Enhancements
2722 Michelson Dr.
Irvine, CA 92715
714-222-6000
714-549-4004 (F)

OmniBus HBA-SXO, $79. ½-length 16-bit ISA board, bus-master.

Data Technology
1515 Centre Pointe Dr.
Milpitas, CA 95035
408-942-4000
408-942-4027 (F)

DTC3282, $285. ¾-length 16-bit ISA board, bus-master, 7H, 4F unit(s) controlled.

Digital Equipment
146 Main St.
Maynard, MA 01754-2571
508-493-5111

PCTAZ-AA, $200. ½-length 16-bit ISA board.

Distributed Processing Technology
140 Candace Dr.
Maitland, FL 32751
407-830-5522
407-260-5366 (F)

SmartConnex/EISA Model PM2012A/90, $655. Full-length EISA board, bus-master.

SmartConnex/ISA Model PM2001/95, $365. ½-length 16-bit ISA board.

First International Computer of America
30077 Ahern Ave.
Union City, CA 94587
510-475-7885
510-475-5333 (F)

FIC EISA SCSI, price not available. EISA board, bus-master, supports 2F drives.

Future Domain
2801 McGaw Ave.
Irvine, CA 92714
714-253-0400
714-253-0913 (F)

MCS-700, $230. Full-length MCA board.

TMC-1670, $165. ½-length 16-bit ISA board.

IBM
Old Orchard Rd.
Armonk, NY 10504
914-765-1900

16-Bit AT Fast SCSI Adapter Kit, price not available. 16-bit ISA board.

Laura Technologies
106 South 54th St.
Chandler, AZ 85226
602-940-9800
602-940-0222 (F)

TNT-4000, $355. ½-length 16-bit ISA board.

MicroNet Technology
20 Mason
Irvine, CA 92718
714-837-6033
714-837-1164 (F)

HA-01, $495. ¾-length 16-bit ISA board, includes floppy disk controller.

NCR
1700 South Patterson Blvd.
Dayton, OH 45479
513-445-5000
513-445-4184 (F)

ADP-37, $250. Full-length MCA board.

Peripheral Land
47421 Bayside Pkwy.
Fremont, CA 94538
510-657-2211
510-683-9713 (F)

QuickSCSI, $399. ½-length 8-bit ISA board; half-length 16-bit ISA board, disk mirroring.

Procom Technology
2181 Dupont Dr.
Irvine, CA 92715
714-852-1000
714-852-1221 (F)

CC-16 Enabler, $349. Full-length 16-bit ISA board.

MC Enabler, $349. Full-length MCA board.

Procomp USA
6777 Engle Rd.
Cleveland, OH 44130
216-234-6387
216-234-2233 (F)

Pro-Val, $199. ½-length 16-bit ISA board.

Sumo Systems
1580 Old Oakland Rd., Suite C103
San Jose, CA 95131
408-453-5744
408-453-5821 (F)

SPI300, $95–$120. 16-bit ISA board, includes floppy disk controller.

UltraStor
15 Hammond, Suite 310
Irvine, CA 92718
714-581-4100
714-581-0826 (F)

Ultra 14F, $210. ½-length 16-bit ISA board, bus-master, includes floppy disk controller.

Ultra 34F, $275. VESA Local Bus, bus-master.

Western Digital
8105 Irvine Center Dr.
Irvine, CA 92718
714-932-4900
714-660-4909 (F)

Model 7000-FASST2, $385. Full-length 16-bit ISA board, provides floppy controller.

Yangs International
44113 Grimmer Blvd.
Fremont, CA 94538
510-651-4036
510-651-4035 (F)

ACME-HSF-I, $98. 16-bit ISA board, supports two 1.44Mb floppy drives.

 # Macintosh SCSI-2 boards

ATTO Technology
1576 Sweet Home Rd.
Baird Research Park
Amherst, NY 14228
716-688-4259
716-636-3630 (F)

SiliconExpress 3D, $995. Bus-master for Macintosh NuBus.

Corporate Systems Center
1294 Hammerwood Ave.
Sunnyvale, CA 94089
408-734-3475
408-745-1816 (F)

Silicon Express, $179. FAST SCSI-2 port that fits any NuBus Mac.

DayStar Digital
5556 Atlanta Hwy.
Flowery Branch, GA 30542
404-967-2077
404-967-3018 (F)

(Other DayStar products are described in Chapter 11)

DataStream, $799–$1,499.

FWB
2040 Polk St.
Suite 215
San Francisco, CA 94109
415-474-8055
415-775-2125 (F)

SledgeHammer SCSI Array, $889 to $14,089. This board is described in Chapter 11.

Loviel Computer
5599 W. 78th St.
Edina, MN 55439
612-828-6880
612-828-6881 (F)

Arrow, $949.

R1 SCSI-2 RAID system. This system is described in Chapter 11.

MicroNet Technology
20 Mason
Irvine, CA 92718
714-837-6033
714-837-1164 (F)

NuPORT II, $600. Macintosh NuBus board.

Raven-040 Disk Array RAID system. This system is described in Chapter 11.

Newer Technology
7803 East Osie St.
Suite 105
Wichita, KS 67207
316-685-4904
316-685-9368 (F)

SCSI-II Dart, $4,700–$34,920. This high-speed SCSI-2 controller with RAM disk is described in Chapter 11.

Procom Technology
2181 Dupont Dr.
Irvine, CA 92715
714-852-1000
714-852-1221 (F)

Nu32 SCSI Enabler, $995. Bus-master capabilities with disk mirroring.

Storage Dimensions
1656 McCarthy Blvd.
Milpitas, CA 95035
408-954-0710
408-944-1200 (F)

Data Cannon MACU-PDS/040, $799.

Data Cannon MDC-PDS/Quadra, $1,199. Bus-master SCSI-2 for Macintosh Quadra tower series.

MacinStor SpeedArray RAID system. This system is described in Chapter 11.

Audio input/output boards

T HIS appendix lists computer adapter boards that allow you to capture and play back sounds. Because of the number of boards on the market, only a representative selection is included in this appendix. The boards listed here, along with many more, are included on the disk that accompanies this book. The listings are in standard ASCII format, and the file is named APPXC.TXT. This file can be loaded into any wordprocessor and searched for specific names, printed out, or read on screen.

In the listing, ISA is the acronym for industry standard architecture, which signifies that the board is compatible with the old IBM PC/XT/AT bus style. Compatible boards also can be installed in EISA (extended industry standard architecture) systems.

MCA and Micro Channel indicate the special non-ISA compatible bus created by IBM for many of its PS/2 systems. Please note that some low-end PS/2s use the old ISA bus.

Macintosh audio boards are listed separately at the end of this appendix. In all listings, the address of the company appears first, followed by one or more of the products that company offers.

PC audio boards

AddTech Research
41332 Christy St.
Fremont, CA 94538
510-623-7583
510-623-7538 (F)

Sound 2000, $595. 16-bit ISA audio processing board based on the Sierra, semiconductor ARIA microprocessor chip, MIDI interface.

AdLib MultiMedia
350 Franquet St.
Suite 80
Sainte Foi, QB, Canada G1P 4P3
418-656-8742
418-656-1646 (F)

Ad Lib Gold 2000MC, $500. ¾-length audio processing board, SCSI interface.

Atlanta Signal Processors
770 Spring St.
Suite 208
Atlanta, GA 30308
404-892-7265
404-892-2512 (F)

Elf-31, $1,195. Full-length 16-bit ISA audio processing board based on the TI TMS320C31 microprocessor chip, MIDI interface.

Aztech Labs
46707 Fremont Blvd.
Fremont, CA 94538
510-623-8988
510-623-8989 (F)

Sound Galaxy NX Pro 16, $269. 16-bit ISA audio processing board, MIDI interface, SCSI interface.

Computer Peripherals
667 Rancho Conejo Blvd.
Newbury Park, CA 91320
805-499-5751
805-499-5742 (F)

ViVa Maestro 16, $299. ¾-length 16-bit ISA audio processing board based on the Sierra, semiconductor ARIA microprocessor chip, MIDI interface, CD-ROM interface.

Creative Labs
1901 McCarthy Blvd.
Milpitas, CA 95035
408-428-6600
408-428-6611 (F)

Sound Blaster 16 ASP, $350. ¾-length 16-bit ISA audio processing board, MIDI interface, stereo digital/analog mixer; microphone and stereo line-in jacks.

Sound Blaster Pro MCV, $399. ¾-length MCA audio processing board, compatible with Micro Channel PS/2 Models, MIDI interface.

IBM
Old Orchard Rd.
Armonk, NY 10504
914-765-1900

Audio Capture/Playback Adapter, $565. MCA audio processing board, compatible with Micro Channel PS/2 Models.

Ultimedia M-Audio Capture/Playback Adapter/A, $370. MCA audio processing board.

Logitech
6505 Kaiser Dr.
Fremont, CA 94555
510-795-8500
510-792-8901 (F)

SoundMan, $289. 16-bit ISA audio processing board, MIDI interface, joystick port.

Media Resources
640 Puente St.
Brea, CA 92621
714-256-5048
714-256-5025 (F)

Multimedia Sound Card MHC-01, $349. 16-bit ISA audio processing board, MIDI interface, SCSI interface.

Multimedia Sound Card MHC-03, $399. 16-bit ISA audio processing board, MIDI interface, joystick port.

Media Vision
3185 Laurelview Ct.
Fremont, CA 94538
510-770-8600
510-770-9592 (F)

Pro Audio Spectrum 16, $299. 16-bit ISA audio processing board, MIDI interface, SCSI interface, joystick port, microphone/stereo input, audio output.

Microsoft
One Microsoft Way
Redmond, WA 98052-6399
206-882-8080
206-883-8101 (F)

Windows Sound System, $289. Full-length 16-bit ISA audio processing board.

Online Computer Systems
20251 Century Blvd.
Germantown, MD 20874
301-428-3700
301-428-2903 (F)

DSA-1640, $1,095. Full-length MCA audio processing board.

DSA-340, $595. Full-length MCA audio processing board, compatible with Micro Channel PS/2 Models.

Orchid Technology
45365 Northport Loop W.
Fremont, CA 94538
510-683-0300
510-490-9312 (F)

Sound Producer Pro, $199. 16-bit ISA audio processing board, MIDI interface, SCSI interface, joystick port.

Roland
7200 Dominion Circle
Los Angeles, CA 90040-3647
213-685-5141
213-722-0911 (F)

LAPC-1, $595. Full-length 16-bit ISA MIDI board.

Sigma Designs
47900 Bayside Pkwy.
Fremont, CA 94538
510-770-0100
510-770-2640 (F)

WinSound, $299. 16-bit ISA audio processing board, MIDI interface, SCSI interface, joystick port.

Turtle Beach Systems
1600 Pennsylvania Ave., Cyber Center
York, PA 17404
717-843-6916
717-854-8319 (F)

MultiSound, $599. Full-length 16-bit ISA audio processing board based on the Motorola 56001 microprocessor chip, MIDI interface, joystick port, stereo input, audio output.

 # Macintosh audio boards

DigiDesign
1360 Willow Rd., Suite 101
Menlo Park, CA 94025
415-688-0600
415-327-0777 (F)

SampleCell II, $1,995. Full-length audio processing board, compatible with Macintosh IIs and Quadras.

Mark of the Unicorn
1280 Massachusetts Ave.
Cambridge, MA 02138
617-576-2760
617-576-3609 (F)

MIDI Express, $349. Macintosh MIDI board.

Media Vision
3185 Laurelview Ct.
Fremont, CA 94538
510-770-8600
510-770-9592 (F)

Pro Audio Spectrum 16 Mac, $495. Audio processing board, compatible with Macintosh IIs, MIDI interface, SCSI interface, joystick port, microphone/stereo input, audio output.

Roland Digital Group
1961 McGaw Ave.
Irvine, CA 92714
714-975-0560
714-975-0569 (F)

SC-7, $399. Macintosh MIDI board.

Video input/output
boards

A P P E N D I X D

THIS appendix includes video capture boards and converters that allow computers to drive a standard television as well as capture video signals from VCRs, camcorders, videodisc players, and other sources. Because of the number of boards on the market, only a selection is listed in this appendix. The boards listed below and many more are included on the disk that accompanies this book. The listings are in standard ASCII format, and the file is named APPXD.TXT. This file can be loaded into any word processor and searched for specific names, printed out, or read on screen.

In general, 8-bit boards usually do not offer the performance that multimedia producers need. Some users will find them powerful enough, however, so a few are listed, along with 16-bit and other boards, such as those that fit in the IBM Micro Channel bus computers (PS/2 Model 80 or 90). Most companies offer other versions of the boards listed.

Macintosh video boards are listed separately at the end of this appendix. In all listings, the address of the company appears first, followed by one or more of the products that company offers.

PC video boards

AdLib MultiMedia
350 Franquet St.
Suite 80
Sainte Foi, QB, Canada G1P 4P3
418-656-8742
418-656-1646 (F)

PC Video, $700. ¾-length 16-bit ISA image capture board with 768K RAM, NTSC or PAL input, live video also displayed in window on computer screen.

AITech International
830 Hillview Ct.
Suite 145
Milpitas, CA 95035
408-946-3291
408-946-3597 (F)

ProVGA/TV Plus, $995. Full-length 16-bit ISA video overlaying/encoding board with 512K RAM, 256 colors, 640 × 480 resolution, genlock, multiple chroma key functions, VGA passthrough, and VGA to NTSC or S-Video conversion.

WaveWatcher-TV, $589. 16-bit ISA motion video board and 640 × 480 resolution, plus audio input, image capture, built-in on-screen remote control, NTSC or PAL video, and VGA overlay.

Creative Labs
1901 McCarthy Blvd.
Milpitas, CA 95035
408-428-6600
408-428-6611 (F)

VideoBlaster, $495. Full-length 16-bit ISA motion video board with 1Mb RAM, 2Mb colors, 640 × 480 resolution, image capture, graphics overlay, audio processing, NTSC and PAL input.

Fast Electronic U.S.
5 Commonwealth Rd.
Natick, MA 01760
508-655-3278
508-650-0447 (F)

Screen Machine-PC, $2,595. Full-length 16-bit ISA motion video board with 512K RAM; 16.7Mb colors; 24 bits per pixel; 1024 × 768, 800 × 600, and 640 × 480 resolutions; frame grabber; NTSC and PAL input; three stereo inputs; S-VHS composite video; video overlay.

Video Machine-PC, $4,000. Full-length 16-bit ISA motion video board with 16.7Mb colors and 24 bits per pixel, supports NTSC and PAL inputs, genlock capabilities, four stereo inputs.

IBM
Old Orchard Rd.
Armonk, NY 10504
914-765-1900

M-Motion Video Adapter/A, $1,435. MCA PS/2 motion video board with 640 × 480 resolution, multiple video windows displayed, image capture, NTSC or PAL video, VGA overlay.

Intel
P.O. Box 58119
2200 Mission College Blvd.
Santa Clara, CA 95052-8119
408-765-8080
408-765-1821 (F)

ActionMedia II Delivery Board/AT, $1,895. Full-length 16-bit ISA motion video board with 16.8Mb colors; still and motion video with audio compression, decompression, video manipulation, and graphics functions; S-VHS video output for NTSC or PAL.

Media Vision
3185 Laurelview Ct.
Fremont, CA 94538
510-770-8600
510-770-9592 (F)

Pro MovieSpectrum, $399. 16-bit ISA motion video board with 32K colors, live video or image capture in window, NTSC or S-Video input.

Orchid Technology
453655 Northport Loop W.
Fremont, CA 94538
800-767-2443

Vidiola, $399. 16-bit ISA full-speed video capture and playback board with NTSC/PAL and S-Video ports.

STB Systems
1651 N. Glenville
Suite 210
Richardson, TX 75081
800-234-4334
214-234-8750
214-234-1306 (F)

TV/GRX, $395. ¾-length 16-bit ISA motion video board with 21 bits per pixel and 640 × 480 resolution, displays NTSC or PAL signal on computer monitor.

Truevision
7340 Shadeland Station
Indianapolis, IN 46256-3925
317-841-0332
317-576-7700 (F)

ATVista, $2,995 (1Mb) to $4,795 (4Mb). 16-bit ISA image capture board with 1Mb to 4Mb RAM; 256 colors; 32 bits per pixel; TI TMS34010 graphics coprocessor; videographic adapter with NTSC encoding, genlock, and overlaying capabilities.

VideoVGA, $995 to $1,195. Full-length 16-bit ISA motion video board with 512K to 1Mb RAM, 256 colors, 1024 × 768 and 800 × 600 resolution, genlock, NTSC and S-Video signals, superimposes computer graphics over television-style video.

Vision Technologies
901 Page Ave.
Fremont, CA 94538
510-683-2900
510-657-0601 (F)

Vision 16, $1,395 to $1,495. Full-length 16-bit ISA image capture board with 32.7K colors, 16 bits per pixel, 512 × 484 resolution, external genlock, RGB and NTSC input

⇨ Macintosh video boards

Advent Computer Products
449 Santa Fe Dr.
Suite 213
Encinitas, CA 92024
619-942-8456
619-942-0648 (F)

Neotech Image Grabber, $1,499. Image capture board with 512K RAM, 256 colors, 8 bits per pixel, 640 × 480 resolution, NTSC or PAL input, compatible with Macintosh IIs.

Computer Friends
14250 N.W. Science Park Dr.
Portland, OR 97229
503-626-2291
503-643-5379 (F)

ColorSnap 32+, $995 to $1,200. Full-length Macintosh II image capture board with 16.8Mb colors, 24 bits per pixel, 640 × 480 resolution, NTSC/PAL input.

Computer Sciences
2 Commerce Dr.
Moorestown, NJ 08057
609-234-1166

VideoDesk 1/32, $4,995. Macintosh II series' motion video board with 640 × 480 resolution, NTSC or PAL input, QuickDraw acceleration, simultaneous image capture and live video in window.

Digital F/X
755 Ravendale Dr.
Mountain View, CA 94043
415-961-2800
415-961-6990 (F)

Video F/X Plus, $15,995. Image capture board with 16.7Mb colors, 640 × 480 resolution, Macintosh to NTSC conversion, MIDI interface, control box for mixing video and sound, compatible with Macintosh II and Quadra.

Intelligent Resources Integrated Systems
3030 Salt Creek Ln.
Suite 100
Arlington Heights, IL 60005-5001
708-670-9388
708-670-0585 (F)

Video Explorer, $7,995–$11,995. Full-length motion video board with 16.7Mb colors, 24 bits per pixel, RGB input/output, real-time video processing board, supports NTSC and PAL signals, compatible with Macintosh IIs and Quandra.

Radius
1710 Fortune Dr.
San Jose, CA 95131-1744
408-434-1010
408-434-0770 (F)

Digital Media Studio, $3,999. Macintosh NuBus motion video board with 16.7Mb colors, 24 bits per pixel, 1152 × 870 and 640 × 480 resolution, built-in JPEG compression accelerator, live video in window, NTSC/PAL video.

RasterOps
2500 Walsh Ave.
Santa Clara, CA 95051
408-562-4200
408-562-4065 (F)

RasterOps 24XLTV, $3,499. Full-length Macintosh II motion video board with 3Mb RAM; 16.7Mb colors; 24 bits per pixel; 1152 × 870, 1024 × 768, and 640 × 480 resolution; interlaced NTSC and/or PAL RGB for external encoding; QuickDraw accelerator board.

SuperMac Technology
485 Potrero Ave.
Sunnyvale, CA 94086
408-245-2202
408-735-7250 (F)

DigitalFilm, $5,999. Macintosh NuBus motion video board with 16.7Mb colors; 24 bits per pixel; 1152 × 870, 1024 × 768, 832 × 624, and 640 × 480 resolution; audio digitizer; JPEG compression; NTSC, PAL, and S-Video; QuickDraw acceleration.

VideoSpigot, $299 to $499. Motion video board with 16.7Mb colors; 24 bits per pixel; 640 × 480 resolution; NTSC or PAL input; compatible with Macintosh LC, IIsi, and NuBus.

Truevision
7340 Shadeland Station
Indianapolis, IN 46256-3925
317-841-0332
317-576-7700 (F)

Bravado 24, $1,995. Full-length Macintosh Quadra series' motion video board with 512K to 1Mb RAM, 16.7Mb colors, 24 bits per pixel, 1152 × 870 and 640 × 480 resolution, audio passthrough, NTSC and PAL video-in-a-window, VGA.

MIDI software

APPENDIX E

IN all these listings, the address of the company appears first, followed by one or more of the products that company offers.

AdLib MultiMedia
350 Franquet St.
Sainte Foi, QB, Canada G1P 4P3
418-656-8742
418-656-1646 (F)

Visual Composer/MIDI Supplement [MS-DOS], $40. 16-channel MIDI software for Ad Lib Personal Computer Music System that provides both sequencing and basic editing capabilities.

Big Noise Software
P.O. Box 23740
Jacksonville, FL 32241
904-730-0754
904-730-0748 (F)

Cadenza [MS-DOS], $200. 64-channel MIDI software that provides professional editing and sequencing; video adapter required.

Cadenza for Windows [Windows 3.X], $300. 64-channel MIDI software that provides sequencing and editing; video adapter required.

Bogas Productions
751 Laurel St.
San Carlos, CA 94070
415-592-5129
415-592-5196 (F)

Studio Session MIDI Utility [Macintosh], $100. Software program that converts songs to standard MIDI format; as many as eight different instruments and more than 40 notes can be played simultaneously, or users can install and play third-party SMF format files.

Dynaware USA
950 Tower Ln.
Foster City, CA 94404
415-349-5700
415-349-5879 (F)

Ballade [MS-DOS], $195. Designed to work with the Roland MT-32, it does both MIDI tone-editing and sequencing.

DynaDuet [MS-DOS], $245. Processes music via both MIDI sequencing and score editing.

Mark of the Unicorn
1280 Massachusetts Ave.
Cambridge, MA 02138
617-576-2760
617-576-3609 (F)

Digital Performer [Macintosh/System 7], $895. MIDI music editing and sequencing software.

Midisoft Corp.
P.O. Box 1000
Bellevue, WA 98009
206-881-7176
206-883-1368 (F)

Midisoft Studio [MS-DOS], $250. 16-channel MIDI multitrack music recording, editing, and sequencing software that links any IBM PC to any MIDI instrument; it can add musical scores to desktop publishing program and multimedia presentations.

Midisoft Studio for Windows [Windows 3.X], $250. 16-channel MIDI software multitrack music recording, editing, and sequencing software that links any IBM PC to any MIDI instrument

OpCode Systems
3950 Fabian Way
Palo Alto, CA 94303
415-856-3333
415-856-3332 (F)

EZ Vision [Macintosh Plus], $100. MIDI sequencing software capable of editing, recording, and playing back music on MIDI synthesizers; designed for both multimedia users and MIDI beginners.

Studio Vision [Macintosh SE/30 and II Series/System 7], $995. MIDI software that combines MIDI sequencing with Vision's digital audio editing/recording ability digital audio.

Vision [Macintosh Plus/System 7], $495. MIDI sequencing software that provides loop recording, onscreen help, and other functions.

Passport Designs
100 Stone Pine Rd.
Half Moon Bay, CA 94019
415-726-0280
415-726-2254 (F)

Audiotrax [Macintosh], $249. MIDI recording software that combines digital audio and MIDI; user can combine dialog/sound effects with MIDI compositions to create complete desktop presentation sound tracks or add narration/sound effects to visual presentations.

Master Tracks Pro 5 [Macintosh Plus and SE/30], $495. MIDI 64-track recording, sequencing, and editing software.

Master Tracks Pro for Windows [Windows 3.X], $395. MIDI 64-track recording, sequencing, and editing software.

MusicTime [Macintosh Plus], $249. Software for desktop music composition and notation that lets users create, play, print out, and record original compositions, played on MIDI-equipped musical instruments, on an IBM PC.

Trax [Macintosh Plus], $99. MIDI 64-track software that acts as a desktop MIDI recording studio; either MIDI instruments (required) or IBM PCs are used to arrange/compose music, add music to multimedia performances, or play along with an orchestra. MIDI interface required.

Trax for Windows [Windows 3.X], $99. MIDI 64-track software that acts as a desktop MIDI recording studio; either MIDI instruments (required) or IBM PCs are used to arrange/compose/edit/play back/record music, add music to multimedia performances, or play along with an orchestra; MIDI sound card or MPU-401 compatible MIDI interface required.

Roland Digital Group
1961 McGaw Ave.
Irvine, CA 92714
714-975-0560
714-975-0569 (F)

Music Editor Scorer and Arranger [MS-DOS], $695. Professional-quality MIDI composing, editing, sequencing, and printing of music manuscripts.

Steinberg/Jones
17700 Raymer St.
Northridge, CA 91325
818-993-4091
818-701-7452 (F)

Cubase Macintosh [Macintosh Plus and II], $495. MIDI 64-track editing and visual sequencing software; users can view song during creation.

Thinkware
130 Ninth St.
San Francisco, CA 94103
415-255-2091

Musicator GS [MS-DOS], price not available. 16-track combination
MIDI editing/notation/sequencing software that can read/write
standard MIDI files and print music notation.

Thoughtprocessors
584 Bergen St.
Brooklyn, NY 11238
718-857-2860
718-398-8411 (F)

Forte II [MS-DOS], $149. 16-channel MIDI track editor and sequencer
that supports MPU-401, C-1 and IBM Music Feature Card MQX-32.

FWAP! [MS-DOS], $59. Editing software that provides a rhythm pattern
generator to be used with drum machines or tone modules.

Note Processor [MS-DOS], $295. MIDI musical notation editing and
sequencing software that has real-time MIDI input and reads/write MIDI
files; compatible with TIFF-file desktop publishing programs.

TwelveTone Systems
44 Pleasant St.
Watertown, MA 02272
617-926-2480
617-924-6657 (F)

Cakewalk Apprentice [MS-DOS], $199. MIDI editing and recording
software that lets users record/edit/play back as many as 256 tracks.

Scanners

T HIS appendix lists only scanners with resolutions greater than 300 dots per inch (dpi), with a few exceptions, such as very high-performance/high-speed specialty scanners and a few popular Macintosh-only scanners with a maximum resolution of 300 dpi. For most professional multimedia applications, a 300 dpi resolution is the absolute minimum, and many systems offering multiple resolutions produce their highest resolutions (such as 300 dpi) only through software manipulation of the images.

Because of the number of products on the market, only a selection is listed in this appendix. All of the products listed here, and many more, are included on the disk that accompanies this book. The listings are in standard ASCII format, and the file is named APPXF.TXT. This file can be loaded into any word processor and searched for specific names, printed out, or read on screen. Most makers also offer a number of other models not listed.

PC-compatible scanners are listed first, with additional compatibility (such as PS/2 or Macintosh), if any, noted for each scanner. If there is no special notation, the scanner is only known to be compatible with standard PCs. SCSI-compatible scanners are generally compatible with all systems having SCSI ports, whether Macintosh, PC, or workstation, but software drivers might not be available for all combinations. Macintosh-only scanners are listed at the end of this appendix. In all listings, the address of the company appears first, followed by one or more of the products that company offers.

⇨ PC scanners

A4Tech
717 Brea Canyon Rd., Unit 12
Walnut, CA 91789
714-468-0071
714-468-2231 (F)

A4Gray AG256, $399. 100- to 400-dpi handheld text and image scanner for continuous tone, half-tone, and gray-scale imaging. Proprietary interface.

AVR Technology
71 E. Daggett Dr.
San Jose, CA 95134
408-434-1115
408-434-0968 (F)

AVR 3000/CL Plus, $1,795 to $1,995. SCSI-2 300- to 600-dpi
flatbed scanner for line art, continuous tone, half-tone, color,
photographs, and gray-scale.

AVR 8800/T, $3,190 to $3,290. SCSI-2 400- to 1,600-dpi flatbed
scanner for line art, color, photographs, transparencies, and gray-scale.

Chinon America
615 Hawaii Ave.
Torrance, CA 90503-9747
310-533-0274
310-533-1727 (F)

DS-3000 B&W, $695 to $895. PC, PS/2, and Macintosh 75- to
300-dpi desktop text and image scanner for line art, continuous tone,
half-tone, and gray-scale. SCSI, parallel, and serial interfaces.

DS-3000 Color, $995 to $1,195. PC, PS/2, and Macintosh 75-dpi
desktop text and image scanner for line art, continuous tone, half-tone,
color, photographs, gray-scale, and 3-D objects. SCSI, parallel, and serial
interfaces.

The Complete PC
1983 Concourse Dr.
San Jose, CA 95131
408-434-0145
408-434-1048 (F)

Complete Half-Page Scanner/400, $199. 200- to 400-dpi handheld
text and image scanner for line art, continuous tone, half-tone,
color, and photographs. Proprietary interface.

Complete Half-Page Scanner/GS, $349 to $399. PC and Macintosh 100-
to 400-dpi handheld image scanner for line art, half-tone, photographs,
and gray-scale. Proprietary interface.

Hewlett-Packard
3000 Hanover St.
Palo Alto, CA 94304
415-857-1501

HP ScanJet IIc, $1,599. PC, PS/2, and Macintosh SCSI 75- to 400-dpi desktop text and image scanner for color and gray-scale.

Hitachi Home Electronics
401 W. Artesia Blvd.
Compton, CA 90220
310-537-8383
310-515-6223 (F)

HS-700, $5,000. PC and Macintosh SCSI 300- to 600-dpi desktop text and image scanner for line art, continuous tone, half-tone, color, and photographs.

Houston Instrument/Summagraphics
8500 Cameron Rd.
Austin, TX 78753
512-835-0900
512-339-1490 (F)

LDS 4000 Plus, $13,995. 400-dpi dedicated scanner for photographs, drawings, and gray-scale; serial interface.

Howtek
21 Park Ave.
Hudson, NH 03051
603-882-5200
603-880-3843 (F)

Scanmaster 3+, $7,995 to $9,195. IBM PC and Macintosh 75- to 1,200-dpi desktop text and image scanner for line art, continuous tone, half-tone, color, art, photographs, reflective art, transparencies, and gray-scale; proprietary interface.

KYE International
2605 E. Cedar St.
Ontario, CA 91761
909-923-3510
909-923-1469 (F)

Genius C105 for Windows, $449. IBM PC and PS/2 100- to 400-dpi handheld text and image scanner for line art, continuous tone, half-tone, color, and gray-scale; proprietary interface.

Genius GS-FC60, $1,095. PC-based 600-dpi desktop text and image scanner for line art, color, and gray-scale.

Logitech
6505 Kaiser Dr.
Fremont, CA 94555
510-795-8500
510-792-8901 (F)

ScanMan Color, $699. PC and Macintosh SCSI 100- to 400-dpi handheld text and image scanner for color and gray-scale.

ScanMan Model 32 for PC, $299. 100- to 400-dpi handheld text and image scanner for line art, continuous tone, half-tone, and color; parallel interface.

Microtek Lab
680 Knox St.
Torrance, CA 90502
213-321-2121
310-538-1193 (F)

ScanMaker 600Z/ZS, $1,995. PC, PS/2, and Macintosh SCSI 600-dpi desktop text and image scanner for line art, half-tone, color, and gray-scale.

Mouse Systems
47505 Seabridge Drive
Fremont, CA 94538
510-656-1117
510-656-4409 (F)

PageBrush Color, $845. PC-based 100- to 400-dpi handheld image scanner for line art, continuous tone, half-tone, color, and gray-scale; proprietary interface.

Mustek
15225 Alton Pkwy.
Irvine, CA 92718
714-833-7740
714-833-7813 (F)

ColorArtist Pro CG-8000, $599. 100- to 800-dpi handheld text and image scanner for line art, continuous tone, half-tone, color, and gray-scale.

Ricoh
3001 Orchard Pkwy.
San Jose, CA 95134-2088
408-432-8800
408-432-8372 (F)

IS510, $17,000. SCSI-2 200- to 400-dpi desktop text and image scanner for line art, half-tone, and color.

➡️ Macintosh-only scanners

Scanners with a maximum resolution of only 300 dpi were eliminated from the PC listings because 300 dpi is not sufficient resolution for professional multimedia production. Apple Computer's scanners of 300 dpi are included here, however, because they are often purchased as part of a Macintosh system. Many of the previously listed scanners are also Macintosh-compatible as indicated in the list.

Apple Computer
20525 Mariani Ave.
Cupertino, CA 95014
408-996-1010
408-996-0275 (F)

Apple Color OneScanner, $1,349. SCSI 300-dpi flatbed text and image scanner suitable for line art and color.

The Complete PC
1983 Concourse Dr.
San Jose, CA 95131
408-434-0145
408-434-1048 (F)

Complete Page Scanner, $999. SCSI 200- to 300-dpi desktop text and image scanner for line art, continuous tone, half-tone, and photographs.

Envisions Solutions Technology
822 Mahler Rd.
Burlingame, CA 94010
415-692-9061
415-692-9064 (F)

ENV24Pro, $1,995. SCSI 1,200-dpi desktop text and image scanner for line art, continuous tone, half-tone, color, photographs, and gray-scale.

Logitech
6505 Kaiser Dr.
Fremont, CA 94555
510-795-8500
510-792-8901 (F)

ScanMan Model 32, $299 to $359. SCSI 100- to 400-dpi handheld text and image scanner for line art, continuous tone, half-tone, photographs, and gray-scale.

Mirror Technologies
2644 Patton Rd.
St. Paul, MN 55113
612-633-4450
612-633-3136 (F)

Model 600 Plus Color, $999 to $1,199. SCSI 600-dpi desktop text and image scanner for line art, color, and gray-scale.

Mouse Systems
47505 Seabridge Dr.
Fremont, CA 94538
510-656-1117
510-656-4409 (F)

True-Color Hand Scanner, $599. SCSI 100- to 400-dpi handheld text and image scanner for line art, half-tone, and color.

Mustek
15225 Alton Pkwy.
Irvine, CA 92718
714-833-7740
714-833-7813 (F)

MacAngelo II MFS-6000CS, $1,099 to $1,595. SCSI 600-dpi desktop text and image scanner for line art, half-tone, color, and gray-scale.

Thunderware
21 Orinda Way
Orinda, CA 94563
510-254-6581
510-254-3047 (F)

LightningScan Pro 256, $649. SCSI 100- to 400-dpi handheld text and image scanner for line art, continuous tone, half-tone, and gray-scale.

Multimedia authoring tools

I N all these listings, the address of the company appears first, followed by one or more of the products that company offers.

AimTech
20 Trafalgar Square
Nashua, NH 03063
800-289-2884
603-883-0220
603-883-5582 (F)

CATS MEOW, $2,525. Sun SPARCstation/SunOS CD multimedia authoring tool. Requires 16Mb RAM and OpenWindows.

IconAuthor, $4,995 to $75,000. HP 9000 Series 700/HP-UX, DEC/VMS, ULTRIX, Unisys, DG AViiON, and MS-DOS multimedia authoring tool. Requires 2Mb RAM and Motif.

IconAuthor for Windows, $4,995. Windows 3.X multimedia authoring tool for nonprogrammers. Requires 2Mb RAM and Windows 3.X.

Aldus
9770 Carroll Center Rd.
Suite J
San Diego, CA 92126-4551
800-888-6293
619-695-6956
619-695-7902 (F)

Aldus SuperCard, $299. Macintosh Plus, SE, SE/30, and II custom applications software for multimedia authoring. Requires 1Mb RAM.

Allen Communication
5225 Wiley Post Way
Lakeside Plaza II, Suite 140
Salt Lake City, UT 84116
800-325-7850
801-537-7800
801-537-7805 (F)

Quest, price not available. MS-DOS multimedia authoring system. Requires 1Mb RAM.

American Training International
12638 Beatrice St.
Los Angeles, CA 90066
310-823-1129
310-827-1636 (F)

Authology: MultiMedia, $4,500. MS-DOS authoring package using Intel's Digital Video Interactive technology.

TourGuide, $2,995. MS-DOS interactive multimedia authoring tool.

TourGuide for Windows, $2,995. Windows 3.X interactive multimedia authoring tool. Requires 4Mb RAM and Windows 3.X.

AskMe Information Center
7100 Northland Circle
Suite 401
Minneapolis, MN 55428
612-531-0603
612-531-0645 (F)

Ask, $495. MS-DOS interactive multimedia authoring program. Requires 2Mb RAM and register-level compatible card.

Asymetrix
110 110th Avenue, N.E.
Suite 700
Bellevue, WA 98004
206-462-0501
206-455-3071 (F)

Multimedia Resource Kit, $300. Windows 3.X multimedia authoring system.

Multimedia ToolBook, $695. Windows 3.X multimedia applications creation tool for Multimedia PC platform.

Boss Logic
1901 Landings Dr.
Mountain View, CA 94043
415-903-7000
415-903-7009 (F)

Document Manager, $1,295. NeXT multimedia document/workflow management program.

Computer Teaching
1713 S. State
Champaign, IL 61820
217-352-6363
217-352-3104 (F)

TenCORE Language Authoring System, $2,400. OS/2 and MS-DOS interactive courseware creation program that supports Windows.

TenCore Producer, $1,800. OS/2 and MS-DOS menu-driven authoring software.

Dataseek
7500 San Felipe
Houston, TX 77063
713-975-5175
713-975-5199 (F)

ProScribe, $2,997. MS-DOS multimedia authoring system. Requires 2Mb RAM, ActionMedia II display card, ActionMedia II capture option, and flatbed scanner or video camera.

Digital Equipment
146 Main St.
Maynard, MA 01754-2571
508-493-5111

DEC MediaImpact, price not available. DEC DECstation/ULTRIX multimedia authoring/presentation creation software. Requires DECwindows.

Discovery Systems International
7325 Oak Ridge Hwy.
Suite 100
Knoxville, TN 37931
615-690-8829
615-690-2913 (F)

Course Builder, $1,495. Macintosh, Plus, SE, and II visual authoring language for multimedia applications. Requires System 7.

Gain Technology
1870 Embarcadero Rd.
Palo Alto, CA 94303
415-813-1800
415-813-8300 (F)

GainMomentum, $15,000 and up. Sun SPARCstation/SunOS; DEC VAX, DECstation/VMS, and ULTRIX; IBM RS/6000/AIX; Hewlett Packard 9000 Series 700 and Apollo/HP-UX; Silicon Graphics/IRIX; and SCO UNIX application development software. Requires 16Mb RAM.

HSC Software
1661 Lincoln Blvd.
Suite 101
Santa Monica, CA 90404
310-392-8441

HSC InterActive Plus, $495. Windows 3.X multimedia authoring tool. Requires 2Mb RAM and sound card.

Humanities Computing Facilities
Duke University
104 Language Building
Durham, NC 27706
919-684-3637
919-681-6485 (F)

WinCALIS, $250. Windows 3.X CALIS (computer-assisted language instructional system) multimedia authoring tool with hypertext help and WinAuthor. Requires 640K RAM, speaker, video overlay board, and laser disc player.

IBM
Old Orchard Rd.
Armonk, NY 10504
914-765-1900

Audio Visual Connection, $571. OS/2 and MS-DOS multimedia authoring tool.

LinkWay Live!, $280 to $1,960. MS-DOS multimedia authoring tool supporting DVI technology.

Storyboard Live!, $395. OS/2 and MS-DOS beginner-level multimedia authoring software. Requires 640K RAM.

Instant Replay
P.O. Box 1750
Saint George, UT 84770-1750
800-388-8086
801-634-1054 (F)

Instant Replay Professional, $795. MS-DOS authoring program with graphical script development editor. Requires 640K RAM.

Interactive Support Group
9420 Topanga Canyon Blvd.
Chatsworth, CA 91311
818-709-7387
818-709-8160 (F)

CdiTools, price not available. Macintosh II Series and Sun SPARCstation/SunOS authoring system for CD-I disks. Requires 8Mb RAM and System 7.

Macromedia
600 Townsend St.
San Francisco, CA 94103
415-252-2000

Authorware Professional for Macintosh, $3,000. Macintosh icon-based multimedia authoring program. Requires 1Mb RAM and System 7.

Authorware Professional for Windows, $3,000. Windows 3.X icon-based multimedia authoring program.

Mathematica
402 S. Kentucky Ave.
Suite 210
Lakeland, FL 33801
800-852-6284
813-682-1128
813-686-5969 (F)

Tempra Media Author, $995. OS/2 and MS-DOS multimedia/video presentation manager with Tempra Pro and Tempra Turbo Animator. Requires 640K RAM.

Tempra Media Author for Windows, $1,985. Windows 3.X multimedia application program.

Tempra Show, $199. AT&T UNIX System V and OS/2 multimedia authoring tool.

Tempra Show for Windows, $199. Windows 3.X multimedia authoring program.

MediaShare
2035 Corte Del Nogal
Carlsbad, CA 92009
619-931-7171
619-431-5752 (F)

Opus, price not available. Windows 3.X multimedia application development tool with Opus Author authoring environment. Requires Windows 3.X.

Microsoft
One Microsoft Way
Redmond, WA 98052-6399
206-882-8080

Multimedia Development Kit, $500. Windows 3.X developers' kit that includes Multimedia Viewer and Multimedia Viewer Author Toolkit. Requires 2Mb RAM, Windows 3.X, a CD-ROM drive, Multimedia PC (MPC) system, and sound board.

Ntergaid
2490 Black Rock Turnpike, Suite 337
Fairfield, CT 06430
203-380-1280
203-380-1465 (F)

HyperWriter! for Windows, $695. Windows 3.X interactive hypermedia/multimedia authoring software.

HyperWriter!, $495. MS-DOS interactive hypermedia/multimedia authoring software. Requires 384K RAM.

Owl International
2800 156th Ave., S.E.
Bellevue, WA 98007
800-344-9737
206-747-3203
206-641-9367 (F)

Guide PC, $795. Windows 3.X authoring system for creation of interactive electronic documents.

Pacific Gold Coast
15 Glen St.
Suite 201
Glen Cove, NY 11542
516-759-3011
516-759-3014 (F)

Take-1, $395. MS-DOS multimedia authoring tool.

Paradise Software
55 Princeton-Hightown Rd.
Princeton Junction, NJ 08550
609-275-4475
609-275-4702 (F)

Mediawrite, $995. Sun SPARCstation/SunOS multimedia authoring software for creation of hypertext/hypermedia applications. Requires OpenWindows.

Q/Media Software
312 E. 5th Ave.
Vancouver, BC, Canada V5T 1H4
800-444-9356
604-879-1190
604-879-0214 (F)

Q/Media Professional for Windows, $495. Windows 3.X interactive multimedia presentation authoring tool for professionals.

Space & Aeronautical Sciences
P.O. Box 62519
Colorado Springs, CO 80962
719-599-8251

Challenger! Desktop Training System, price not available. Windows 3.X multimedia authoring tool that includes Challenger/Author, Challenger/Manager, and Challenger/Tutor.

UniSQL
9390 Research II
Suite 200
Austin, TX 78759
512-343-7297
512-343-7383 (F)

UniSQL/X Database Management System, $3,995. IBM RS/6000/AIX, Sun SPARCstation/SunOS, and Solbourne combined object-oriented/relational client/server database system.

Pointing devices

THE products listed in this appendix control the movement of the cursor. Although cursor movement is not very important for most nongraphical user interface programs (such as word processors or spreadsheets) virtually all multimedia production requires such a pointing device, either to speed editing or as part of a graphics-creation package.

Mice are often bundled with new computers now that Windows is becoming a popular preloaded environment, but many older systems still do not have a mouse or other pointing device and need one added. While the mice supplied with Windows systems are usually adequate for operating Windows itself, they often lack features demanded by those who do extensive graphics creation or editing. Not many specialized keyboards have built-in pointing devices; thus, these specialized keyboards are only listed in Chapter 12 and not repeated here.

Because of the number of products on the market, only a select few are listed in this appendix. These pointing devices and many more, are included on the disk that accompanies this book. The listings are in standard ASCII format, and the file is named APPXH.TXT. This file can be loaded into any word processor and searched for specific names, printed out, or read on screen.

In all these listings, the address of the company appears first, followed by one or more of the products that company offers.

 # Mice

Amazing Technologies
1050 W. Beacon St.
Brea, CA 92621
714-255-1688
714-255-1686 (F)

AAR-500, $200. Wireless, three-button serial-port mouse; 100- to 800-dpi resolution. PC-compatible.

Advanced Gravis Computer Technology
7400 MacPherson Ave.
Suite 111
Burnaby, BC, Canada V5J 5B6
800-663-8558
604-431-5155 (F)

Gravis SuperMouse, $130. Three-button mouse; self-cleaning ball
mechanism; 320-dpi resolution; Gravis Utilities software required.
Macintosh-compatible.

Kraft Systems
450 W. California Ave.
Vista, CA 92083
619-724-7146
619-941-1770 (F)

Kraft Mouse, $80. Three-button mouse; 10- to 1150-dpi resolution.
PC-compatible.

Logitech
6505 Kaiser Dr.
Fremont, CA 94555
510-795-8500
510-792-8901 (F)

3-D Mouse, $999. Five-button pointing device; a "suspend" button
(designed for applications and multidimensional, spatial graphics-
supporting hardware, such as CAD/CAM and virtual reality). Becomes
a standard three-button mouse in 400-dpi mode; built-in microphone
connects to speech/sound recognition systems; serial port mouse.

Mouse Systems
47505 Seabridge Dr.
Fremont, CA 94538
510-656-1117
510-656-4409 (F)

A3 Mouse, $135. Optomechanical, three-button mouse; 300-dpi
resolution. PC- and PS/2-compatible.

NewMouse Cordless, $130. Three-button, optomechanical mouse; 400-
dpi resolution. PCs and PS/2s.

PC Mouse 3D-6D, $400. Multidimensional, three-button mouse; either
300- or 600-dpi resolution; Microsoft, Mouse Systems, and Mouse
Systems 3-D compatible. PC-compatible.

⇨ Trackballs

A trackball can be thought of as an inverted mouse. They are sometimes built into keyboards (see Chapter 12). Selected standalone trackballs are listed below.

Amazing Technologies
1050 W. Beacon St.
Brea, CA 92621
714-255-1688
714-255-1686 (F)

AAK-300, $59. Three-button trackball; 50- to 800-dpi resolution; serial interface. PC-compatible.

A4Tech
717 Brea Canyon Rd.
Unit 12
Walnut, CA 91789
714-468-0071
714-468-2231 (F)

A4Trac Model AT-5P, $89. Optomechanical trackball; 600-mm-per-second tracking speed; 300- to 1,450-dpi resolution; Image72 paint program included. PC-compatible.

CTI Electronics
200 Benton St.
Stratford, CT 06497
203-386-9779
203-378-4986 (F)

T12X3, $695. Trackball with 2"-diameter. PC- and Macintosh-compatible.

DynaPoint
1016-B Lawson St.
City of Industry, CA 91748
818-854-6440
818-854-6444 (F)

DynaTrak, $70. Right- or left-handed trackball; serial and IBM PS/2 mouse port connectors; adjustable tilt for angle positioning; breakaway clamp assembly; drivers for DOS and Windows applications. PC- and PS/2-compatible.

Kensington Microware
2855 Campus Dr.
San Mateo, CA 94403
415-572-2700
415-572-9675 (F)

Expert Mouse, $150–$180. Right- or left-handed two-button trackball; three-button, optomechanical technology; 200-dpi resolution; bus and serial versions; Windows 3.0 version with software designed for custom acceleration and double-click control. PC- and PS/2-compatible.

Key Tronic
N. 4424 Sullivan Rd.
Spokane, WA 99216-0687
509-928-8000
509-927-5248 (F)

TrakMate, $149. Trackball built into an adjustable, free-standing wrist pad; two extra LED buttons for changing pointing speed and engaging drag lock. PC- and PS/2-compatible.

KYE International
2605 E. Cedar St.
Ontario, CA 91761
909-923-3510
909-923-1469 (F)

GeniTrac HiTrak, $75. Trackball with 350- to 1,050-dpi resolution; autodetection mode between two- and three-button mouse mode; PC Paintbrush IV software. PC- and PS/2-compatible.

Microsoft
One Microsoft Way
Redmond, WA 98052-6399
206-882-8080
206-883-8101 (F)

Ballpoint, $175. Two-version (right- and left-handed) clip-on laptop mouse/trackball; two programmable keys on each side; user-adjustable angles.

MicroSpeed
44000 Old Warm Springs Blvd.
Fremont, CA 94538
510-490-1403
510-490-1665 (F)

FastTrap, $149–$169. Trackball (bus or serial version), for X/Y axis; with a Z-axis fingerwheel; 3-D input. PC- and PS/2-compatible.

Multipoint Technology
319 Littleton Rd.
Suite 201
Westford, MA 01886
508-692-0689
08-692-2653 (F)

Multipoint Z 3-D Mouse, $250. Three-button mouse with mouse ball underneath, 3-D trackball on top, and side thumbwheel; allows six degrees of freedom for pan, zoom, and view rotation. PC- and Macintosh-compatible.

Winner Products
821 S. Lemon Ave.
Suite A-9
Walnut, CA 91789
909-595-2490
909-595-1483 (F)

T2+ Trackball, $60. Three-button trackball; 115- to 1,150-dpi resolution; automatically adjusted resolution; window lock. PC- and PS/2-compatible.

⇨ Joysticks

Advanced Gravis Computer Technology
7400 MacPherson Ave.
Suite 111
Burnaby, BC, Canada V5J 5B6
604-431-5020
604-431-5155 (F)

Gravis Analog Joystick, $60. Joystick with eight-position centering tension; three microswitch fire buttons; pistol grip handle with fire button. PC-compatible.

Gravis GamePad, $30. Control pad/joystick combination with detachable handle to convert to pad; four-button option. PC- and Macintosh-compatible.

IMSI
1938 4th St.
San Rafael, CA 94901
415-454-7101
415-454-8901 (F)

IMSI Joystick, $80. Two-button, free-floating joystick with spring-centering control modes; permits right- and left-handed play. PC-compatible.

Measurement Systems
777 Commerce Dr.
Fairfield, CT 06430
203-336-4590
203-336-5945 (F)

Model JTX Joystick, price not given. Joystick, in quadrature square wave and serial outputs, that emulates common mouse formats; has an impact-resistant case; designed for industrial and professional applications. PC- and PS/2-compatible.

⇨ Graphics tablets

Chisholm
910 Campisi Way
Campbell, CA 95008
408-559-1111
408-559-0444 (F)

ColorWriter CW2, $3,495. Electronic chalkboard with eight-color projection; works with any color projection device; supports VGA, EGA, CGA, Macintosh video, or 640 × 480 resolution; PC-compatible.

Kurta
3007 E. Chambers St.
Phoenix, AZ 85040
602-276-5533
602-276-7823 (F)

IS/ADB, $495–$965. Graphics tablet in several sizes (8.5" × 11", 12" × 12", or 12" × 17" surface); 23 programmable function keys; comes with either a corded pen/cursor or a cordless pen/cursor; requires Apple System Tools Release 6; Macintosh-compatible.

MicroTouch Systems
300 Griffin Park
Methuen, MA 01844-9867
508-659-9000
508-659-9100 (F)

PC UnMouse, $199. Small glass graphics tablet; attaches to serial port; 1,000 × 1,000 resolution; power key pad for macros. Users can position cursor or trace images by moving a stylus or their finger around the 3" × 4.5" active area. PC- and PS/2-compatible.

Mouse Systems
47505 Seabridge Dr.
Fremont, CA 94538
510-656-1117
510-656-4409 (F)

PenMate, $350. Graphics tablet; uses a 9" × 6" work area; two-button pointing system; Microsoft Mouse protocol support; PC- and PS/2-compatible.

Summagraphics
60 Silvermine Rd.
Seymour, CT 06483-3907
203-881-5400
203-881-5367 (F)

SummaScribe, $499. Graphics tablet for pen-based computing; uses a 6" × 6" active area; comes with pen stylus to edit documents and/or enter handwritten data; Microsoft Windows for Pen Computing software; PC-compatible.

Standard file formats

BIN	Driver, overlay
BIT	Lotus
BMP	OS/2
BMP	Windows
CDR	Corel Draw vector graphics
CE	Computer Eyes (video)
CEB	Continuous Edge bitmap (for users of CEG video boards)
CEG	Edsun Continuous Edge Graphics
CGM	CGM vector graphics
CLP	Windows Clipboard files
CUT	Dr. Halo
CVP	Kodak's Color Video Printer
DIB	Windows
DLL	Dynamic link library
DRW	Micrografx Designer vector graphics
DWG, **DXF**	AutoCAD vector formats
EPS	Encapsulated PostScript
FLC, **FLI**	AutoDesk animation
GED	Arts & Letters graphics
GEM	GEM vector graphics
GIF	CompuServe raster graphics
GRF	Micrografx Charisma vector graphics
GX1, **GX2**	Show Partner raster graphics
HEX	Generic hexadecimal format
IFF	Amiga/Video Toaster
IMG	Aurora (Data Translation)
IMG	DT-Iris (Data Translation)
IMG	GEM Paint raster graphics
IMG	Ventura
LBM	Deluxe Paint
MCP	MacPaint
MID	MIDI
MSP	Microsoft Paint
PCC	PC Paintbrush Clipboard files
PCT	Macintosh Color bitmap
PCX	ZSoft PC Paintbrush
PPM	Unix portable pixmap
RAS	Sun Raster
RGB	Silicon Graphics
RLE	Compressed Windows bitmap

SLD	AutoCAD slide
SVW	Super Video Windows
TGA	Targa
TIF	Tagged Image File Format
VOC	Creative Labs (SoundBlaster) VOiCe file
WAV	Windows sound file format
WMF	Windows Metafile
WPG	WordPerfect Raster format

Glossary

ADPCM Acronym for adaptive pulse code modulation. The digital audio compression technique used to store up to 16 hours of narration-quality audio information on a CD-ROM disc using CD-ROM XA specification.

AFTRA Acronym for American Federation of Television and Radio Artists. A broadcast talent workers' union.

all rights The rights to use text, sound, or images in all markets. A distributor or publisher buying "all rights" to a work can sell it to TV, cable, home video, and foreign markets or include it in other creations.

Alpha A high-performance 64-bit microprocessor made by Digital Equipment that runs Windows NT programs.

analog Continuously varying signal.

ANSI Acronym for American National Standards Institute. Designates a U.S. standard. ANSI standards are available from ANSI, 1430 Broadway, New York, NY 10018; 212-642-4900.

ANSI labeled tape One of the standard formats for data stored on 9-track tapes. CD-ROM files are placed on 9-track tapes for processing because much of the data comes from mainframe computers, which commonly have this capability. This format uses ANSI-standard volume labels and contains extensive information about the files on the tape.

ANSI tape standards Physical specifications for the magnetic tape used to hold mastered CD-ROM data, such as ANSI X3.39 (1600 bpi) or ANSI X3.54 (6250 bpi). Make sure you supply a tape that your production facility (pressing plant) can use.

anti-aliasing Automatically inserting tiny intermediate color or gray elements to smooth transition on the boundary of jagged diagonal lines.

AppleTalk Apple Computer's built-in network that links two or more Macintoshes or PCs together to share files and devices.

artifact Distortion caused by over-processing a video or audio signal.

ASCAP Acronym for the American Society of Composers, Arrangers, and Performers, which registers and licenses music created in the United States.

ASCII Acronym for the American Standard Code for Information Interchange. A near-universal file format used to share text between different programs.

aspect ratio The ratio of height to width in an image. Displaying an image created in one aspect ratio in a window that is not a multiple (both height and width multiplied by the same number) of the ratio can cause distortion.

AT bus (or PC AT) The 16-bit computer architecture invented by IBM. Also referred to as the ISA (industry standard architecture) bus.

autotrace A utility that outlines raster graphics images and converts them into vector graphics.

A/V Abbreviation of audio/visual. Equipment used in electronic media.

binary The two-element (base-2) numbering system used by digital computers.

bit A single binary digit.

bitmapped Images defined by individual pixel elements (i.e., dot-by-dot). Paint programs create bitmapped images.

blackout Fade to blank screen.

browse mode The ability to page through the data on a CD-ROM like a book instead of looking up various items using the search mode.

buffer Hardware or software device used to speed data transfer.

byte The common unit of measuring computer data. One byte of data represents one letter, symbol, or number from 0 to 9. Thus, a 1,000-byte word processing file would contain about 1,000 letters, numbers, spaces, punctuation marks, or special characters. A byte is usually 8 bits (i.e., 10110001).

CAD Acronym for computer-aided design. Vector image creation software.

capture board An interface card installed in the computer motherboard and used to capture and process sound or video signals.

CCD Acronym for charge coupled device. The photo-sensitive element used in place of film to record an image and convert it into a digital signal.

CD Acronym for compact disc. The shiny 12-cm (4.72") diameter discs that contain up to an hour of music digitally recorded and are capable of far higher fidelity than analog records. Most laser-scanned media discs are digital in nature; CD is the name of the

product physically identical to CD-ROM discs but containing digitally encoded music/sound exclusively. Also known as the Red Book standard.

CD-DA Acronym for compact disc-digital audio. Another term for the CD audio or music disc.

CD-I Acronym for compact disc-interactive. A proposed CD-ROM data format standard that goes beyond Red and Yellow Book standards to include hardware and software standards that allow data, audio, and video images to be placed on the same disc and accessed as a single unit. Also known as the Green Book standard. Philips and Sony are responsible for CD-I.

CD-recordable Also CD-WO, the writable, CD-ROM-compatible system that allows users to create CD-ROM discs on desktop recorders.

CD-ROM Acronym for compact disc-read-only memory. Physically identical with the CD audio disc but contains text/data information instead of audio information. A minimum of 550Mb of data fit on a 12-cm disk. Also the defining standard for the CD- ROM (sometimes referred to as the Yellow Book standard) refers to the physical size and structure of the media. Does not specify any data file structures, such as High-Sierra.

CD-ROM disc player Essentially the same as an audio CD player except for the read-laser head positioning mechanism. Some CD-ROM players have the capability of playing CD audio discs, but not vice versa.

CD-ROM XA (Extended Architecture) The latest standard proposed by Microsoft, Philips, and Sony. Includes both graphics (CD-I) and data (CD-ROM) as well as audio on the same disc. The proposed XA players will read CD-ROM discs, but CD-ROM players will require modification or new adapter cards to play CD-ROM XA discs. The advantage of this standard is that it allows simultaneous access of data and audio because XA allows audio and other data to reside on the same track. CD-ROM XA also allows audio compression techniques.

CD-WO CD write-only or recordable. CD-ROM compatible discs that can be created on a desktop drive and played back on any standard CD-ROM drive.

cel Slang for the celluloid plastic sheets once used to create all animation. In software, refers to an image clipped from a video frame.

CIRC Acronym for cross-interleaved Reed-Solomon code. The base error-correction code used on CD and CD-ROM discs. *See* Levels and Modes.

CMYK (Cyan, Magenta, Yellow, and blacK) Color model used in four-color process printing.

color cycling Using rapidly changing colors to liven up a still image or make it appear animated. Used judiciously, this can be an easy way to improve animation appearance at little cost.

color models Systems by which color is defined for various media. RGB color is often used in computers; the CMYK model, based on reflected light, is used in printing; and the HSB model uses hue (the part of the spectrum), saturation (the intensity of color), and brightness (the amount of light).

compression Any of a number of techniques used to pack more data into the same number of data blocks. These algorithms place more information in the same number of bytes of data; the CD-ROM physical standard remains the same.

cue channel Videotape track used to store time-related signals.

cut Attaching two frames or sequences end-to-end with no transition effects.

device driver The software needed to link a computer with any external device such as a CD-ROM. Device drivers run printers, serial ports, and other computer hardware and form the intermediary between the computer and the outside world. An example of a driver is HITACHI.SYS used for Hitachi and Amdek

drives. Other drivers include ANSI.SYS, which provides enhanced monitor displays and FASTDISK.SYS, which creates a RAM disk in memory. Drivers are installed as a part of the CONFIG.SYS file. E.g., DEVICE=HITACHI.SYS /D:MSCD001 /N:1.

digital A yes/no-, on/off-type signal used by computers and easily stored as binary data.

digital camera A camera that captures an image electronically on a CCD instead of traditional film. Also called a filmless or still video camera.

DIN Acronym for Deutsche Industrie-Norm. German electronic connection plug standard. MIDI uses a 5-pin DIN connector.

dithering A smoothing technique where boundaries of images are blended together slightly to reduce unnatural sharpness of images.

dpi Acronym for dots per inch. The number of pixel elements recorded for every inch of an image. The higher the dpi, the finer the resolution.

DSP Acronym for digital signal processor. Specialized microprocessor devoted to high-performance audio signal processing.

DV-I Acronym for digital video-interactive. General Electric's contribution to CD-ROM standards. Fits up to one hour of video on a CD-ROM. The major difference between DV-I and CD-I is in the amount of full-motion video encoded on the disc. DV-I discs play on standard CD-ROM players with the addition of two video processor chips in a new controller board. The 30-frame/second DV-I has been endorsed by Bill Gates (Chairman of Microsoft), as well as Intel Corp. and Lotus Development Corp. (DV-I for an AT-compatible costs about $6,000.)

ECC/EDC Error-correction coding and data correction used to supplement the base CIRC error coding on all CDs. This extra error-correction provides the data quality needed by computers.

The ECC/EDC information is calculated and added to the data during the premastering step.

ELV Acronym for edit-level video. The 10-frame/second development-level video for DV-I that can be compressed and stored on a microcomputer using a special compression board from Intel.

error-correction codes *See* CIRC and ECC/EDC.

error-correction quality Although CIRC and ECC/EDC are specified for CD-ROM recordings, some drives make more extensive use of the built-in error-correction codes.

ESDI Acronym for enhanced system device interface. A nearly obsolete type of high-performance hard drive and drive controller. Modern SCSI-2 drives have almost entirely replaced ESDI.

file formats The data stored by programs.

first rights The right to the first use of a copyrighted work. Provides an exclusive right to use the image or document only once.

flatbed scanner A digitizer that converts drawings and other flat images to computer files.

flic Autodesk's term for a video clip or sequence of frames.

fractals Special mathematical creations from the field of chaos research that enhance images, especially natural objects, such as trees, clouds and rivers.

frame A single complete image from which a movie or animation is made.

frame grabber A video capture board.

gigabyte One billion bytes.

Green Book standard *See* CD-I.

gray scale A range of gray tones between black and white.

HSB Color model that uses hue, saturation, and brightness to define a color.

hue Color.

index CD-ROM discs must be indexed just as a book because of the amount of data they contain and, as in a large reference book, the quality of the index determines how usable a specific CD-ROM is. Typically, a CD-ROM index is a full-text database that includes the location of each occurrence of all but the most common words (a concordance). Some discs, mainly those containing shareware and public domain software, are organized in standard directories with no special indexing of any sort.

ISO 9660 Essentially the High-Sierra Group standard for CD-ROM file formats. The International Standards Organization logical file format standard that specifies a consistent volume table of contents and directory structure. This standard lets discs be accessed, at least to the extent of displaying the disc's contents, on different computer systems such as MS-DOS and Macintosh.

jewel case The plastic case often used to store CD and CD-ROM discs.

JPEG A standard for image compression devised by the Joint Photographic Experts Group, experts sanctioned by the International Standards Organization (ISO) and the CCITT. Provides for 20:1 to 30:1 data compression with little loss or up to 100:1 for lower-quality reproduction.

jukebox An automatic storage and loading device that permits remote/automatic access to large quantities of data stored on multiple optical discs, usually the larger laser discs. It holds various discs in indexed positions and can sequentially or randomly load them into the scanning drive, just as its namesake can store, select, and play records.

Kaleida A joint venture between Apple and IBM to create multimedia products.

kilobyte (K) Roughly used to mean 1,000 bytes, although it is actually a binary number equaling 1,024 bytes. In typical use, there is not enough difference to make any effort to be precise, especially because kilobyte is almost always used in a technical sense where it does mean 1,024 bytes and any one who cares about the details would understand the possible confusion.

Level 0 A track on a CD disc having only the base CIRC error-correction code. Level 0 uses EFM and CIRC only and can be read by any CD (audio, ROM, etc.) player.

Level 1 Every CD-ROM drive can read Level 1, which includes further error-correction coding layered over CIRC. Level 1 has two modes; *see* Mode 1 and Mode 2.

mastering Transferring data to create the master glass form which is used to "press" the plastic discs that are the actual CD-ROMs. Mastering also involves producing metal production forms used to make final distribution discs. (Cost range of $2,000 to $12,000.)

MCI Acronym for media control interface. A programming interface from IBM/Microsoft for controlling multimedia devices.

megabyte Either 1,000,000 bytes or 1,048,576 bytes. The odd number is due to the nature of binary arithmetic and generally it doesn't matter which precise definition is being used.

metallizing Vapor deposition of aluminum on the newly pressed plastic (polycarbonate) disc. Places the reflective surface on the plastic which is then overcoated to prevent corrosion and physical damage.

Microsoft Extensions MSCDEX.EXE is the program first announced by Microsoft Corp. in September of 1986 which lets MS-DOS 3.1 or higher access 550Mb of data on a CD-ROM disc as a single drive, eliminating the 32Mb file limitation that existed in DOS until DOS 4.00. These were High-Sierra compatible

extensions and are only available on an OEM basis. You can copy from or run programs directly from the CD-ROM drive but can't perform any operation that requires writing to the device. By convention, a DIR always shows "0 bytes free" at the end because none of the empty space can be used for anything.

MO Acronym for magneto-optical. The technology used for some erasable drives (Sony and Ricoh drives use this method), where a strong magnetic field is used to change the magnetic orientation of tiny spots on the disc when the spots are heated using a laser beam. The optical characteristics of the disc are changed in these areas, allowing a weaker laser beam to "read" the spots as data.

Mode 1 A CD-ROM track format standard implementing an error-correction code. (Level 1)

Mode 2 A CD-ROM track format lacking error correction. (Level 1)

morphing The video special effect that takes a beginning and end image and creates a smooth series of transition images that make one image appear to slowly change into the other. The more intermediate steps involved, the smoother the transition. Morphing is used in TV commercials to change one car into another and so forth, but is especially well-known from the movie *Terminator 2*, where the villain regularly transformed from a silver blob into various people and objects. Some documentation calls this tweening, but it is generally called morphing, short for metamorphosing.

MPC Multimedia standard managed by the Multimedia PC Marketing Council but essentially defined by Microsoft and requiring Microsoft Windows. MPC trademark licensing costs $250,000, while upgrade kit makers can stick the MPC label on their ads and products by shelling out $100,000.

MPEG Motion Picture Experts Group video compression technique that saves space by only noting changes between adjacent frames.

NTSC Acronym for National Television Standards Committee. North American standard for the generation, transmission, and reception of television communication using a 525-line picture.

offline Working on copy of the video footage, for reference only.

online editing Actual editing on the original source material. This can be done manually or automatically, using timing signals created during offline editing.

Orange Book The writable CD specification, developed and licensed by Sony and Philips, allowing developers to lay down digital data streams on a writable optical disc also known as CD-WO (write-once) or CD recordable.

OS/2 IBM's 32-bit operating system for the PC that was intended to compete with the advanced Windows environment (at least after Microsoft pulled out of OS/2 codevelopment).

PAL Color TV standard used in Western Europe having 625 lines.

PCM Acronym for pulse code modulation. Speech-digitizing system.

phono cable Inexpensive wiring often used with audio and video signals and ending in RCA-style plugs.

ping-pong Creating animation by having an object bounce back and forth, usually in the same path.

overhead The amount of storage space lost to the index of a full-text database, typically up to one-half of the storage space required for the information contained in the database.

Photo CD The Kodak system of storing photographic images on CD-ROM discs.

pixels Abbreviation for "picture elements," the dots that build up bitmapped images. These are the smallest visual elements stored or processed.

PLV Acronym for presentation-level video. The full, high-quality, 30-frame/second DV-I video signal that must be compressed using a mainframe computer at a special DV-I processor center.

premastered tape A 9-track tape with the data ready for transfer to the glass master disc.

premastering Formatting and otherwise preparing the data for transfer to the master disc, including the addition of error-correction information.

pressing/replication Injection molding of the CD-ROM discs, using the metal masters created from the glass master.

QuickTime Multimedia extensions to the Macintosh System 7 operating system that adds sound and video capabilities.

RAID Acronym for redundant arrays of inexpensive disks. Mass storage system using multiple hard drives.

raster A bitmapped image.

raw footage Original (unedited) video.

Red Book The CD audio physical standard specifying a 12-cm disc containing 72 minutes of high-quality sound stored on a three-mile-long spiral track, played back using the constant linear velocity (CLV) method. Same physical standard used by CD-ROM discs and drives.

RGB Red/Green/Blue. The second major way of specifying colors and editing different sequences together so the colors are not jarringly different. The other method of defining colors is HLS.

RIFF Acronym for resource interchange file format. The multimedia data format jointly introduced by IBM and Microsoft.

RS-232, RS-422 Serial communication standards that allow computer control of VCRs. Typically used to connect computers to modems for data transfer.

runtime Special software included with some multimedia productions that help run the program.

SCSI Acronym for small computer system interface, pronounced SCUZZY. The SCSI specification available from ANSI. SCSI is a relatively fast interface for scanners, CD-ROM, and hard drives. Few PCs come with SCSI built in, but Macintosh computers come with SCSI. SCSI is notorious for being a nonstandard; that is, while it is supposed to be easy to use to interface different devices, it often doesn't work. The 8-bit SCSI (or SCSI-1) supports up to eight devices per port and allows up to five megabytes per second data transfer speed.

SCSI-2 A 16-bit SCSI which is faster than the original SCSI and also much more compatible. Eight-bit SCSI-2 provides double the transfer speed of SCSI-1, but a full 16- or 32-bit SCSI-2 port and cable provides for up to 40 megabytes per second data transfer rate.

SCSI-3 A proposed SCSI standard that would allow the user to daisy-chain more devices than do SCSI and SCSI-2 ports.

search and retrieval software There is little standardization here; different publishers use different retrieval programs and different user interfaces. BlueFish, SilverPlatter, and TMS use menu-driven and command-line interfaces, while MicroBASIS and DIALOG are command languages.

SECAM TV standard used in France and former French colonies.

second rights Permission to use images or text after the more expensive and exclusive first-time use.

SGML Acronym for standard generalized mark-up language. A set of descriptive mark-up standards for manuscripts developed by the Association of American Publishers. A guideline for data preparation to simplify transfer to CD-ROMs, but only one of several such standards. SGML is popular in the Federal Government.

SIGCAT Acronym for Special Interest Group on CD-ROM Applications and Technology. A group started in 1985 and based at the U.S. Geological Survey Headquarters in Reston, Virginia, but open to nongovernment members. Its purpose is to serve as a focus group and information forum for government personnel interested in how the technology could be applied to their departments.

stop words The words (such as *and*, *but*, *a*, etc.) that are not indexed when producing full-text database indexes.

sync generator Provides a signal that allows smooth video editing.

terabyte One thousand billion bytes.

transition effects Various ways of changing from one image to another very different one (not animation where the change is between very similar images). This includes fade-in/fade-out, dissolves, wipes, and so forth.

true color 16,777,216 (24-bit) color.

Ultimedia IBM's term for multimedia.

vector image As opposed to a bitmapped image, this type consists of equations that define starting and end points of image elements along with descriptions of how the line curves between points. Vector images are much more precise than paint (bitmap) images and can be enlarged to any arbitrary size.

videodisc A standard 12"-diameter disc used to store video programs and associated audio tracks in an analog form. This format has won out over RCA's CED (Capacitance Electronic Discharge) movie disc format but is an analog storage device as used to store images. The same disc or the 8" size is also used for storing computer data in digital form. The video and computer discs may be identical but the drives and circuitry are quite different, unlike CD and CD-ROM drives which are both digital.

video RAM Special memory (RAM) used to speed performance of video imaging.

wireframe A transparent outline of an image element usually showing *every* edge, even those hidden in a certain view. Wireframe animation is used as a shortcut drawing technique, which is then filled in by the software to create an image.

WORM Acronym for write once-read many. This is a writable laser disc that differs from CD-ROM discs in several ways. First, the smaller WORM discs are 5.25" in diameter, so they won't even fit in a CD-ROM drive, and, second, the disk is not metallized in the same way. A WORM disc can be written to and the data (up to 800Mb or so) can also be destroyed by overwriting, but the overwritten area can't be reused to store new data, unlike an erasable magneto-optical disc. Larger WORM discs also exist holding proportionally more data (in the gigabytes).

Yellow Book The CD-ROM standard that specifies the way data are actually recorded and the Reed-Solomon error-correction method.

Sources

⇨ Books

Grotta, Sally Wiener and Daniel Grotta. *Digital Imaging for Visual Artists*. Blue Ridge Summit, PA: Windcrest/McGraw-Hill, 1994.

Heimlich, Richard with David M. Golden, Ivan Luk, and Peter M. Ridge. *Sound Blaster, The Official Book*. Berkeley, CA: Osborne/McGraw-Hill, 1993.

Juliussen, Karen Petska, and Egil Juliussen. *The 6th Annual Computer Industry Almanac, 1993*. Lake Tahoe, NV: Computer Industry Almanac, Inc.

McCormick, John A. *A Guide to Optical Storage Technology*. Burr Ridge, IL: Dow Jones-Irwin, 1990.

McCormick, John A. *The New Optical Storage Technology, Including Multimedia, CD-ROM and Optical Drives*. Burr Ridge, IL: Irwin Professional Publishing, 1994.

Microsoft Corporation. *Microsoft Windows Multimedia Programmer's Reference*. Redmond, WA: Microsoft Press, 1991. Included with the Microsoft Windows Multimedia Development Kit.

Microsoft Corporation. *Microsoft Windows Multimedia Programmer's Workbook.* Redmond, WA: Microsoft Press, 1991.

Moss, Julian. *Upgrading, Maintaining, & Servicing IBM PCs & Compatibles.* San Marcos, CA: Microtrend Books, Slawson Communications, Inc., 1992.

Sheldon, Tom. *Windows 3.1, the Complete Reference, 2nd Ed.* Berkeley, CA: Osborne/McGraw-Hill, 1993.

Vaughan, Tay. *Multimedia, Making it Work.* Berkeley, CA: Osborne/McGraw-Hill, 1993.

Yankelovich, N., K.E. Smith, L.N. Garrett, and N. Meyrowitz. "Issues in Designing a Hypermedia Document System." *Interactive Media,* eds. Ambron, S. and K. Hooper. Redmond, WA: Microsoft Press, 1988.

Electronic Computer Glossary. The Computer Language Co. Inc., 1993.

Newton's Telecom Dictionary. Harry Newton, 1993.

⇨ Software documentation

Adobe Illustrator, Adobe Corp.

Advanced PRO-PATH 6, SoftCorp.

Aldus Freehand, Aldus Corp.

Ami Professional, Lotus Development Corp.

Arts & Letters, Computer Support Corp.

Authorware Professional for Windows, Macromedia.

Autodesk Animator Pro, Autodesk.

Autodesk 3D Studio, Autodesk.

Cakewalk Professional, Twelve Tone Systems.

Electric Image Animation System, Electric Image Corp.

IBM OS/2 2.1, International Business Machines and Microsoft Corp.

Instant Replay Professional, Instant Replay Inc.

HyperWriter!, Ntergaid.

Microsoft Windows 3.0, Microsoft Corp.

Microsoft Windows 3.1, Microsoft Corp.

MS-DOS 3.11, 4.0, 5.0, and 6.0, Microsoft Corp.

Photofinish, ZSoft Corp.

Photomagic for Windows, Micrografx.

Project Scheduler 5, Scitor.

Publisher's Paintbrush, ZSoft Corp.

Q/Media Professional for Windows, Q/Media.

Studio Vision, Opcode.

Tempra Media & Tempra Pro, Mathematica.

TimeLine, Symantec.

⇨ Video

Note Newsbytes is an electronic news service available from a number of sources, including archival CD-ROM from the publisher and through online services including: GEnie, CompuServe (Ziffnet), America Online, Internet (Clarinet), and Prodigy.

Blankenhorn, Dana. 1992. "COMDEX: A Big Show Surprise: SuperMac Videospigot." *Newsbytes News Network*, 20 November 1992.

——. 1993. "Compression Labs Vs. PictureTel." *Newsbytes News Network*, 3 February 1993.

——. 1993. "Digital Video Announcements." *Newsbytes News Network*, 26 April 1993.

Buckler, Grant. "IBM Foresees Many Uses for Compression Chip." *Newsbytes News Network*, 17 August 1993.

Buckler, Grant and Wendy Woods. "New Special Effects Firm Due Tomorrow from IBM." *Newsbytes News Network*, 24 February 1993.

Computer Currents. "MovieWorks Creates QuickTime Movies on Mac." *Newsbytes News Network*, 12 March 1993.

Cross, Jerry. "Playing Live Digital Video under Windows." *Windows/DOS Developer's Journal*, 3 (3), 1992: 39–48.

Emigh, Jacqueline. "Software Dev't '93—Morph's Outpost Mag Debuts." *Newsbytes News Network*, 30 August 1993.

Fulco, William. "The QuickTime/AVK Connection: Building a Beautiful Relationship." *Dr. Dobb's Journal*, 17 (7), 1992: 28–29.

Green, James L. "Capturing Digital Video Using DVI; Multimedia and the i750 Video Processor." *Dr. Dobb's Journal*, 17 (7), 1992: 16–26.

Kalman, Audry. "Virtual World for Windows." *Newsbytes News Network*, 25 January 1993.

Karney, James. "Learn to Animate from the Experts at Disney." *PC Magazine*, 11 (4), 1992. p.454.

LeVitus, Bob. "QuickTime Believer." *MacUser*, 8 (6), 1992: 239–242.

Mallory, Jim. "Microsoft Announces Data Compression Standard." *Newsbytes News Network*, 28 January 1993.

———. "Low Cost PC-To-TV Adapter." *Newsbytes News Network*, 9 April 1993.

———. "Morphing Software for Windows Arrives." *Newsbytes News Network*, 2 June 1993.

———. "Video Software Developers Kit." *Newsbytes News Network*, 25 June 1993.

McCormick, John. "Senators Criticize Violent Sega Video Games." *Newsbytes News Network*, 10 December 1993.

McQuillin, Lon. "Multimedia and Video." *MacUser*, 7 (2), 1992: S4–17.

———. "Authoring, Modeling and Animation." *MacUser* 7 (2), 1991: S52–62.

Miyazawa, Masayuki. "New Technology Stores 3 Hours of Color Motion Data." *Newsbytes News Network*, 15 March 1993.

Petzold, Charles. "Video for Windows Brings Interleaved Audio and Full-motion Digital Video to the PC." *Microsoft Systems Journal*, 8 (1), 1993: 43–52.

Ratcliff, John W. "Audio Compression: Digitized Sound Requires its own Compression Algorithms." *Dr. Dobb's Journal*, 17 (7), 1992: 32–39.

———. "Examining PC Audio: Welcome to the Wild and Wooly World of PC Sound." *Dr. Dobb's Journal*, 18 (3), 1993: 78–86.

Rohrbough, Linda. "Consumer Electronics Show: Digital 'VCR' from 3DO." *Newsbytes News Network*, 8 January 1993.

———. "Truevision Bundles HSC with Bravado Video Boards." *Newsbytes News Network*, 26 January 1993.

———. "Intel Sells PLV Video Compression Business to HTI." *Newsbytes News Network*, 11 February 1993.

———. "Full-Motion MPEG Real-Time Compression Chip." *Newsbytes News Network*, 12 April 1993.

———. "New Quicktime Faster, Needs Less Memory." *Newsbytes News Network*, 22 April 1993.

———. "Lowest Priced Full-Motion Video Board from Sigma." *Newsbytes News Network*, 10 June 1993.

———. "Media Vision to Intro PC Video Graphics Boards." *Newsbytes News Network*, 21 June 1993.

———. "Digital World—Virtualcinema." *Newsbytes News Network*, 25 June 1993.

———. "Supermac Video Editing/Authoring Bundle." *Newsbytes News Network,* 6 July 1993.

Rosenbaum, Andrew. "Cirrus GUI Accelerator Chip, Multimedia Designs." *Newsbytes News Network*, 2 March 1993.

———. "Autodesk Intros Cyberspace Developer Kit." *Newsbytes News Network*, 8 March 1993.

Rosenthal, Steven. "Set Up Your MPC System to Capture Video." *MPC World*, June 1992. p.47.

———. "Plethora of PC Video." *MPC World*, June 1992: 75–76.

Said, Carolyn. "Kodak Hopes to Click with Photo CD." *MacWEEK* 6 (4), 1992. p.30.

Schroeder, Erica. "HSC Readies Video Editor for Mac, Windows." *PC Week*, 9 (6), 1992. p.42.

Stokell, Ian. "RasterOps Video Board For Mac Centris." *Newsbytes News Network*, 12 February 1993.

Torgan, Emerson Andrew. "PC Animate Plus Makes Animation More Affordable." *PC Magazine*, 11 (5), 1992. p.66.

Trespasz, Nancy. "Game Makers Build 'Virtual Reality'; Publishers Blend TV, Film, and Graphics in *Computer Reseller News*, 3 February 1992, #458. p.S11–12.

Volkman, Victor R. "The Digital Video Interface for Windows Multimedia." *Windows-DOS Developer's Journal*, 3 (9), 1992: 5–13.

Woods, Wendy. "Digital, Online Video Production on a Mac." *Newsbytes News Network*, 29 July 1993.

Zientara, Marguerite and Computer Currents. "Convert Videos to Interactive PC Applications." *Newsbytes News Network*, 8 June 1993.

⇨ Video (authors unknown)

"Desktop Video Market Study." *Multimedia Computing & Presentations*, 2 (5), 1990: 10–11.

"Optibase Inc. Debuts Workshop Technology for Adding JPEG Image Compression to MS-DOS and Microsoft Windows Applications." *Multimedia Computing & Presentations*, 4 (4), 1992. p.10.

"XGA Video Standard: Phoenix Technologies Partnership With INMOS." *EDGE: Work-Group Computing Report*, 3 (87), 1992. p.49.

"Autodesk Ships Autovision Rendering for Windows." *Newsbytes News Network*, 15 December 1993.

"Controlling Pioneer LaserDisc Players from MCI." *Microsoft Systems Journal*, 8 (1), 1993: 56–57.

"Video-in-a-Window with the Video Blaster Board." *Microsoft Systems Journal*, 8 (1), 1993: 52–56.

"Apple Announces Video Production Bundle for Quadra." *Newsbytes News Network*, 3 January 1994.

"High-Res, Color Immersive Monitor for VR Viewing." *Newsbytes News Network*, 6 January 1994.

"Prodigy Interactive TV & Cable Delivery Demo at CES." *Newsbytes News Network*, 4 January 1994.

"Radius Intros PrecisionColor Pro 24XK 24-bit Graphics Card." *Newsbytes News Network*, 3 January 1994.

"TV/VCR Controller Battle Continues." *Newsbytes News Network*, 7 January 1994.

⇨ Sound

Arnett, Nick. "Audio Synthesis: Will Yamaha's Hold on the Low End Be Broken by an Expiring Patent and New Technology?" *Multimedia Computing & Presentations*, 4 (4), 1992: 4–5.

Bertolucci, Jeff. "DSPs Sow Seeds of New Products." *PC World*, 10 (12), 1992: 70.

Bindra, Ashok. "DSP Coprocessors Move to Motherboards, but to Take Advantage, Better Software Support is Needed." *Electronic Engineering Times*, 27 January 1992, #677: 35–36.

Davis, Andrew W. and Joe Burke. "Digital Signal Processing." *BYTE*, 17 (8), 1992: 269–273.

Flynn, Mary Kathleen and Charles Petzold. "Sampling Sound." *PC Magazine*, 11 (12), 1992: 32.

Grech, Christine. "How to Buy a Sound Card." *PC-Computing*, 5 (10), 1992: 274–277.

Gruberman, Ken and Lon McQuillin. "Multimedia and Audio." *MacUser*, 7 (2), 1991: S38–46.

Gwennap, Linley. "First Mwave DSP Provides High Integration; Texas Instruments' TMS320M500 Aims to Bring Multimedia to the Masses." *Microprocessor Report*, 6 (16), 1992: 1–4.

Keizer, Gregg. "Sound Investments: PC Audio Products." *Computer Shopper*, 13 (2), 1993: 376–378.

Lawrence, Danny. "A MIDI Device Driver for XENIX." *C Users Journal*, 10 (12), 1992. pp.61–72.

Louderback, Jim. "DSP Technology is Giving New Voice to Sound Cards." *PC Week*, 10 (7), 1993: 88.

Mallory, Jim. "Logitech's Soundman 16, Alliance With Media Vision." *Newsbytes News Network*, 8 February 1993.

McCormick, John. "Crystal Semi Intros New Multimedia Audio Chips." *Newsbytes News Network*, 22 February 1993.

Petzold, Charles. "Exploring waveform audio: Building a digital tape recorder." *PC Magazine*, 10 (22), 1993: 371–376.

———. "An Introduction to the Musical Instrument Digital Interface." *PC Magazine*, 11 (5), 1993: 427–430.

———. "Making Music: an Introduction to MIDI Sequencing." *PC Magazine*, 11 (7), 1992: 393–397.

———. "Playing a MIDI Synthesizer from your PC Keyboard." *PC Magazine*, 11 (8), 1992: 403–406.

———. "Exploring the Low-Level MIDI Input Functions." *PC Magazine*, 11 (13), 1992: 467–473.

———. "Buffered Input and Output of MIDI Short Messages." *PC Magazine*, 11 (14), 1992: 488–490.

———. "Recording and Playing Back MIDI Sequences." *PC Magazine*, 11 (15), 1992: 439–345.

———. "MCI, MIDI, and the Nature of Time." *PC Magazine*, 11 (16), 1992: 395–398.

———. "Playing MIDI Files Using the Media Control Interface." *PC Magazine*, 11 (17), 1992: 380–386.

———. "Exploring the Structure of MIDI files." *PC Magazine*, 11 (18), 1992: 377–379.

———. "Saving your Music in a MIDI File." *PC Magazine*, 11 (19), 1992: 395–398.

Rohrbough, Linda. "CES Show: Creative Labs' 16-Bit Sound, Supermac Deal." *Newsbytes News Network*, 7 January 1993.

———. "Media Vision Intros Sound Compression, Contest." *Newsbytes News Network*, 19 January 1993.

———. "Intel Promotes Sound Capability In Pentium-based PCs." *Newsbytes News Network*, 14 April 1993.

Rosenbaum, Andrew. "Media Vision Intros PC Audio Card With Music Synthesis." *Newsbytes News Network*, 9 August 1993.

———. "Creative Labs Intros Sound Blaster 16 Basic For PC." *Newsbytes News Network*, 30 August 1993.

———. "Logitech Intros SoundMan Audio PC Boards." *Newsbytes*

Rowell, Dave. "The Sound of a Spreadsheet." *PC Sources*, 3 (12), 1992: 95–96.

Trivette, Don. "The Magnificent Ninth Goes Multimedia." *PC Magazine*, 11 (3), 1992: 451.

Venditto, Gus. "Disney and Phoenix to Provide $20 MPC Sound for Laptops." *PC Magazine*, 11 (2), 1992: 32.

Wallach, Naor. "Sigma Designs Monitor; Multimedia Kit." *Newsbytes News Network*, 22 January 1993.

⇨ General

Banet, Bernard A. "CD-ROM Expo 1990: More Titles, More Tools." *The Seybold Report on Publishing Systems*, 20 (5), 1990: 12–22.

Bass, Steve. "Multimedia for the Rank and File." *PC World*, 10 (11), 1992: 344.

Blankenhorn, Dana. "AT&T, Novell In Strategic Partnership 01/06/93." *Newsbytes News Network*, 6 January 1993.

Booker, Ellis. "Enabling Multimedia; As Prices of Digital Signal Processors Fall, Applications Emerge." *Computerworld*, 26 (46), 1992: 28.

Buckler, Grant. "IBM Launches Multimedia Business Unit." *Newsbytes News Network*, 21 January 1993.

Canning, Jim. "IconAuthor 4.0 Builds Multimedia with 'Hotspot' Approach." *InfoWorld*, 14 (5), 1992: 97.

Caruso, Denise and Bernard Banet. "Everybody's Doin' It: CD-ROM Expo is an Orgy of Industry Alliances." *Digital Media: A Seybold Report*, 1 (10), 1992: 15–16.

Colossi, Dawn. "Goldstar's CD-ROM Bundles." *PC Sources*, 3 (2), 1992: 80.

Cook, Rick. "Multimedia Moves to the Motherboard." *Datamation*, 38 (20), 1992: 57–59.

Crabb, Don. "Authorware: Breathtaking Multimedia." *InfoWorld*, 14 (5), 1992: 97.

Dyson, Peter E. "Making Sense of the Digital World." *The Seybold Report on Desktop Publishing*, 4 (12), 1990: 3–15.

Emigh, Jacqueline. "Unix Gets Multimedia and More." *Newsbytes News Network*, 10 February 1993.

———. "MacWorld—Apple Demonstrates AV Multimedia Computers." *Newsbytes News Network*, 9 August 1993.

Flynn, Mary Kathleen. "Multimedia: Looking for the Killer App." *PC Magazine*, 11 (5), 1992: 31.

Gold, Steve. "UK—IBM Ships PS/1 Media Exploration Multimedia PC." *Newsbytes News Network*, 15 December 1993.

Janson, Jennifer L. "Computer-based Training Helps Firms Trim Budgets; Managers Tailor Courses for Specific Needs." *PC Week*, 9 (4), 1992: 90–91.

Loeb, Shoshana. "Architecting Personalized Delivery of Multimedia Information." *Communications of the ACM*, 35 (12), 1992. 39(10).

Lynch, John F. and Narciso Mera. "Signal Processing for Multimedia." *BYTE*, 17 (2), 1992: 105–108.

Mallory, Jim. "Two Firms to Develop Holographic Storage Products." *Newsbytes News Network*, 18 February 1993.

———. "CD-ROM Drive Performance Improver." *Newsbytes News Network*, 2 April 1993.

Masud, S.A. "Multimedia Network Will Integrate Defense Traffic." *Government Computer News*, 11 (2), 1992: 37–38.

McCarthy, Vance. "MacWorld Vendors Push Multimedia." *PC Week*, 9 (3), 1992: 19–20.

McCormick, John. "Integrated Circuit Systems Forms Multimedia Division." *Newsbytes News Network*, 24 August 1993.

———. "Xplor 1993 Technology Directions Survey Results." *Newsbytes News Network*, 21 December 1993.

McLachlan, Gordon. "Breaking the Bottleneck: Three High-Bandwidth Systems Have Emerged to Address the Impending Multimedia Boom." *LAN Computing*, 3 (9), 1992: 12.

Miller, Michael J. "Multimedia: Pong for the Nineties." *PC Magazine*, 11 (5), 1992: 81–82.

Miyazawa, Masayuki. "Ricoh Creates Multimedia Association for Unix." *Newsbytes News Network*, 24 January 1992.

———. "Multimedia Device Developed By Fujitsu." *Newsbytes News Network*, 11 January 1993.

———. "Japan—Multimedia Market Set to Explode." *Newsbytes News Network*, 9 February 1993.

———. "Japan: Fujitsu to Set Up Multimedia Unit; New PC Debuts." *Newsbytes News Network*, 17 February 1993.

———. "IBM Japan's Multimedia Developers Club." *Newsbytes News Network*, 3 March 1993.

———. "Japan to Set Up Int'l Standard on Multimedia." *Newsbytes News Network*, 7 May 1993.

———. "Mitsubishi Develops Multimedia DRAM." *Newsbytes News Network*, 3 June 1993.

Moore, D.J. "Multimedia Presentation Development Using the Audio Visual Connection." *IBM Systems Journal*, 29 (4), 1990: 494–508.

O'Donnell, Craig. "Apple Leading New CD-ROM Pack" *MacWEEK*, 6 (4), 1992: 40–51.

Petzold, Charles. "Experimenting with Additive Synthesis in Multimedia Windows." *PC Magazine*, 11 (4), 1992: 373–377.

———. "Building a Multimedia PC without MPC-Trademark Hardware." *PC Magazine*, 11 (6), 1992: 144.

———. "Exploring the Resource Interchange File Format." *PC Magazine*, 11 (11), 1992: 387–391.

Quain, John R. "Practical Multimedia." *Computer Shopper*, 12 (11), 1992: 396.

Reisman, S. and W.A. Carr. "Perspectives on Multimedia Systems in Education." *IBM Systems Journal*, 30 (3), 1991: 280–295.

Rohrbough, Linda. "New Multimedia CD-ROM Title Helps Children Read." *Newsbytes News Network*, 5 February 1992.

———. "Poor Man's CD-ROM Intros Multimedia Sports Adventure." *Newsbytes News Network*, 27 January 1993.

———. "Media Vision Intros Macintosh Multimedia Kit." *Newsbytes News Network*, 12 April 1993.

———. "Multimedia Market Barely Tapped, Huge Growth By 1997." *Newsbytes News Network*, 13 August 1993.

———. "New Evidence Forces Reexamination Of Compton's Patent." *Newsbytes News Network*, 20 December 1993.

Rooney, Paula. "Microsoft Weds Windows WP to Multimedia." *PC Week*, 9 (7), 1992: 4.

Rosenbaum, Andrew. "Creative Labs Intros Multiple Products." *Newsbytes News Network*, 30 June 1993.

——. "Surge of Multimedia Sales Expected in Europe." *Newsbytes News Network*, 6 January 1993.

——. "Motorola Announces Multiple Chip Technology Breakthroughs." *Newsbytes News Network*, 23 August 1993.

Scisco, Peter. "Two Presentation Packages Bring Multimedia to the Masses for Under $200." *PC Magazine*, 11 (5), 1992: 38–39.

Simone, Luisa. "Sound and Fury: Presentations in the Multimedia Age." *PC Magazine*, 11 (5), 1992: 118–119.

Sprague, David. "How Will Multimedia Change System Storage?." *BYTE*, 17 (3), 1992: 164–165.

Stokell, Ian. "Apple, Macromedia In Multimedia Deal." *Newsbytes News Network*, 12 February 1993.

Sullivan, Eamonn. "Adobe Multimedia Tool Makes Nimble Partner for QuickTime." *PC Week*, 9 (4), 1993: 34.

——. "Multimedia Duo Aids Presentations." *PC Week*, 9 (5), 1992: 67–70.

Torgan, Emerson Andrew. "KnowledgePro Windows Adds Multimedia Support." *PC Magazine*, 11 (5), 1992: 64.

Walsh, Aaron E. "Programming QuickTime: Multimedia to the Macs." *Dr. Dobb's Journal*, 17 (7), 1992: 76–82.

Woods, Wendy. "Symantec PC Cache Software Speeds CD-ROM Access 3000%." *Newsbytes News Network*, 25 March 1993.

⇨ General (authors unknown)

"Issues of the Future." *Release 1.0*, 89 (8)l, 1989: 18–20.

"Publishing without Paper." *The Seybold Report on Publishing Systems*, 18 (14), 1989: 17–25.

"HyperCard 2.0 Spawns New Products." *Multimedia Computing & Presentations*, 2 (9), 1990: 9.

"Industry profile: CD-ROM is Muscling Microfilm Aside." *Tech Street Journal*, 9 (4–5), 1990: 12–16.

"Lessons in Document Interchange at NIST: a Look at Current Options." *The Seybold Report on Desktop Publishing*, 4 (12), 1990: 38–40.

"IBM Makes Multimedia its Main Chance; Unlike Tandy, IBM Has Gone Whole-Hog into Multimedia." *P.C. Letter*, 8 (6), 1992: 3–6.

"The Imagination Station Delivers Comprehensive Multimedia Capabilities at an Affordable Price." *Computer Shopper*, 12 (2), 1992: 858.

"MediaTree Manages Multimedia in Outlines." *MacWEEK*, 6 (5), 1992: 30.

"MIDI, CD-ROM XA, and DSP: The Handmaidens of Multimedia." *P.C. Letter*, 8 (7), 1992: 8–10.

"Multimedia Authoring System for Windows." *Computing Canada*, 18 (2), 1992: 58.

"Understanding Multimedia." *Dr. Dobb's Journal*, 17 (2), 1992: 105–107.

"Videologic and IBM Working on Something 'Big'." *Digital Media: A Seybold Report*, 2 (3), 1992: 15.

"Collaborator II & Scriptware for Scriptwriting." *Newsbytes News Network*, 15 December 1993.

"Multimedia: AT&T joins Matsushita, Time Warner, MCA & Electronic Arts as Investor in the 3D0 Company; Will License 3D0 Technology." *EDGE on & about AT&T*, 8 (233), 1993: 1.

"CES—Casio Rolls Out the Gadgets." *Newsbytes News Network*, 7 January 1994.

"Corel Launching Clip Art CD-ROM at CES." *Newsbytes News Network*, 4 January 1994.

"Double-, Triple-Speed MM Kits Aimed at Apple Market." *Newsbytes News Network*, 3 January 1994.

"India—Multimedia Network Project Planned." *Newsbytes News Network*, 4 January 1994.

"Mac PowerPC Upgrade Path, Developer Tools Announced." *Newsbytes News Network*, 3 January 1994.

"$100 Million in CD-ROM Sales for First Part of 1993." *Newsbytes News Network*, 7 January 1994.

⇨ Additional suggested reading

Anderson, Carol and Mark D. Ljaov. *Authoring Multimedia*. Glenview, IL: Scott, Foresman, 1990.

Bove, Tony and Cheryl Bove. *Que's Macintosh Multimedia Handbook*. Carmel, ID: Que Corporation, 1990.

Brand, Stuart. *The Media Lab: Inventing the Future at MIT*. New York, NY: Viking Press, 1987. A chronicle of several months at the think tank for media technology at MIT.

Brown, Michael. *Desktop Video Production*. Blue Ridge Summit, PA:

Windcrest/TAB Books, 1991. Using the Commodore Amiga and Macintosh computers to create video productions. Considers hardware, software, and project management issues.

Efreim, Joel Lawrence. *Video Tape Production and Communication Techniques.* Blue Ridge Summit, PA: TAB Books, 1972.

Martin, James. *Hyperdocuments and How to Create Them.* Englewood Cliffs, NJ: Prentice Hall, 1989.

Roncarelli, Robi. *The Computer Animation Dictionary.* New York, NY: Springer-Verlag, 1989.

Sosinsky, Barrie. *Beyond the Desktop: Tools and Technology for Computer Publishing.* New York, NY: Bantam Books, 1991.

Wilson, Stephen. *Multimedia Design with HyperCard.* Englewood Cliffs, NJ: Prentice Hall, 1990.

Videomaker. Chico, CA: Videomaker, Inc., 1994.

Index

Illustration page numbers are in **boldface**

GEnie®
The most fun you can have with your computer on.

No other online service has more cool stuff to do, or more cool people to do it with than GEnie. Join dozens of awesome special interest RoundTables on everything from multimedia to Microsoft to food and wine, download over 200,000 files, access daily stock quotes, talk to all those smart guys on the internet, play the most incredible multi-player games, and so much more you won't believe your eyeballs.

And GEnie has it all at a standard connect rate of just $3.00 an hour.   That's one of the lowest rates of all the major online services! Plus -- because you're a reader of *Create Your Own Multimedia System* -- you get an even cooler deal. If you sign up before March 31, 1995, we'll waive your first monthly subscription fee (an $8.95 value) and include ten additional hours of standard connect time (another $30.00 in savings). That's fourteen free hours during your first month – *a $38.95 value!*

You can take advantage of this incredible offer immediately -- just follow these simple steps:

1. Set your communications software for half-duplex (local echo) at 300, 1200, or 2400 baud. Recommended communications parameters 8 data bits, no parity and 1 stop bit.
2. Dial toll-free in the U.S. at 1-800-638-8369 (or in Canada at 1-800-387-8330). Upon connection, type **HHH** (Please note: every time you use GEnie, you need to enter the HHH upon connection) At the U#= prompt, type **JOINGENIE** and press <Return>
3. At the offer code prompt enter GAF225 to get this special offer.
4. Have a major credit card ready. In the U.S., you may also use your checking account number.
5. (There is a $2.00 monthly fee for all checking accounts.) In Canada, VISA and MasterCard only.

Or, if you need more information, contact GEnie Client Services at 1-800-638-9636 from 9am to midnight, Monday through Friday, and from noon to 8pm Saturday and Sunday (all times are Eastern).

1 U.S. prices. Standard connect time is non-prime time: 6pm to 8am local time, Mon. - Fri., all day Sat. and Sun. and selected holidays.
2 Offer available in the United States and Canada only.
3 The offer for six additional hours applies to standard hourly connect charges only and must be used by the end of the billing period for your first month. Please call 1-800-638-9636 for more information on pricing and billing policies.

FLEXCAM

Color video camera and microphone:

- 1/3" CCD
- 18" flexible wand
- Focuses 1/4" to infinity
- 50:1 magnification
- Stereo microphones

Great for multimedia uses:

- videoconferencing
- presenting
- image capture
- security

FlexCam is an exciting new multimedia camera for desktop video production and eye-to-eye videoconferencing. Its sleek, flexible 18-inch gooseneck wand lets you direct the swivel-head camera at any subject for precise positioning.

FlexCam is available in both NTSC and PAL versions.

VideoLabs, Inc.
5270 West 84th Street
Minneapolis, MN 55437
612-897-1995
612-897-3597 FAX

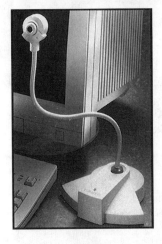

VIDEOLABS

$50 Off COUPON

Present this coupon to VideoLabs with your order to receive $50 off FlexCam or FlexCam Pro

I want to order FlexCam

Please have a VideoLabs marketing representative contact me

Name _____

Title _____

Company _____

Address _____

City _____ State _____ Zip _____

Telephone ( ) _____ Fax ( ) _____

ORDER FORM

(U.S. PRICES)

FlexCam $595.00 *($50 less with coupon)*	Qty. _____	$ _____
FlexCam Pro $795.00 *($50 less with coupon)*	Qty. _____	$ _____
Minnesota Residents Add 6.5% Sales Tax		$ _____
Shipping(UPS Ground)		$10.00
	Total	

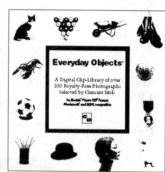

Disk Instructions

The included diskette contains MS-DOS files, all in automatic extraction compressed format. The appendix text files are in ASCII and can be read on any computer, but the rest require MS-DOS or Windows.

To use the files, copy the master file to another diskette or a hard disk subdirectory and then run the file. For example, the CONVERT.EXE file contains both VOC2WAV.EXE and WAV2VOC.EXE. These two utilities convert between the Creative Labs (SoundBlaster) file format .VOC used in many MS-DOS applications and the Microsoft Windows .WAV sound file format. To access these files, copy CONVERT.EXE to another disk, then type CONVERT and press Enter.

The file GIF-JPG.EXE contains a set of $20 shareware files that convert between JPEG and GIF file format.

WHATPIC2.EXE contains a program that identifies a number of graphics file formats and produces a report providing information about the format, size, and resolution of the file.

HISS.EXE contains a freeware program that removes some of the background noise (hiss) in sound samples saved in VOC, SND, SOU, or any 8-bit raw data format.

TEXTCN.EXE contains the program and documentation files for TEXTCON, a useful ASCII file conversion utility that removes extra carriage returns from the TEXT-OUT files produced by many word processors.

FRACTAL.EXE contains files needed to run Fractal Paint, a $25 shareware program that lets you create fractal images in Windows.

WINJAM.EXE contains a $50 shareware WindJam MIDI editor.

CD-AUDIO.EXE contains a neat MS-DOS and Windows utility that lets you play audio CDs on your CD-ROM drive.

MIDSUM.EXE contains a simple example of a document created using Ntergaid HyperWriter! Many of the fancier features were left out of this demo due to space considerations. The Ntergaid software can be used to produce royalty-free multimedia programs (such as this sample) for distribution or sale. The HyperWriter! authoring system offers full animation, video, and sound links for true multimedia in a rich text environment.

APPENDIX.EXE contains ASCII text files for expanded versions of the listings appearing in appendices A, B, C, E, and H.

DISK WARRANTY

This software is protected by both United States copyright law and international copyright treaty provision. You must treat this software just like a book, except that you may copy it into a computer in order to be used and you may make archival copies of the software for the sole purpose of backing up our software and protecting your investment from loss.

By saying "just like a book," McGraw-Hill means, for example, that this software may be used by any number of people and may be freely moved from one computer location to another, so long as there is no possibility of its being used at one location or on one computer while it also is being used at another. Just as a book cannot be read by two different people in two different places at the same time, neither can the software be used by two different people in two different places at the same time (unless, of course, McGraw-Hill's copyright is being violated).

LIMITED WARRANTY

Windcrest/McGraw-Hill takes great care to provide you with top-quality software, thoroughly checked to prevent virus infections. McGraw-Hill warrants the physical diskette(s) contained herein to be free of defects in materials and workmanship for a period of sixty days from the purchase date. If McGraw-Hill receives written notification within the warranty period of defects in materials or workmanship, and such notification is determined by McGraw-Hill to be correct, McGraw-Hill will replace the defective diskette(s). Send requests to:

Customer Service
Windcrest/McGraw-Hill
13311 Monterey Lane
Blue Ridge Summit, PA 17294-0850

The entire and exclusive liability and remedy for breach of this Limited Warranty shall be limited to replacement of defective diskette(s) and shall not include or extend to any claim for or right to cover any other damages, including but not limited to, loss of profit, data, or use of the software, or special, incidental, or consequential damages or other similar claims, even if McGraw-Hill has been specifically advised of the possibility of such damages. In no event will McGraw-Hill's liability for any damages to you or any other person ever exceed the lower of suggested list price or actual price paid for the license to use the software, regardless of any form of the claim.

McGRAW-HILL, INC. SPECIFICALLY DISCLAIMS ALL OTHER WARRANTIES, EXPRESS OR IMPLIED, INCLUDING, BUT NOT LIMITED TO, ANY IMPLIED WARRANTY OF MERCHANTABILITY OR FITNESS FOR A PARTICULAR PURPOSE.

Specifically, McGraw-Hill makes no representation or warranty that the software is fit for any particular purpose and any implied warranty of merchantability is limited to the sixty-day duration of the Limited Warranty covering the physical diskette(s) only (and not the software) and is otherwise expressly and specifically disclaimed.

This limited warranty gives you specific legal rights; you may have others which may vary from state to state. Some states do not allow the exclusion of incidental or consequential damages, or the limitation on how long an implied warranty lasts, so some of the above may not apply to you.